IMAGES
of America

CATALINA BY SEA
A TRANSPORTATION HISTORY

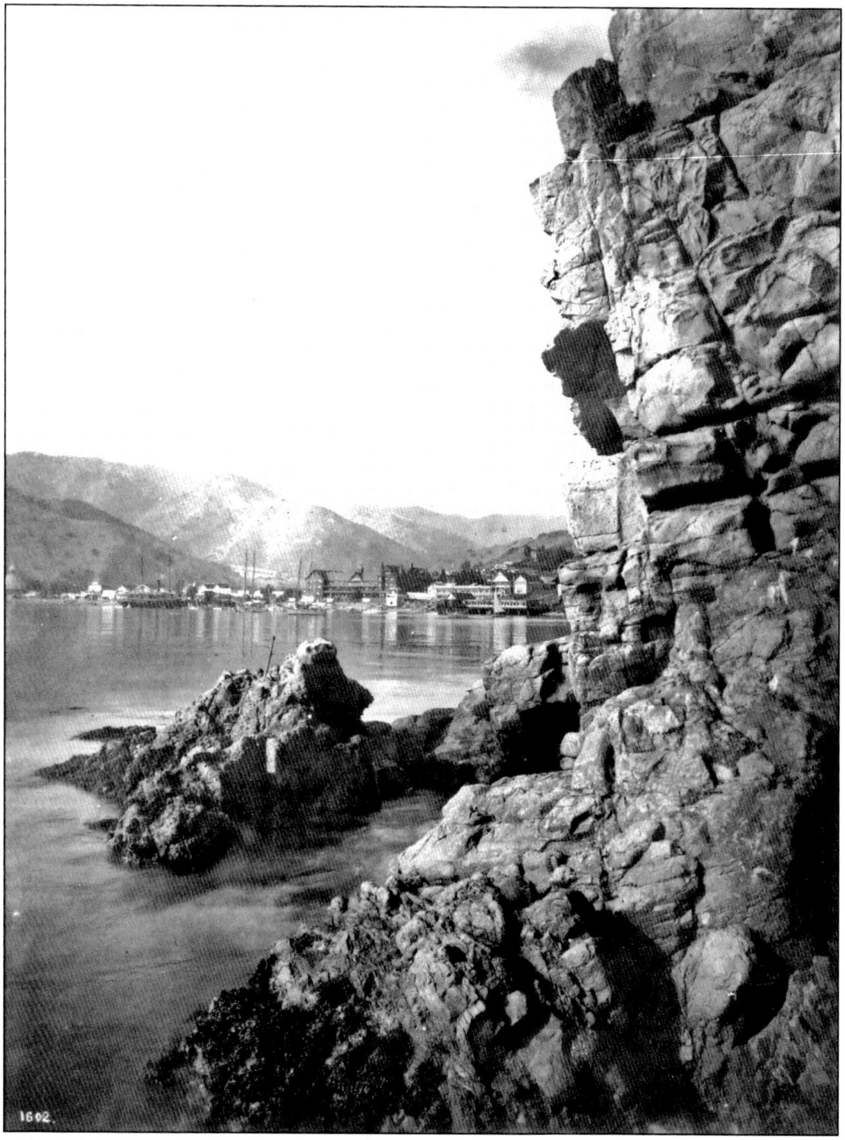

Catalina Island is an enchanting Pacific isle just off the coast of Los Angeles. The island has a fascinating history dating back over 7,000 years, which recently includes the development of the world-renowned resort community of Avalon and the millions of visitors who have been lured by its charm. One of the most interesting aspects of this history is transportation. Since Catalina Island lies in the middle of the ocean, how did visitors first access the island and how long did it take? Crossing the San Pedro Channel by steamship was the most common way. The channel crossing could be quite exciting and was a memorable part of the Catalina experience.

ON THE COVER: Avalon Bay is the primary port for Catalina Island, and for 80 years the steamships docked at the center of the bay on the steamer pier. Once passengers disembarked the ship, they would explore the small town of Avalon and its many attractions. Over the years, the resort town of Avalon has offered visitors a variety of sights and tours, such as glass-bottom boats, the Casino building, and Catalina's Bird Park.

IMAGES
of America

CATALINA BY SEA
A TRANSPORTATION HISTORY

Jeannine L. Pedersen and
the Catalina Island Museum

ARCADIA
PUBLISHING

ISBN 978-0-7385-3116-8

Published by Arcadia Publishing
Charleston, South Carolina

Printed in the United States of America

Library of Congress Catalog Card Number: 2005937820

For all general information contact Arcadia Publishing at:
Telephone 843-853-2070
Fax 843-853-0044
E-mail sales@arcadiapublishing.com
For customer service and orders:
Toll-Free 1-888-313-2665

Visit us on the Internet at www.arcadiapublishing.com

Contents

ACKNOWLEDGMENTS

The photographs, brochures, and postcards in this volume represent a significant aspect of Catalina Island history. The Catalina Island Museum is dedicated to collecting, preserving, and interpreting every aspect of Catalina's unique history. Since the museum opened its doors in 1953, it has accepted over 100,000 artifacts from hundreds of generous donors used for exhibition, research, educational purposes, and publication. This book would not be possible without the generosity of these donors and the assistance of the museum staff and several community members. I would like to personally thank Ivonne Cachu, Carol Hendersen, and Stacey Otte for their assistance with research, scanning, and editing. Thank you to Roy Rose, Ada Blanche Wrigley Schreiner, Hugh T. Smith, and Rudy Piltch for sharing their wonderful memories. And a very special thank you to Doug Bombard, whose extensive knowledge of Catalina's water transportation added significant material and insight to this project.

FOREWORD

This volume marks our second publication with Arcadia. The first was a general history of Catalina Island told primarily through images from our extensive collection. We knew we had only skimmed the surface of the collection for that book, so when Arcadia approached us for a second volume, we leaped at the chance.

We initially thought to focus on both air and water transportation to the island, but our collection of steamship photos and ephemera was so rich, we decided to narrow our focus to "Catalina by sea"—and save our great airplane collection for perhaps another volume in the future.

The museum's curator, Jeannine Pedersen, has spent countless hours researching this topic, combing through our archives and conducting meetings and interviews with several longtime residents of the island, including Ada Blanche Wrigley Schreiner, the granddaughter of island owner and chewing-gum magnate William Wrigley Jr. She is a truly delightful lady who carries on the family legacy of caring and stewardship for her island home.

Another rich human resource was Doug Bombard, who was a fearless driver of the *Miss Catalina* speedboats as a young man and later founded and operated today's primary cross-channel carrier, *Catalina Express*. Jeannine's meetings with Doug filled in many knowledge gaps and have helped to expand our research files.

There are many aspects to the story of cross-channel transportation to our island. While on the surface it may sound like a topic of interest only to the nautical-minded, in fact the human side of the story is compelling to anyone who cares about the island.

The first people who lived on Catalina were the Native Americans who, after European contact, became known as the Gabrielino (today many descendents prefer the names Tongva or Pimuvit). These people used plank canoes to ply the waters to and from the mainland and other Channel Islands. Their sturdy canoes allowed them to develop a sophisticated trade system that augmented the resources they made use of on the island.

During European exploration of the seas, large sailing ships came near the island and the first documented landing was by Juan Rodriguez Cabrillo in 1542. Sailing ships continued to be the primary mode of transport for centuries, although there wasn't much need of regular service to the island until later in the 19th century.

When the island was first being developed as a resort by entrepreneur George Shatto in 1887, transportation to it was primarily limited to steamships. The Banning Brothers, who later purchased the island in 1892, quickly began offering their ships to augment Shatto's limited fleet. Early advertising makes it clear that the ocean voyage was as much a part of the experience as the actual visit to the island. For the vast majority of visitors, no doubt the two-or-so-hour trip was their first ocean voyage and was an enticing and exotic attraction on its own.

Early on, a tradition of greeting the steamship passengers developed. Every day—sometimes twice a day during the height of the season—the townspeople would close their shops temporarily to come down to the steamer pier entrance and give the passengers a warm island welcome. Kids dove for coins thrown by passengers as they waited to disembark. Steamer greetings became more elaborate and sing-alongs became part of the ritual, as did gentle razzing and joking as a kind of right of passage for passengers. This warm and friendly greeting made quite an impression on visitors and is an often-recalled story we hear today at the museum from our visitors who remember those days.

In this volume, Jeannine will be sharing with you both the history of the ships that have delivered visitors to the island for over 100 years and the human side of that story as well. I can think of nowhere else in the world that has such a history of steamship greetings, enacted day after day, year after year.

We hope you will enjoy this exploration of a unique and special part of our history. No doubt many of you will have some of your own memories of voyaging to Catalina. Maybe you were treated to the sight of a large pod of dolphins or migrating whales, or danced to a band on the SS *Catalina*, or maybe met the love of your life while you both were waiting for your first sighting of the island. We'd love to hear your stories and hope you will share them with us. Please visit our website at www.catalinamuseum.org and you will find a link to share a story with us and be able to read others' reminiscences.

The Catalina Island Museum is a private, nonprofit organization, and we rely on our members and supporters for the funds to do our work in preserving the stories, memories, and artifacts of our past. Please consider supporting our vital work. Donations are tax deductible and can be sent to: Catalina Island Museum, PO Box 366, Avalon, CA 90704.

Happy reading!

—Stacey Otte, Executive Director
Catalina Island Museum

One

The Early Days

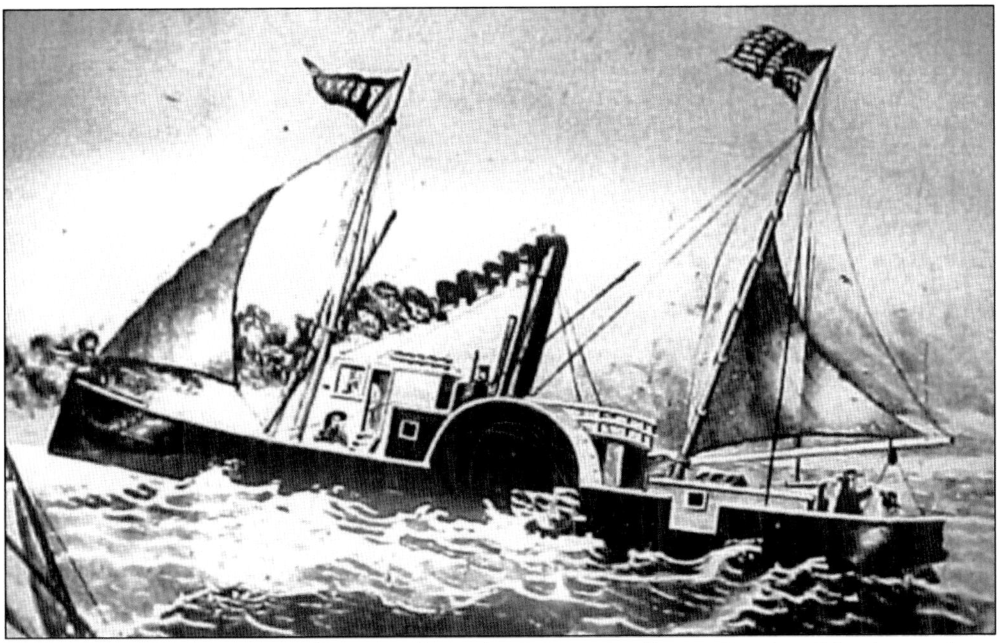

Sailing vessels and steamers began making the crossing to Santa Catalina Island as early as 1860 to serve the miners and ranchers on the island. At this time, steamships were increasingly becoming the common mode of transport in maritime technology. The first steamer to make a regular crossing was the *Cricket*, operated by Phinneas Banning. The *Cricket*, a wooden steamship built in the early 1860s, crossed the channel from the mainland to Catalina in four hours, which was typical of the early steamers. By the early 1880s, Banning, who also played a key role in the development of Los Angeles Harbor, started offering a regularly scheduled service to Catalina. The Banning family established the Wilmington Transportation Company in 1884 and began to develop a fleet of vessels that would serve a growing number of people interested in visiting and exploring Catalina Island.

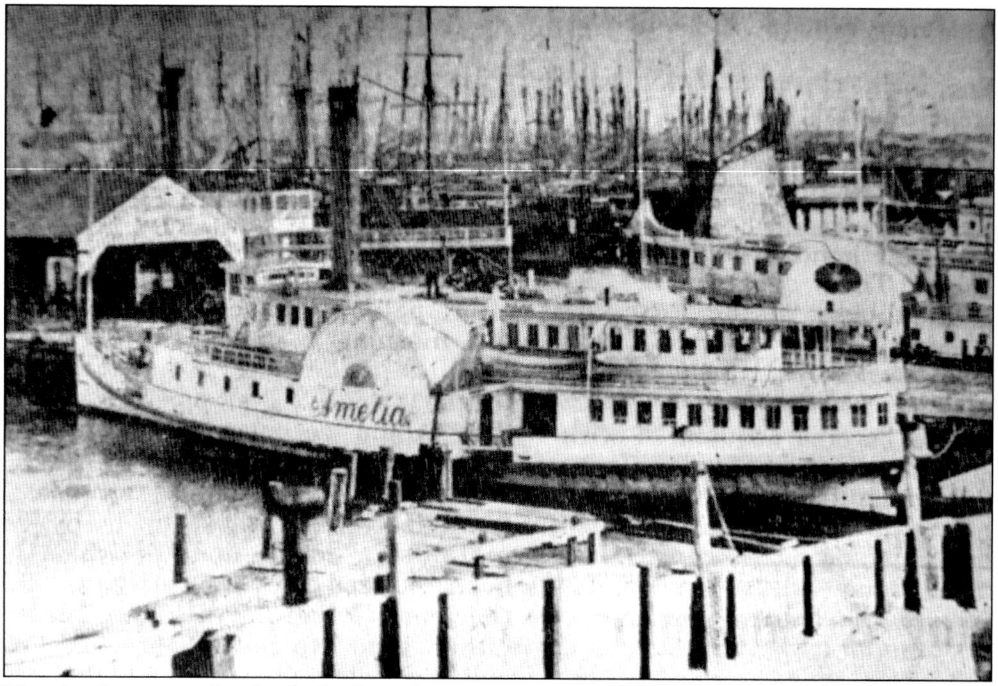

The *Amelia* was a side-wheeler built in Sacramento in 1860 and purchased in 1880 by Phinneas Banning for the Catalina run between Los Angeles Harbor and Avalon. The 147-foot, wooden ship was well appointed with a restaurant and salon. Entertainment was provided to passengers during the three-hour crossing. The *Amelia* served Catalina Island for three years until she was sold to a firm in Northern California in 1883.

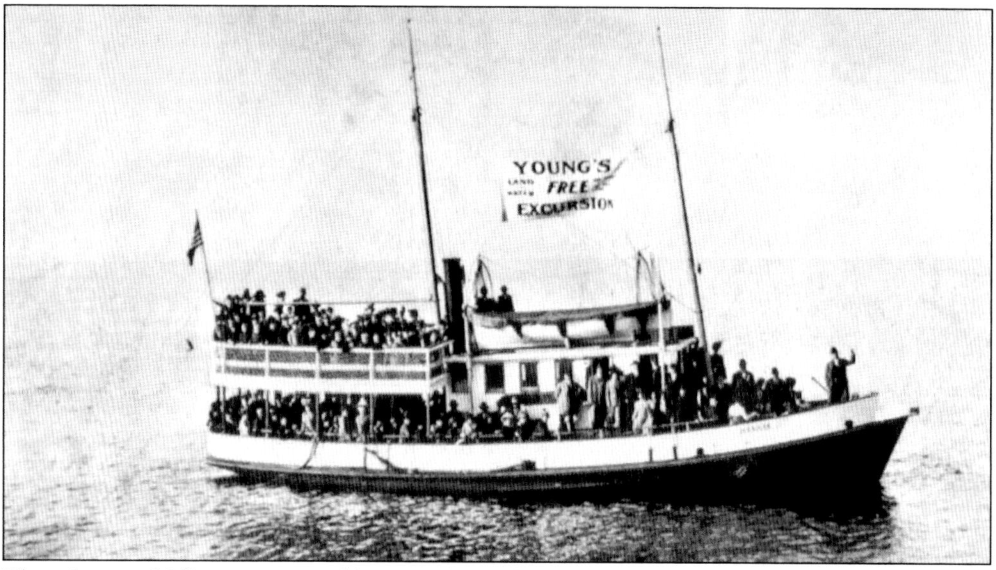

The schooner *Nellie* was operated by an independent service and was used for excursion cruises around the Channel Islands at the turn of the 20th century. Avalon was a popular stop on these extended day cruises. According to an article printed in the *Los Angeles Times* in 1899, "The schooner *Nellie* returned from her cruise about the Channel Islands yesterday. Much of the time there was no wind and the vessel was two days longer in making the trip than had been expected."

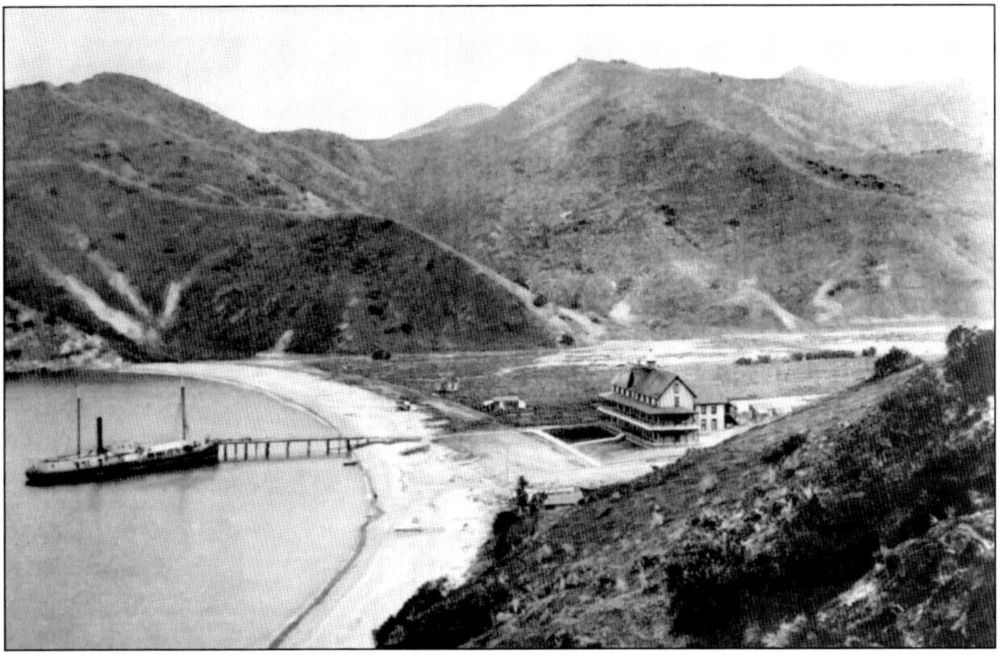

The development of Catalina Island as a vacation destination was the initial vision of George Shatto, a businessman from Grand Rapids, Michigan. Shatto was given the opportunity to purchase Catalina Island in 1887. His plan was to develop the bay, now known as Avalon, into a pleasure resort. He quickly began the construction of a hotel and steamer wharf and purchased the SS *Ferndale* in 1888. The *Ferndale* operated between San Pedro and Avalon once daily.

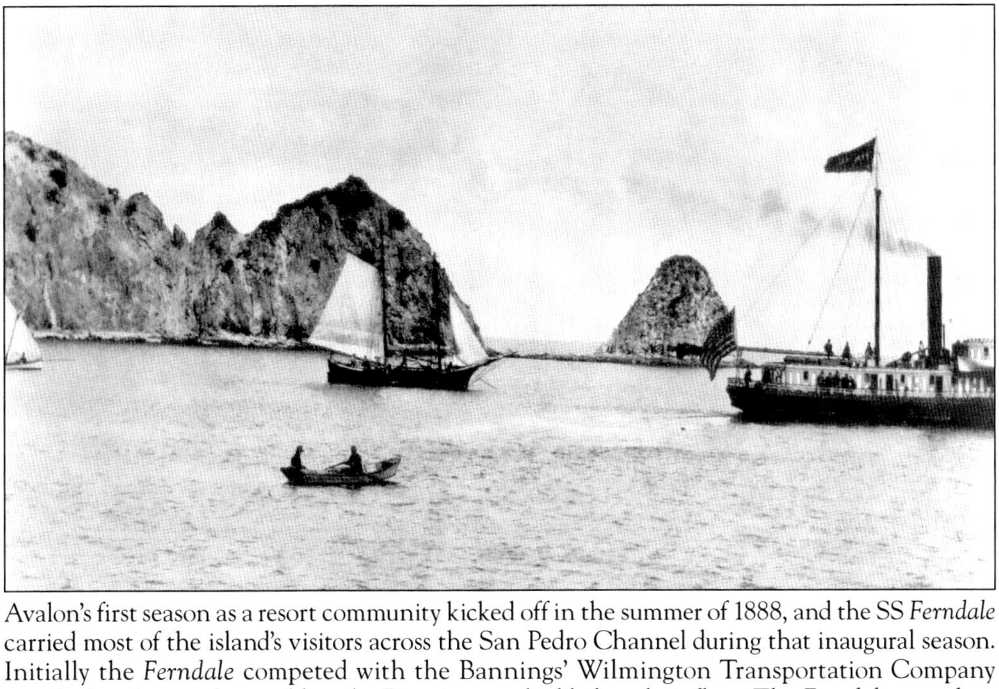

Avalon's first season as a resort community kicked off in the summer of 1888, and the SS *Ferndale* carried most of the island's visitors across the San Pedro Channel during that inaugural season. Initially the *Ferndale* competed with the Bannings' Wilmington Transportation Company vessels, but she was later sold to the Bannings and added to their fleet. The *Ferndale* served on the Catalina run for just a few short years.

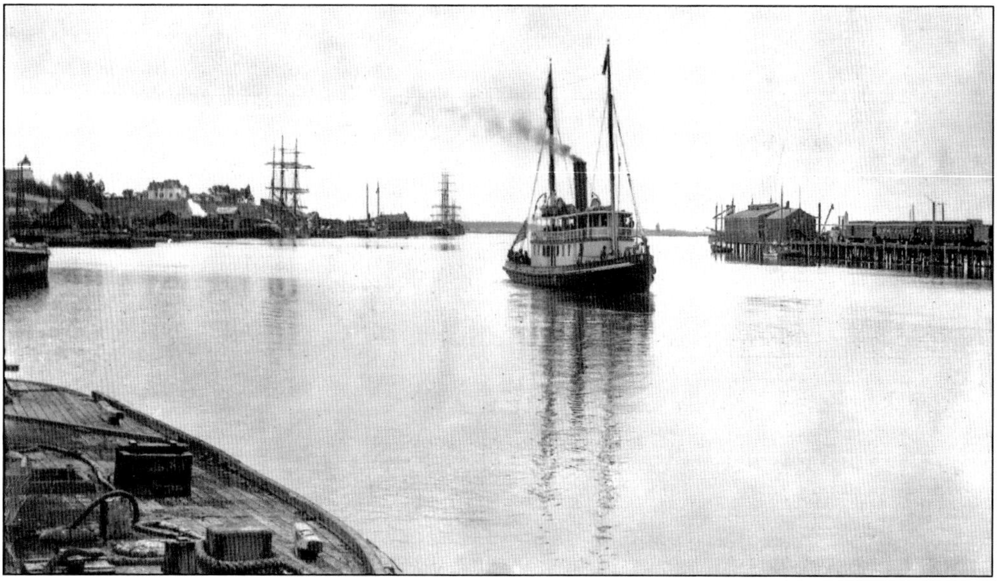

The SS *Falcon* was built in San Francisco in 1886 for the Wilmington Transportation Company. The wooden lumber schooner and cargo carrier was 100 feet in length and operated with a crew of seven. The *Falcon* was a multipurpose vessel originally used as a tug and later rebuilt to carry passengers.

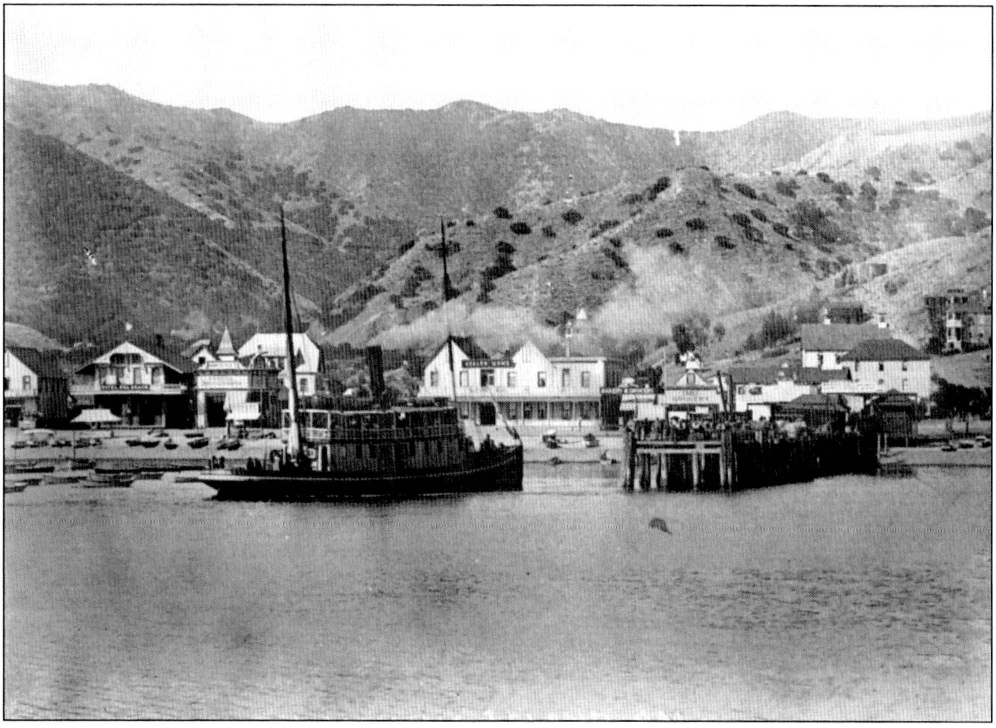

As a passenger vessel, the *Falcon* was a staple on the Catalina run throughout the 1890s. She was remodeled twice during the decade to increase her speed and comfort for passengers. The *Falcon* was often mentioned in the *Los Angeles Times* "Shipping News" as having crossed the channel with passengers and merchandise for the Wilmington Transportation Company.

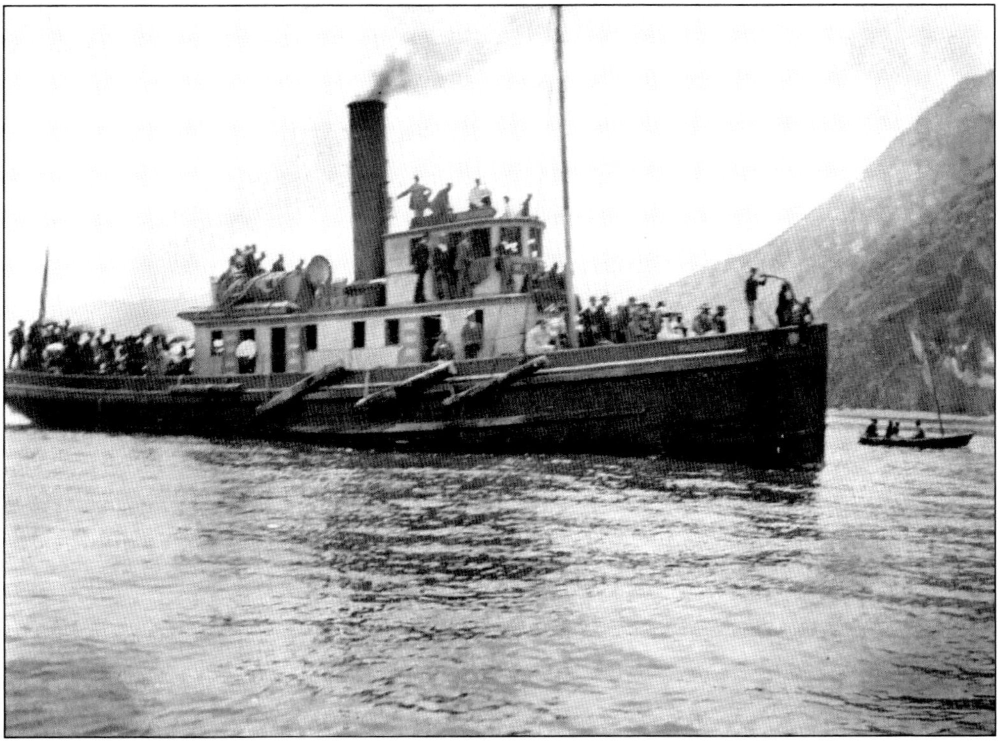

The original SS *Warrior* was built in the 1880s for the Wilmington Transportation Company and served on the Catalina run throughout the 1890s. The *Warrior* was a multipurpose vessel used to carry passengers, freight, and rock from the island's quarries. The *Warrior* was dismantled in 1900 and replaced by the *Warrior II*.

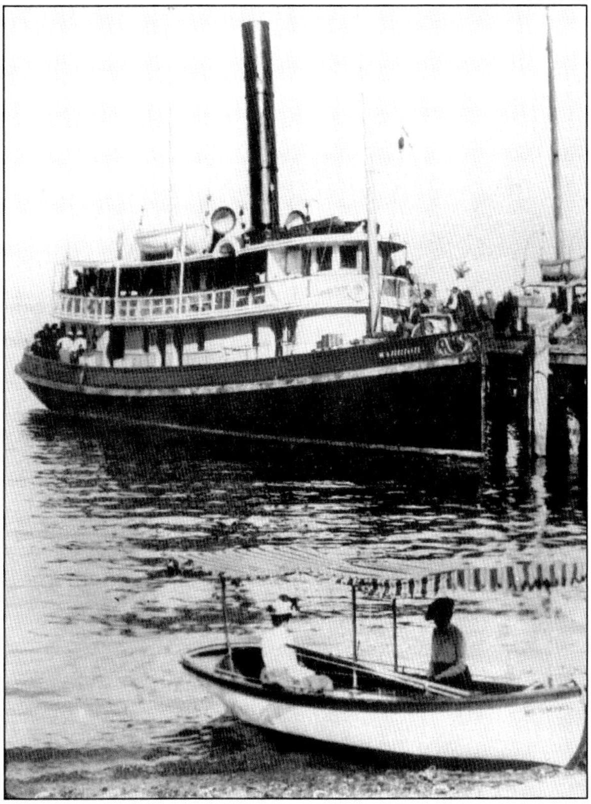

The SS *Warrior II* was launched in December 1900. The *Los Angeles Times* printed a description of the new vessel in 1901, "The *Warrior II* is five feet longer than the *Falcon*, and built on pretty much the same plan, excepting that she has a cabin on the upper deck, and the after deck below, is much more spacious. She stands nearly two feet higher than the *Falcon* and has greater horsepower. She is expected to cut the time of the other boats at least 20 minutes." The *Warrior II* served on the Catalina run for 17 years.

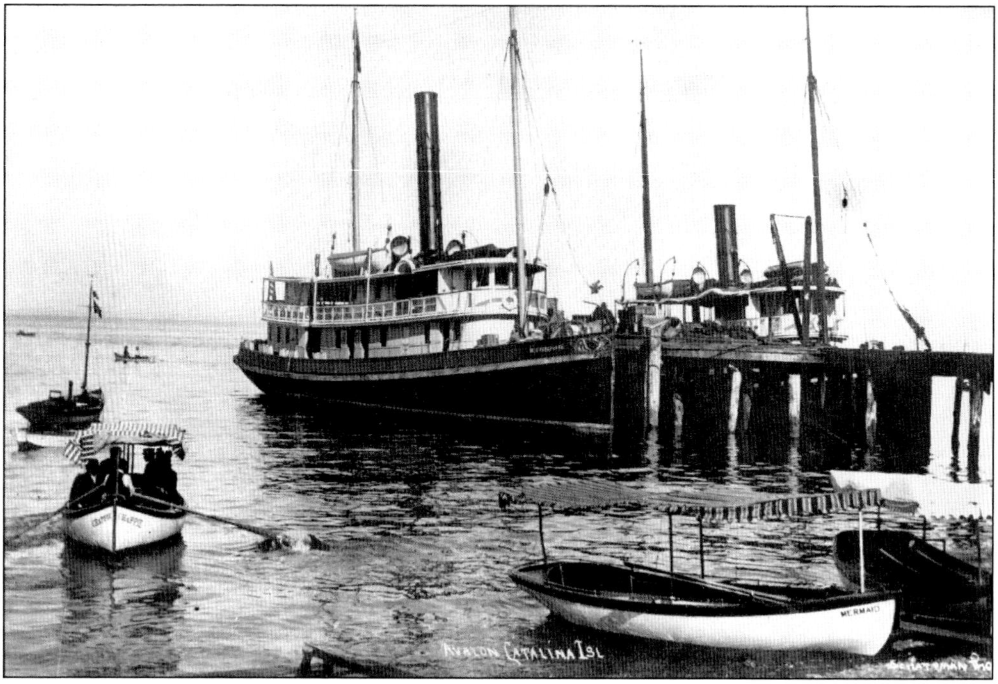

The SS *Warrior* and SS *Falcon* played significant roles in the island's early transportation history. They were an important part of the Wilmington Transportation Company fleet for many years. They carried hundreds of passengers across the channel to Catalina Island as well as freight and fresh water for the residents. The SS *Warrior* and SS *Falcon* served well, and it is only fitting that pieces of the vessels can still be found on the island.

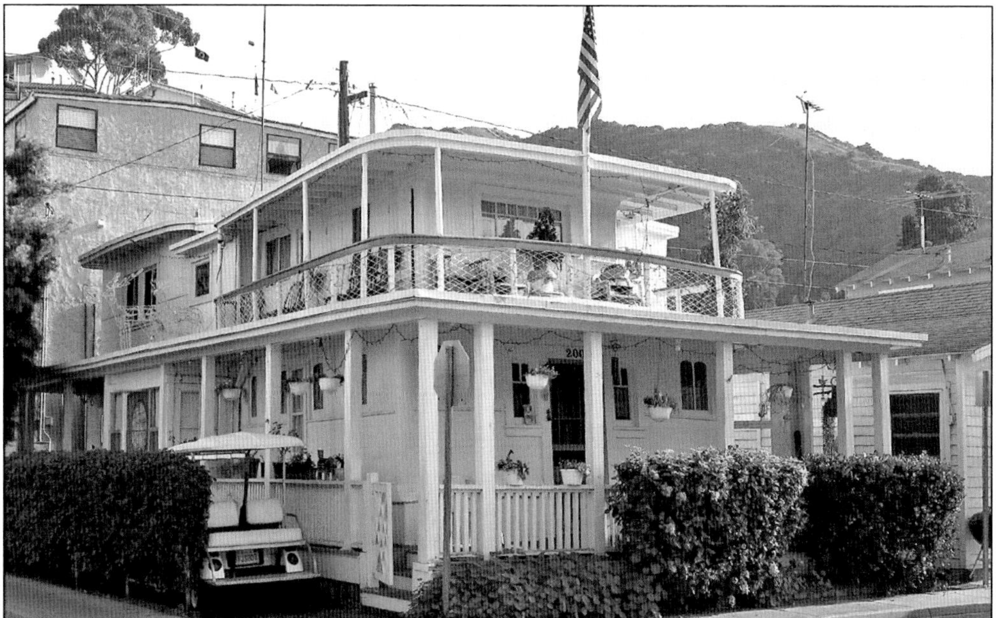

This house, located on the corner of Third Street and Descanso Avenue in Avalon, was built in the early 1900s using dismantled pieces from the *Warrior* and the *Falcon*.

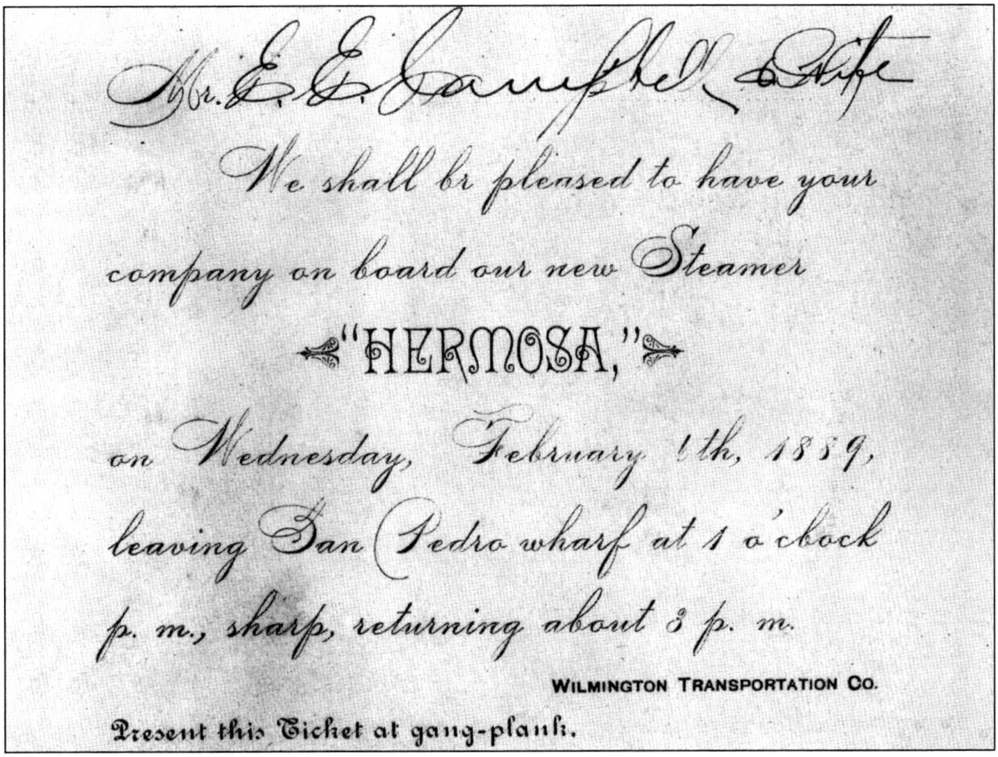
Mr. E. E. Campbell & Wife

We shall be pleased to have your company on board our new Steamer

"HERMOSA,"

on Wednesday, February 6th, 1889, leaving San Pedro wharf at 1 o'clock p. m., sharp, returning about 3 p. m.

WILMINGTON TRANSPORTATION CO.

Present this Ticket at gang-plank.

The SS *Hermosa* was launched in 1888 by the Wilmington Transportation Company. At the time, it was the largest and most elegant vessel of its kind on the West Coast. This ticket was an invitation to attend the maiden voyage of the *Hermosa* to Catalina Island in February 1889.

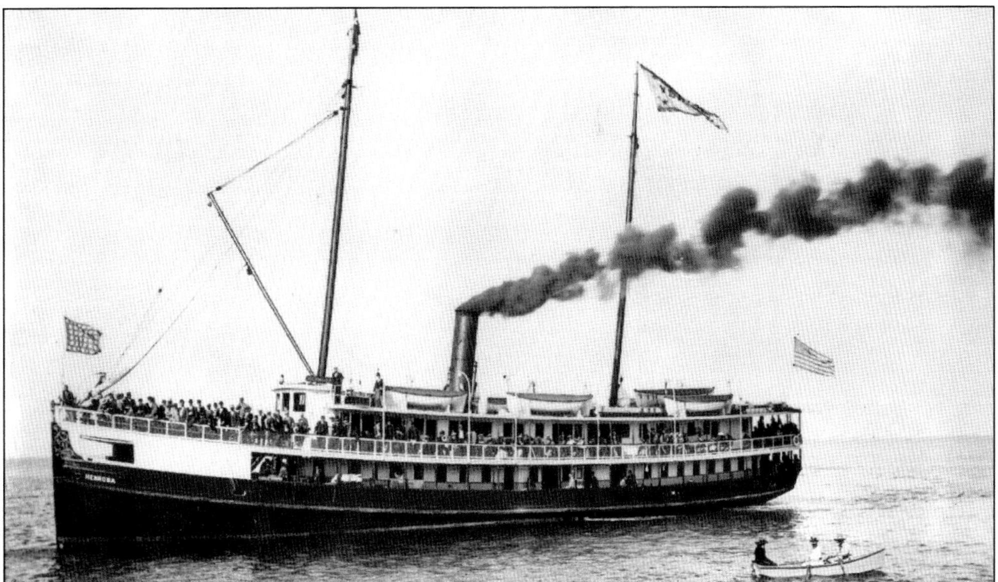

The *Hermosa* was a wooden ship, 141 feet in length, and carried up to 150 passengers. She was elegantly appointed with incandescent lights and maple and mahogany woodwork. The well-known Hungarian Orchestra usually accompanied passengers on the almost three-hour crossing.

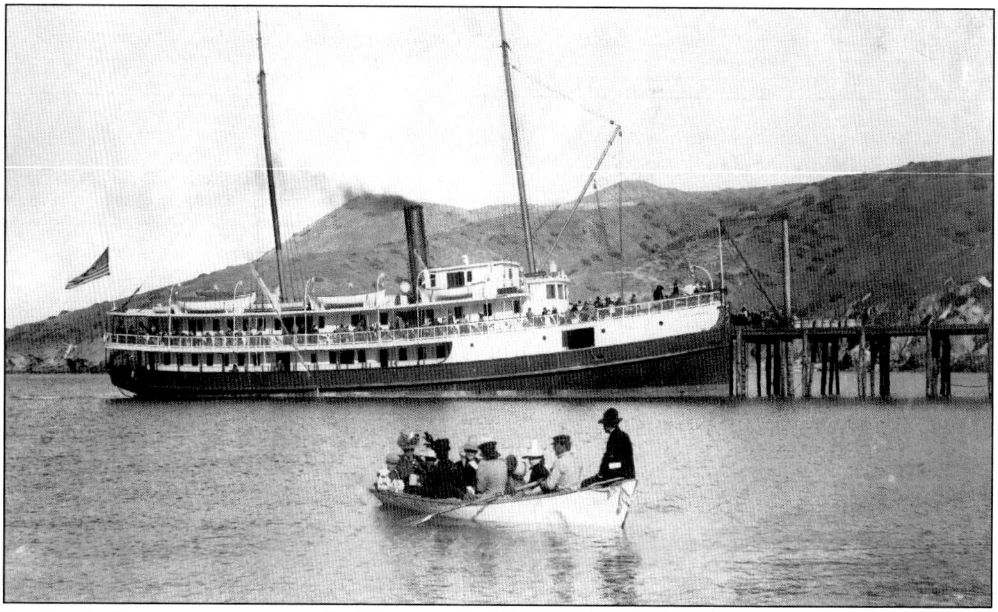

During the busy summer season, the *Hermosa* proudly served as the primary vessel of the Wilmington Transportation Company's fleet. She made three trips weekly from San Pedro to Catalina Island and daily trips during the summer season. The *Hermosa* also served the Isthmus and is pictured here at the Isthmus Pier in 1901.

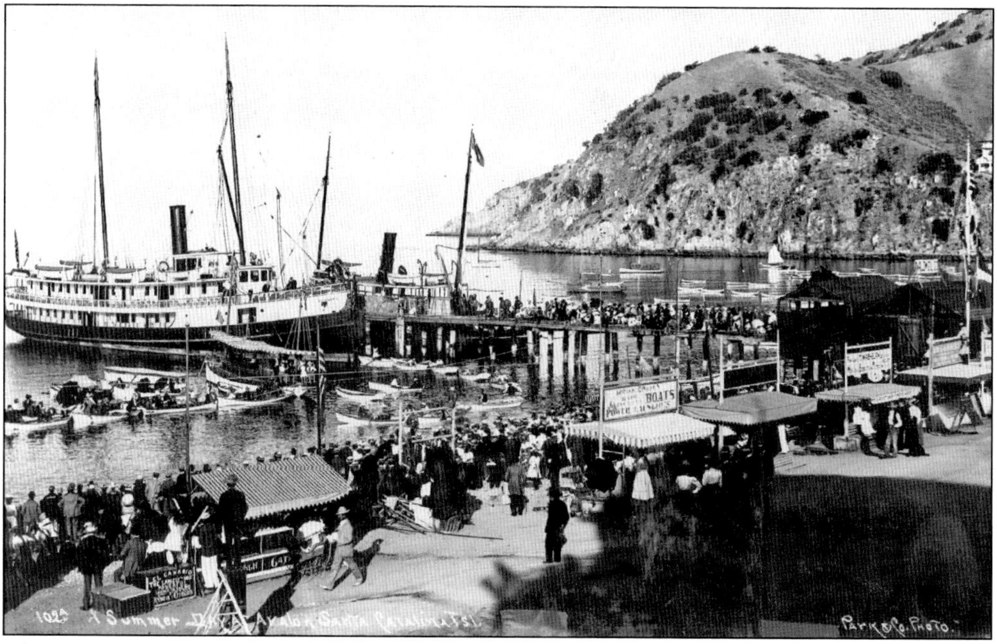

The *Hermosa* carried thousands of passengers to the island throughout her 14 years on the Catalina run. She was also leased on occasion during the winter season, spending the winter of 1890 ferrying people in Puget Sound and the winter of 1898 carrying passengers between Seattle and Skagway, Alaska. The *Hermosa* was decommissioned from the fleet in 1902, stripped of her luxuries, and burned in Avalon Bay during a Fourth of July celebration to make way for the SS *Hermosa II*.

By the turn of the 20th century, the Banning brothers not only owned the Wilmington Transportation Company, which operated a regularly scheduled steamer service to Catalina, they also owned the island itself. After seven successful years operating their company, the Bannings jumped on the opportunity to purchase Catalina in 1891.

Santa Catalina Island

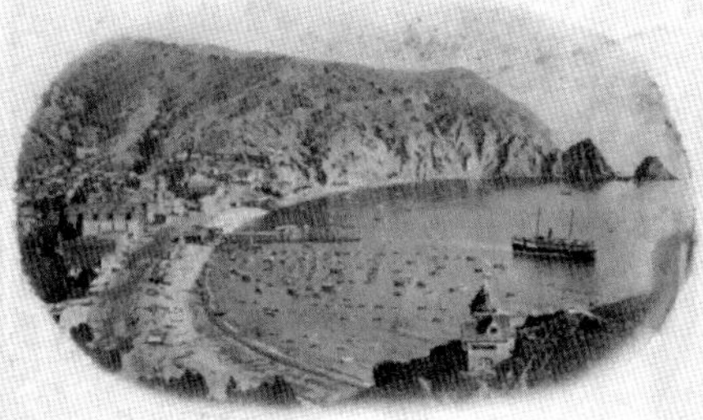

AVALON BAY

SANTA CATALINA ISLAND, three hours from Los Angeles; a park in the Pacific Ocean, off the Coast of Southern California. It is 22 miles long and contains 40,000 acres. A bit of the world by itself. Its climate, natural beauty and opportunity for sport perfect. Situated Lat. 32½ deg. N. long. 118½ W. Twenty-seven miles from the harbor of San Pedro, where steamer connection is made.

Banning Company

Pacific Electric Building, Sixth and Main Streets

Both Phones 36 Los Angeles, Cal.

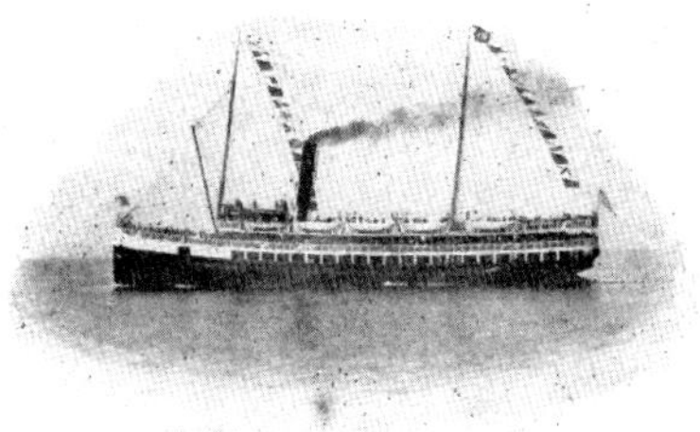

Time Card in Effect Sept. 21, 1909

Trains Leave Los Angeles	Daily	Saturdays Only
S. P. (Arcade Depot)	9 05 a.m.	
Salt Lake Railway (1st Street)	8 50 a.m.	
Pacific Electric Railway (6th and Main)	9 15 a.m.	5 00 p.m.
STEAMER Leaves SAN PEDRO	10 00 a.m.	5 45 p.m.
STEAMER Arrives AVALON	12 30 p.m.	8 00 p.m.
STEAMER LVS. AVALON	3 15 p.m.	
TRAINS ARRIVE		
S. P. (Arcade Depot)	6 35 p.m.	
Salt Lake Railway (1st Street)	6 30 p.m.	
Pacific Electric Railway (6th and Main)	6 35 p.m.	

REGULAR fare from Los Angeles to Catalina Island and return $2.75, good for sixty days.

EXCURSION rates, good going Saturday or Sunday, returning same day or the following Monday, $2.50.

The Wilmington Transportation Company reserves the right to change steamers and time of sailing without notice.

Santa Catalina Island Ticket Office

104 Main Entrance, Pacific Electric Building

Los Angeles, Cal. :: or Railway Depots

Phones: Sunset Main 4492, Home F-6576

The Banning brothers produced a variety of brochures and other literature that advertised the island to potential visitors. Each brochure listed an array of activities for the adventurous traveler, including the "world's best fishing grounds," submarine gardens, golf, boating, and bathing. The brochures also included timetables for the steamers. This card from 1909 advertises a round-trip fare of $2.75.

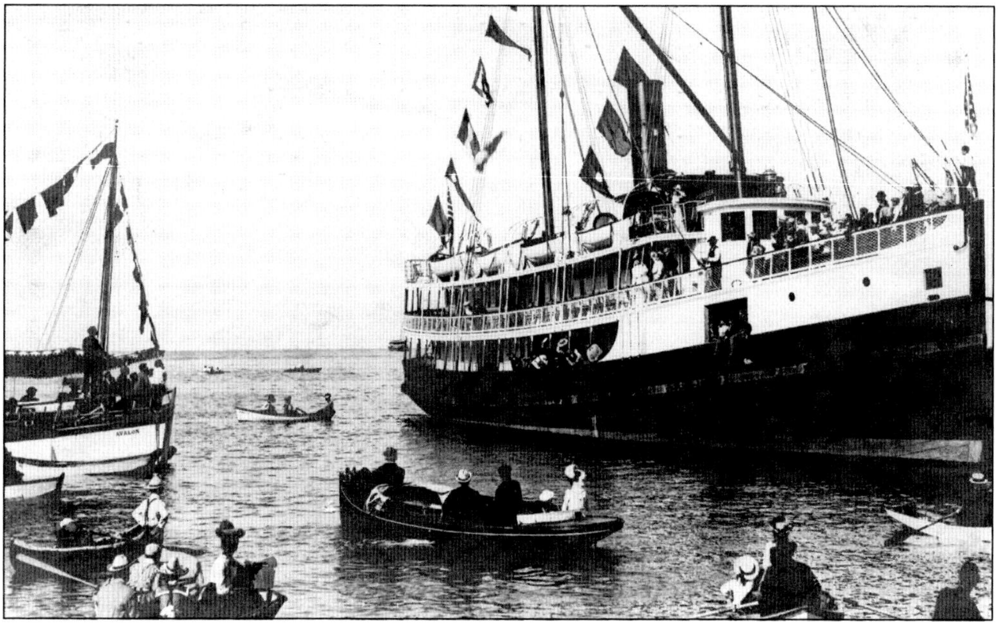

As the island's popularity increased, so did the need for bigger ships. The *Hermosa II* was launched in 1902 to replace the *Hermosa I*. The new, beautifully appointed vessel drastically increased its passenger limit to 700 from the 150 on the previous *Hermosa*. The *Hermosa II* was 145 feet in length with 325 horsepower and could do up to 12 knots.

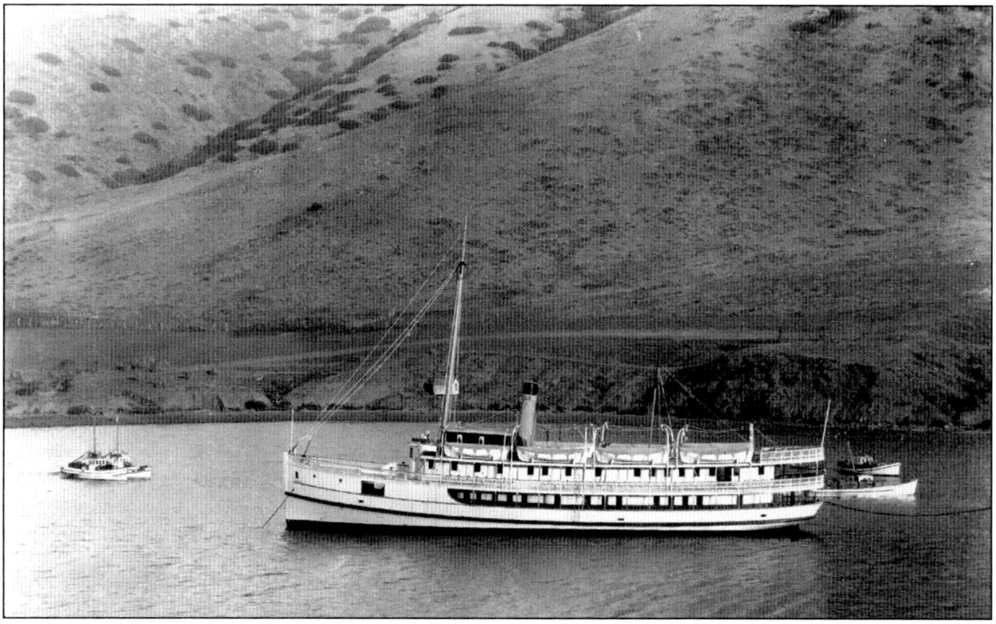

The *Hermosa II* served on the Catalina run from 1902 until 1920 when the SS *Avalon* replaced her as the primary ship. However, the *Hermosa II* continued to serve Catalina for several more years. She was used as a standby vessel for overflow passengers and made runs to the Isthmus. The *Hermosa II*, painted white, is pictured here in the Isthmus Cove in 1923. In 1928, she was sold and converted into a fishing vessel. While on a fishing expedition in Costa Rica in 1935, the *Hermosa II* was destroyed by fire.

The *Hermosa II* and the SS *Cabrillo* were both built specifically for the Catalina run by the Wilmington Transportation Company. The Banning brothers constructed the vessels in an effort to increase their fleet's size, as well as comfort for passengers. The trip across the channel is described in this brochure from the 1910s as "the two hour trip across the San Pedro Channel is delightful, intensely interesting and one long to be remembered."

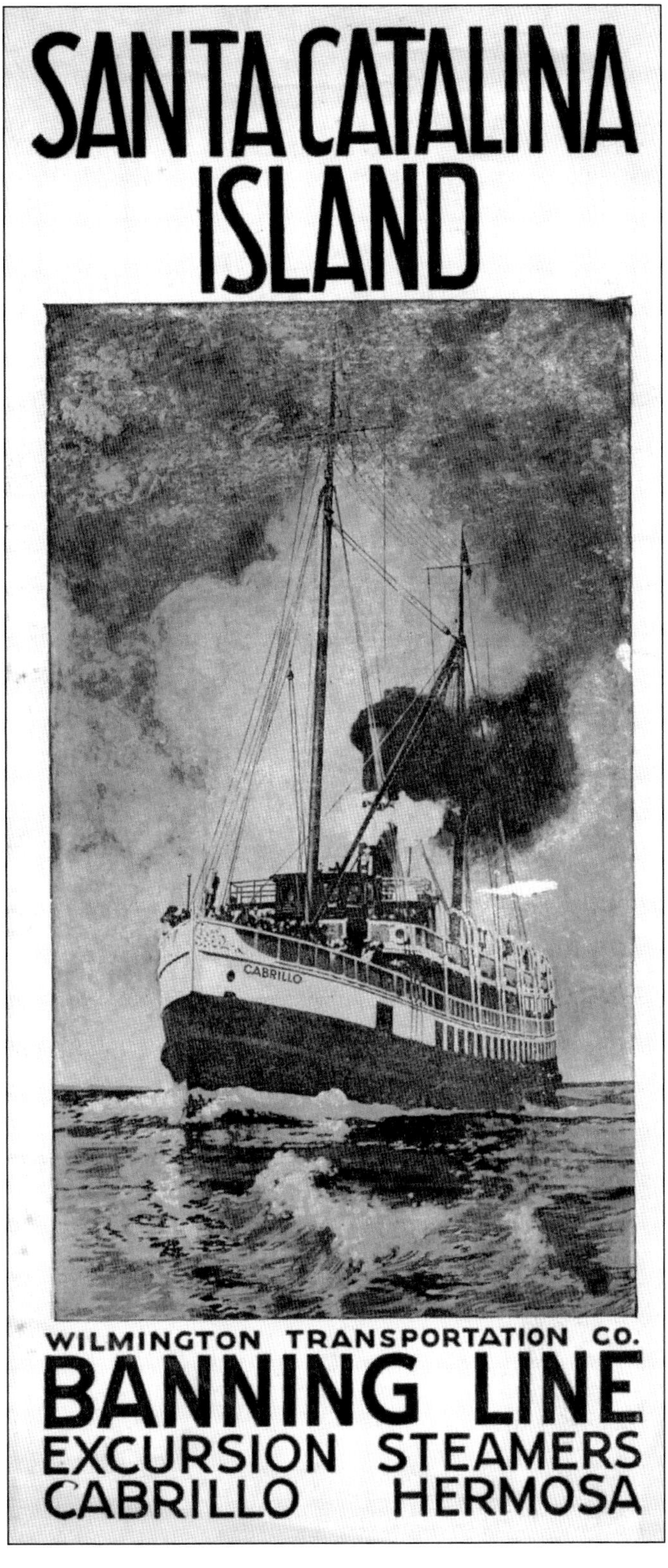

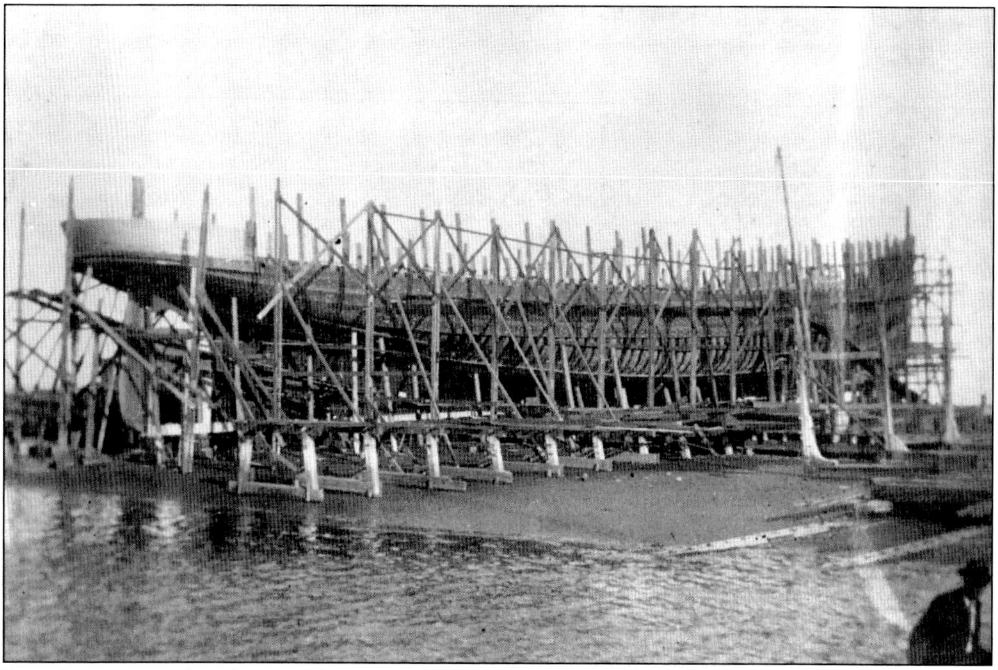

Less than a year after the completion of the *Hermosa II*, the Banning brothers realized that it was not big enough and they needed to build yet another bigger, more luxurious ship. The *Cabrillo* was planned and construction soon began in the Mormon Island Shipyards of Wilmington Transportation Company in San Pedro, California. This photograph shows the *Cabrillo* under construction in 1903.

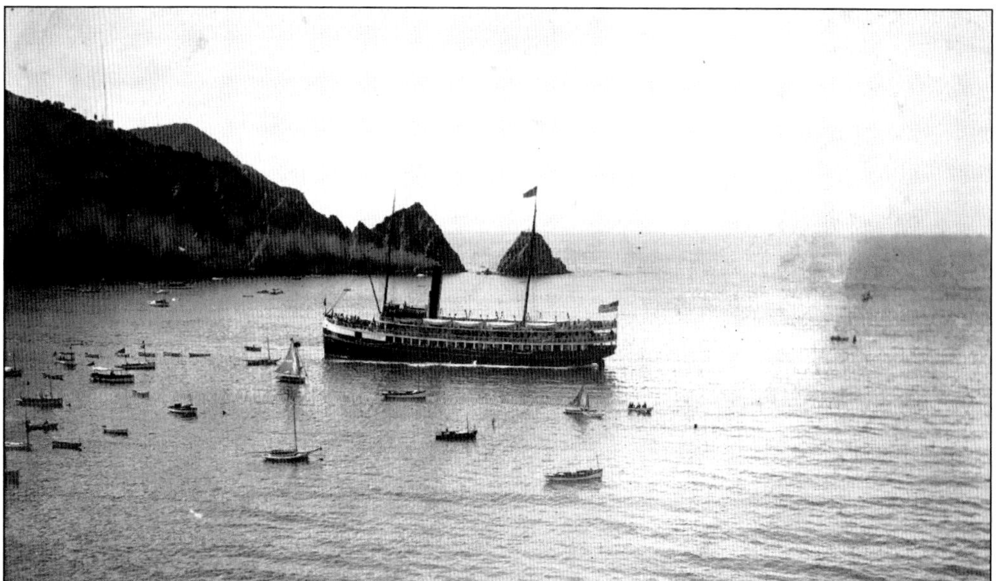

The *Cabrillo* was launched on the morning of February 15, 1904, by the Wilmington Transportation Company. She was christened by Margarethe Muller, the 11-year-old daughter of ship designer and builder William Muller, with a bottle of special christening champagne. Her superstructure was then added and by May 1904 the *Cabrillo* was delivered and placed on the Catalina run.

When launched, the *Cabrillo* was the most luxurious ship on the Catalina run. She was equipped with Javanese teak decks, a rosewood staircase, deep-pile carpeting, mahogany paneling, and a tiered-glass mahogany bar. She had 10 staterooms, a social hall, and a grillroom on the main deck for food service.

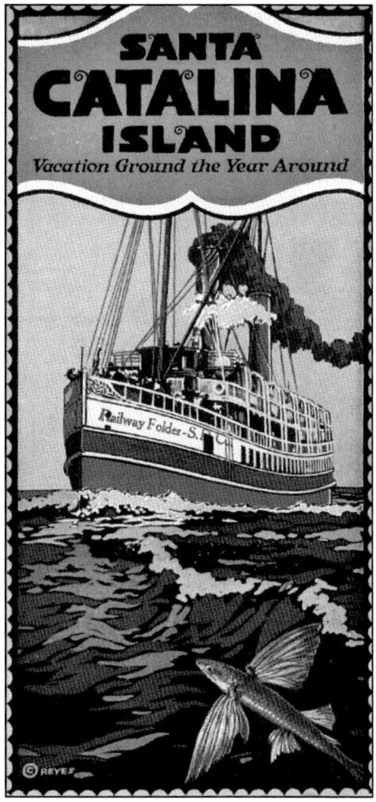

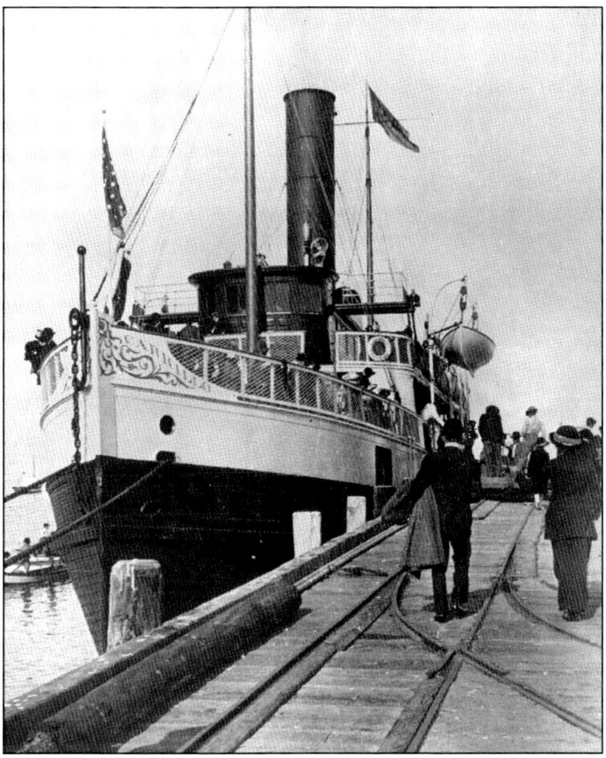

The *Cabrillo* quickly became the favorite vessel for visitors and residents alike. She was often called the "Queen of the South Coast" and lived up to this reputation. Beautifully appointed, she could make the trip across the channel in two hours. The *Cabrillo* continued to delight passengers for over 40 years and was a staple on the Catalina run until the beginning of World War II.

Time Table in Effect Apr. 2, 1914

Trains Leave Los Angeles	DAILY
Pac. Elec. Sta. (6th and Main Sts.)	9 15 a.m.
Salt Lake Route (East 1st St.)........	8 45 a.m.
Going Steamers	
Steamer Leaves San Pedro	10 05 a.m.
Steamer Arrives Avalon.	12 30 p.m.
Returning Steamers	
Steamer Leaves Avalon	3 15 p.m.
Steamer Arrives San Pedro	5 45 p.m.
Trains Arrive Los Angeles	
Pac. Elec. Sta. (6th and Main Sts.)	6 45 p.m.
Salt Lake Route (East 1st St.)........	7 10 p.m.

The Wilmington Transportation Co. reserves the right to change steamers and time of sailing without notice.

Baggage will be received for checking at Los Angeles: P. E. Ry. before 8:15 a. m.; Salt Lake Ry. before 8:30 a. m.

Regular fare from Los Angeles to Catalina Island and return, $2.75, good sixty days.

EXCURSION rates, good going Saturday or Sunday, returning the same day or the following Monday, $2.50.

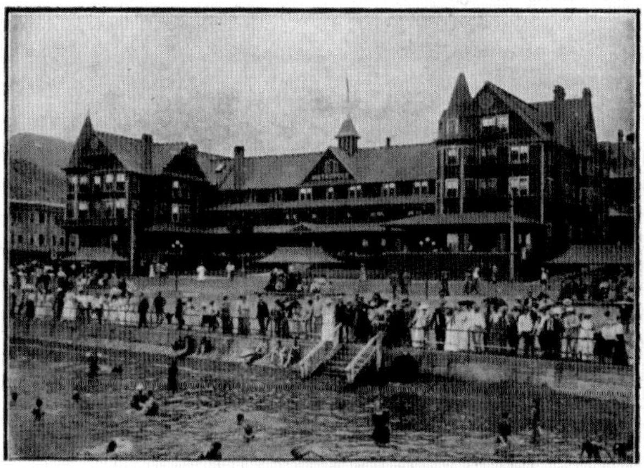

HOTEL METROPOLE

Now open for the Season

FORM C10 I 10 M-5-18-14 CADMUS PRESS

The *Cabrillo* was advertised as an "ocean going excursion steamer" by the Wilmington Transportation Company and made daily trips to the island. This timetable for 1914 provides the daily schedule for the vessel. Visitors who made day trips to the island only had about two and a half hours in Avalon, and the rest of the day was spent riding the steamer.

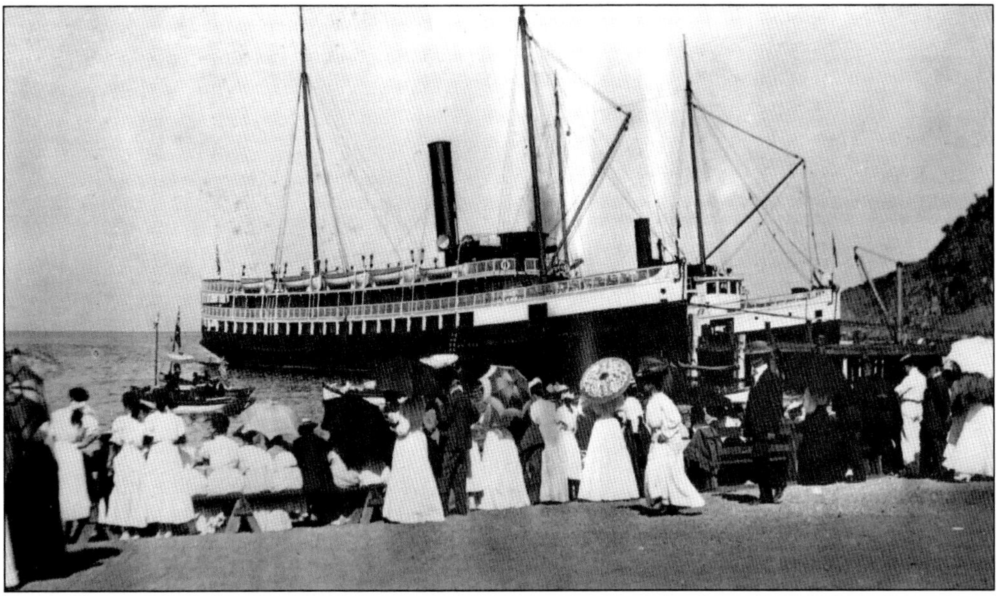

The *Cabrillo* was equipped with a triple-expansion steam engine that was oil-fired and built by United Engineering Works of San Francisco. Long time island resident Doug Bombard remembers that the engine "had a little thump to it and if you rode the boat very much you would never forget it."

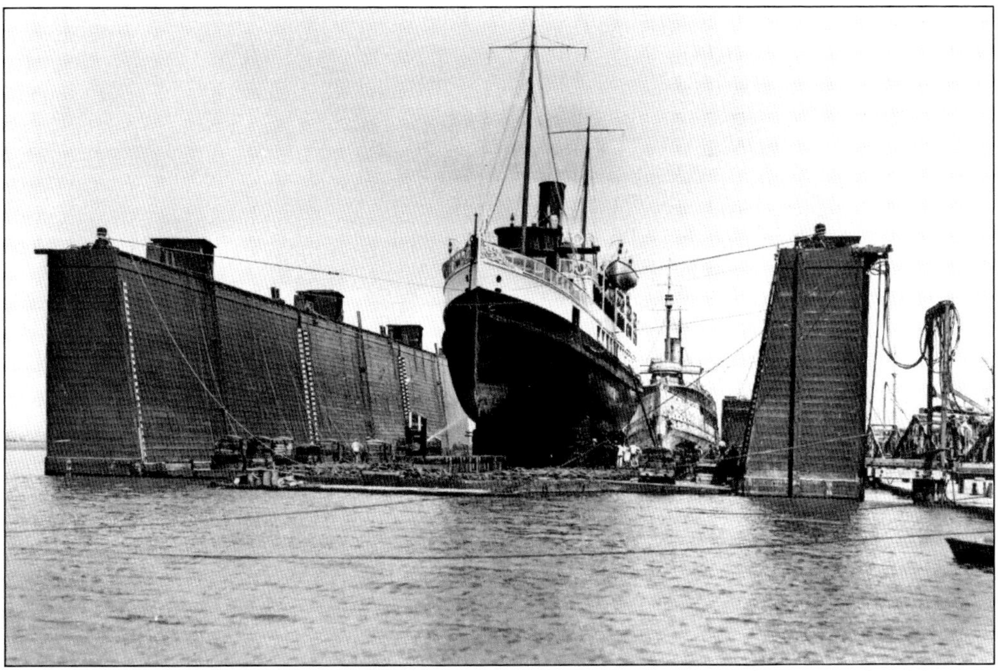

The well-designed, 194-foot vessel could carry up to 1,200 passengers. She was made of Oregon pine and Australian ironwood, and the bottom of the ship was covered with plates of copper sheath. She had a 13-and-a-half-foot propeller and could do up to 16 knots with 1,500 horsepower. The *Cabrillo* is pictured here in dry dock in San Pedro, California.

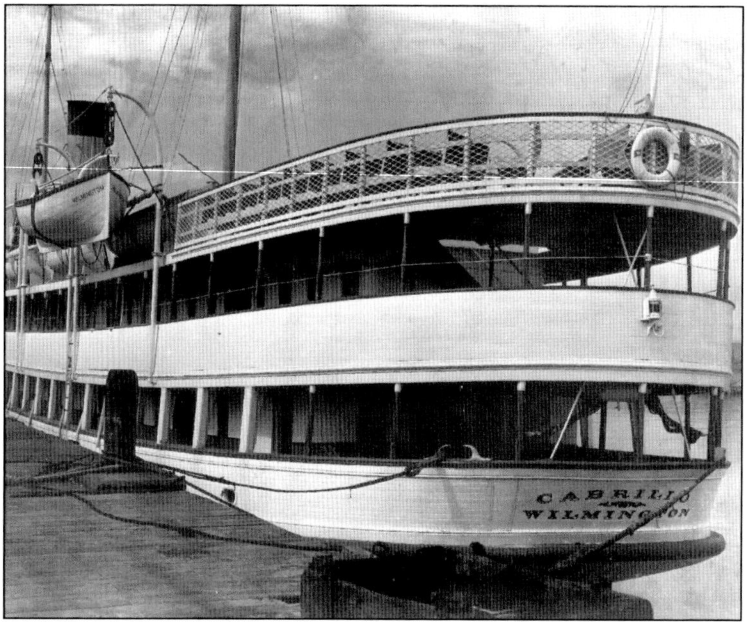

In the early 1920s, the *Cabrillo* was painted white and was joined on the Catalina run by the SS *Avalon* and SS *Catalina*. The iron and steel *Avalon* and *Catalina* soon took over as the primary vessels on the Catalina run, and the *Cabrillo* remained the last of the wooden excursion ships. She continued to carry thousands of passengers and delight them with her luxurious appointments.

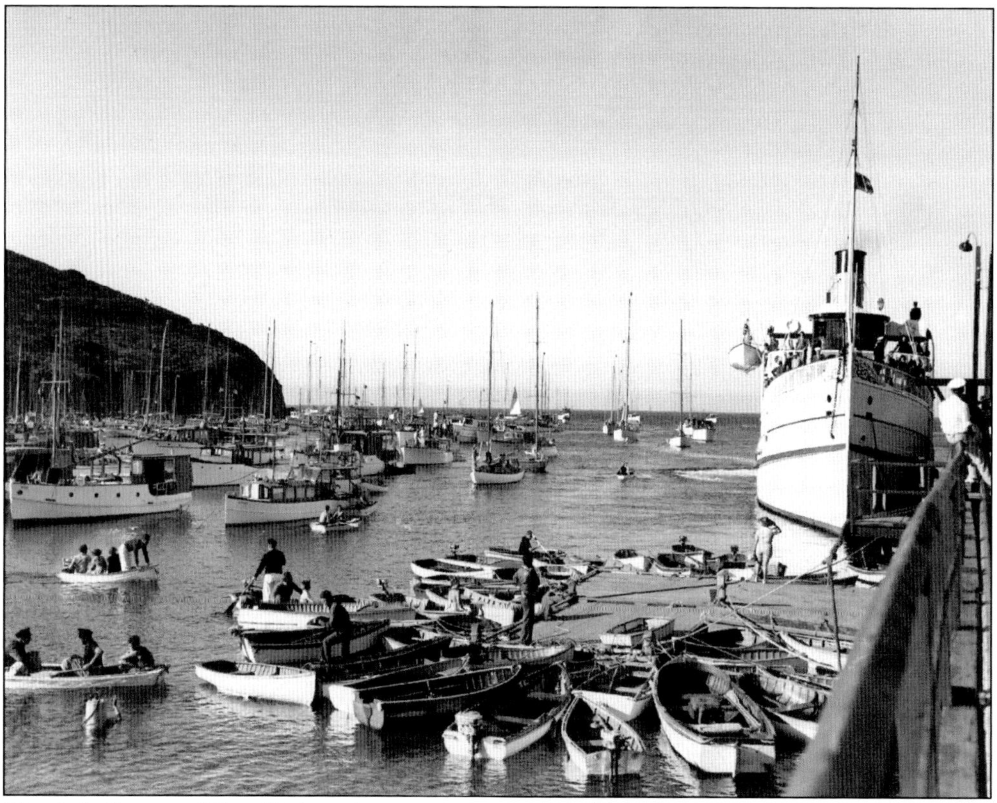

The *Cabrillo* served Two Harbors for many years and could dock at the Isthmus Pier, which was originally built as a steamer pier. During the 1920s and 1930s, the Isthmus was a popular yachting destination as it is today, but it was also known as the Isthmus Movie Colony because it served as the location for several motion picture productions.

The officers of the *Cabrillo* are pictured at the terminal in Wilmington. At center is the captain Frank Pennoyer, and to his right is chief engineer C. A. Harrison.

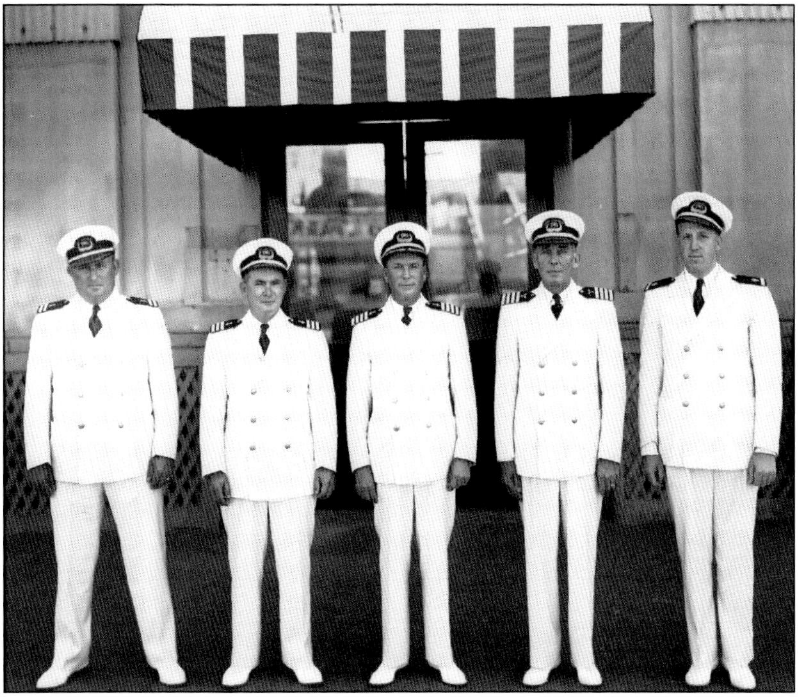

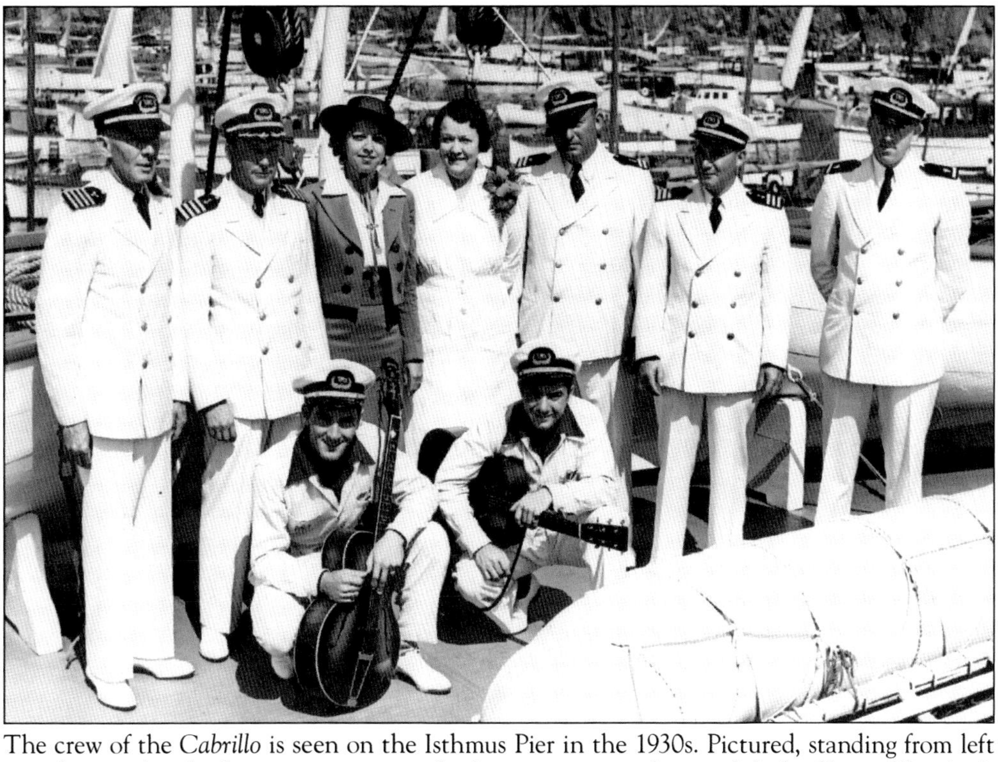

The crew of the *Cabrillo* is seen on the Isthmus Pier in the 1930s. Pictured, standing from left to right, are the chief engineer, captain, ship's courier, stewardess, and deck officers. The ship's entertainment crew are pictured in front. The crew was dedicated to providing passengers with every level of comfort and speed in crossing the channel.

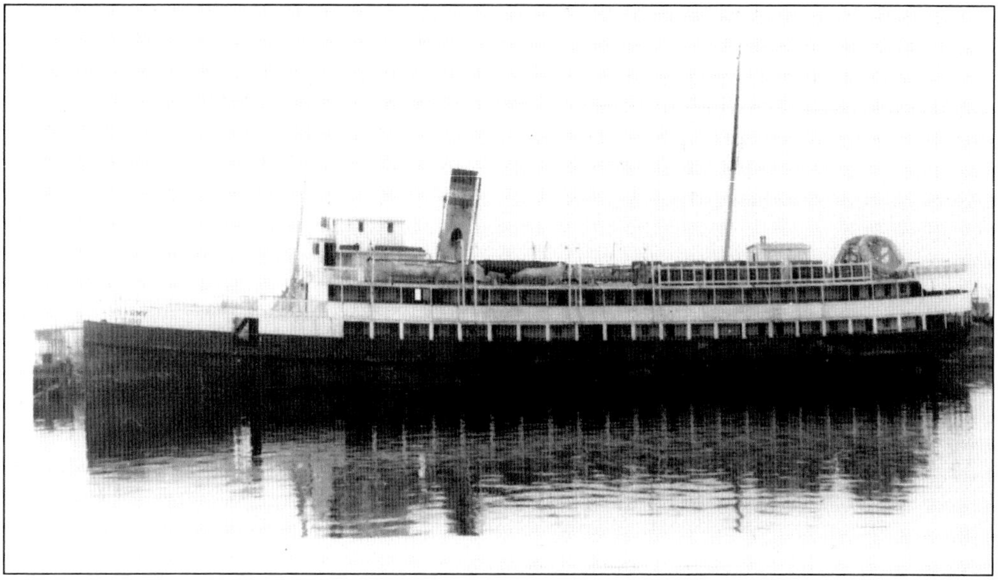

After the breakout of World War II, the *Cabrillo* was requisitioned by the United States War Shipping Administration and taken to San Francisco. She served as troop transport, carrying soldiers to Camp Stoneham in Stockton, California, and to points in San Francisco Bay. The U.S. Army later purchased the *Cabrillo* and operated her until January 1947. She was then moved to Cuttings Wharf in Napa, California. The *Cabrillo* is pictured here at Cuttings Wharf in 1948.

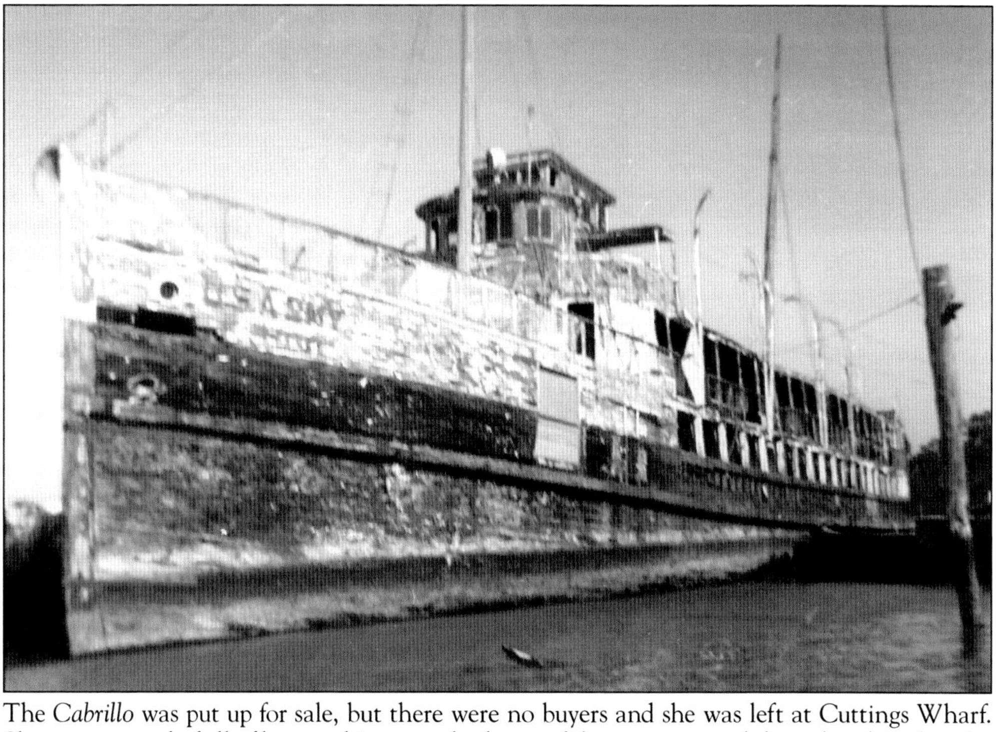

The *Cabrillo* was put up for sale, but there were no buyers and she was left at Cuttings Wharf. She was stripped of all of her machinery and other useful equipment and then abandoned to the elements. The *Cabrillo* is pictured here at Cuttings Wharf in 1961.

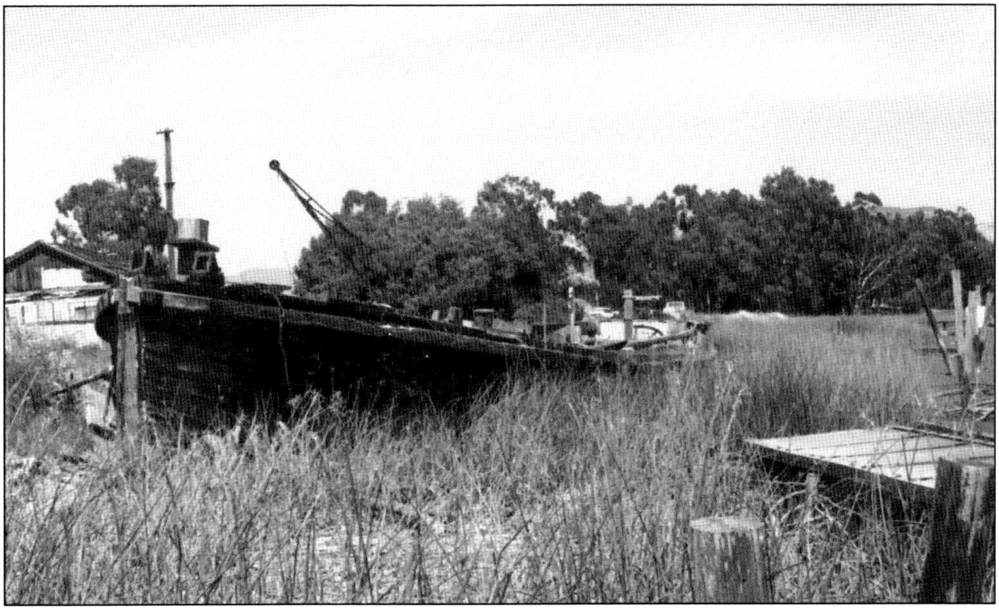

The SS *Cabrillo* slowly deteriorated over the years and is pictured here on the Napa River in 1986. The entire superstructure has been stripped and not much remains but the hull. Today, little if anything remains of the once graceful, wooden excursion ship that served Catalina so well for so many years.

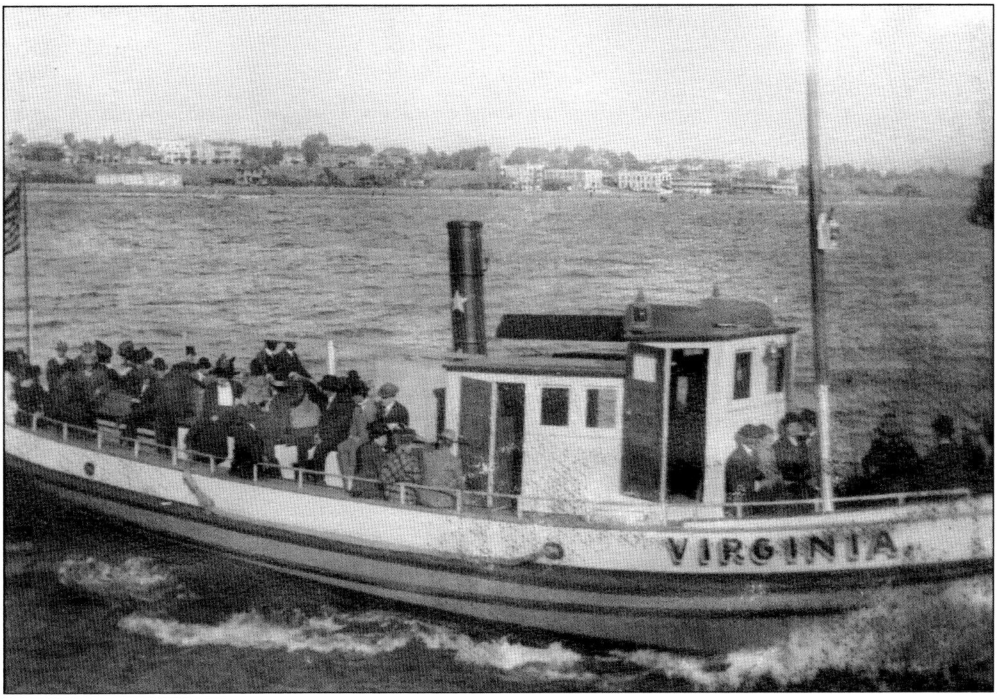

Little is known about the steamer *Virginia* except that she provided independent service to Catalina Island from Long Beach in 1910. There was no covered seating on the *Virginia*, so passengers spent three hours soaking up the sun and sea air as they crossed the San Pedro Channel to Catalina Island.

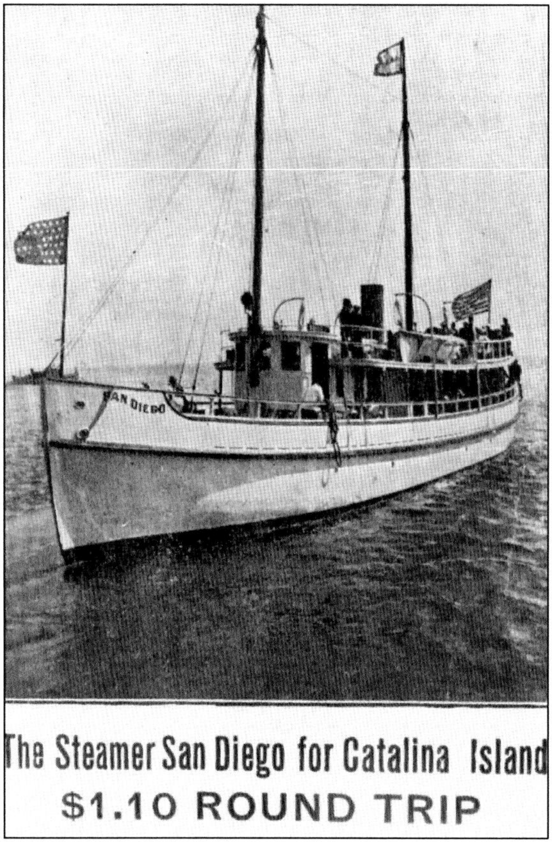

The steamer SS *San Diego* offered trips to Catalina Island between 1913 and 1914. The *San Diego* was an independent service that operated from the Pine Avenue Pier in Long Beach. The *San Diego* provided daily trips to Catalina Island during the summer season, departing Long Beach at 10:00 a.m. and leaving from Avalon at 3:00 p.m.

The *San Diego* was 107 feet long and well appointed with staterooms, cabins, and a piano. The ship was advertised as the largest and only boat offering safety and comfort running between Long Beach and Catalina. The round-trip fare to Catalina was $1.10.

Daily Excursions to Catalina Island

ON THE RELIABLE STEAMER "SAN DIEGO"

$1.10 Round Trip From Long Beach

Leave PINE AVENUE PIER at 10 a. m. Daily, weather permittfng. Returning, Leave CATALINA at 3 p. m.

The Steamer SAN DIEGO is 107 feet long, 105 tons, modern in equipment with piano, state rooms, cabins, etc., under government inspection, provided with enough life boats, life rafts and life preservers to carry all passengers and crew. Plenty of room, safety and comfort.

The largest boat and the only boat so equipped running between Long Beach and Catalina.

The right is reserved to land passengers at the municipal wharf inside Long Beach Harbor when the sea is too rough to land at the pier. Street car connections to all points.

TICKETS on sale at booth No. 4, end of pier, and Hotel Arlington cigar stand, 200 W. Ocean avenue, Long Beach.

PHONES: PIER, Home 369, Sunset 667-W; OFFICE, Home 9, Sunset 499-J

☞ Make Reservations in Advance

CATALINA TRANSPORTATION LINE

OFFICE NO. 2 SOUTH PACIFIC AVE.

CAPT. E. E. NAPIER, MGR. L. W. FOLSOM O. O. OUTCALT, SEC.

Two

SS Avalon

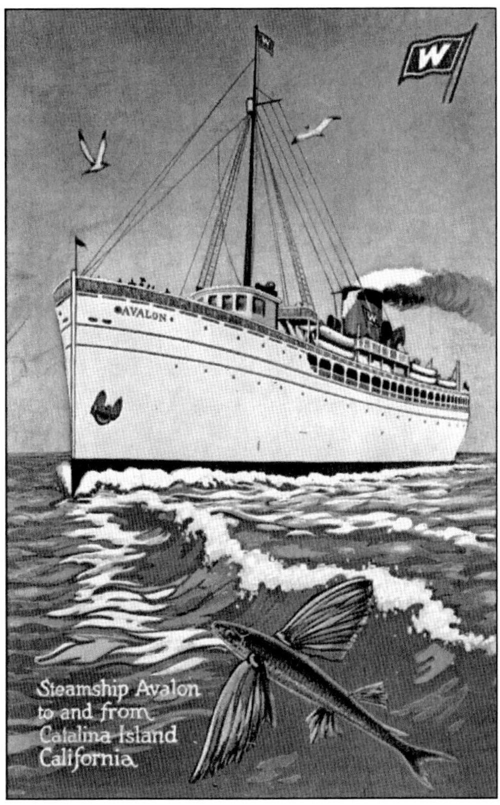

Upon his purchase of Catalina Island and Wilmington Transportation Company in 1919, William Wrigley Jr. understood the crucial importance of water transportation to the success of the island. He felt that the passengers should be comfortable and the trip should not be too long. Wrigley immediately sought to increase the amenities and size of the Wilmington Transportation Company fleet. The first ship introduced by Wrigley was the SS *Avalon*. Originally built as the SS *Virginia*, the ship made the run between Chicago and Milwaukee on Lake Michigan between 1891 and 1918. The U.S. Navy requisitioned her during World War I and Wrigley later tracked her down in a navy yard in Boston in 1919. The ship sailed for Los Angeles and received extensive alterations and refitting. The *Avalon* was soon ready to carry passengers to Catalina Island, which she did for 31 years.

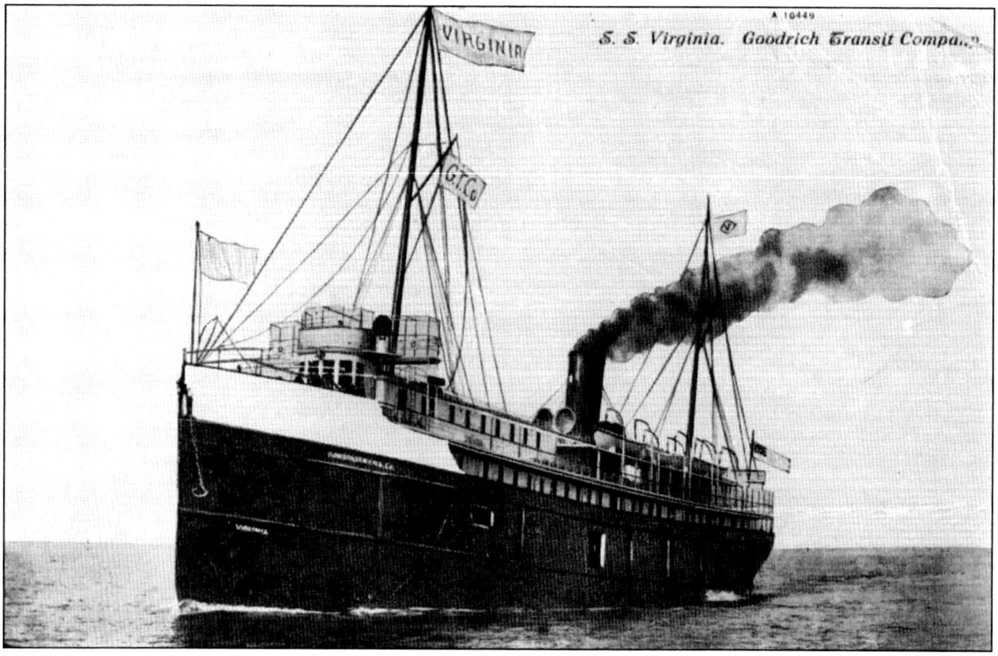

The Goodrich Transfer Company launched the *Virginia* in 1891. She served on the run between Milwaukee and Chicago on Lake Michigan. The *Virginia* was built of iron by Globe Iron Works of Cleveland, Ohio. She was 278 feet in length and equipped with twin reciprocating steam engines. Under full throttle she could do 16 knots. The vessel was elegantly appointed and very popular with the traveling public because of her speed and comfort.

The • Virginia

THIS steel passenger steamer, built to order by the Globe Iron Works, is pronounced by the *Marine Review* (a recognized authority in all matters relating to the construction and equipment of vessels) to be not only "the trimmest, neatest, handsomest and most elegantly appointed passenger steamship built, but more than that, the finest ship that flies the American flag." The none too extravagant expressions about her yacht-like lines and sylph-like mold (it adds) are all contained in the fact that her per cent. of fullness, or co-efficient is .61, fully .15 less than any large steamer on the lakes, and equal to the finest lined ocean steamship. The dimensiones of hull are 278 feet over all, 260 feet keel, 38 feet beam and 25 feet deep. The water bottom (divided into 6 sections, 3 on either side) contains a tank that will hold 4,500 gallons of fresh water.

The *Virginia* was pronounced "a floating palace and the finest steamer that flies the American flag" by the *Chicago Tribune* in 1891. She was magnificently appointed with polished mahogany woodwork and decorated plate-glass windows. She had several large staterooms, a dining room, and salon. The *Virginia* was later requisitioned by the U.S. Navy in 1918, and renamed the USS *Blueridge*. She was decommissioned in 1919, having seen no action.

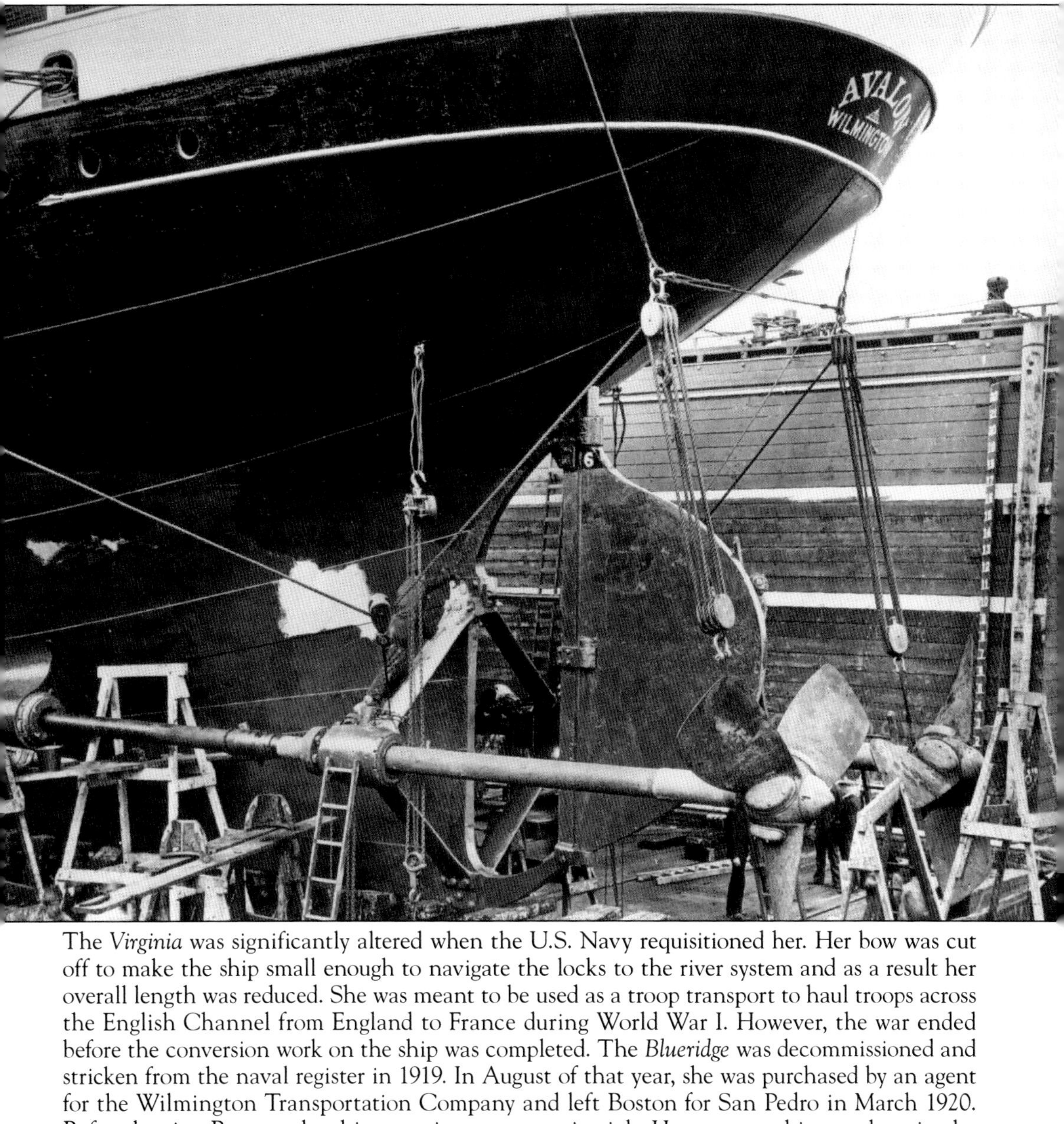

The *Virginia* was significantly altered when the U.S. Navy requisitioned her. Her bow was cut off to make the ship small enough to navigate the locks to the river system and as a result her overall length was reduced. She was meant to be used as a troop transport to haul troops across the English Channel from England to France during World War I. However, the war ended before the conversion work on the ship was completed. The *Blueridge* was decommissioned and stricken from the naval register in 1919. In August of that year, she was purchased by an agent for the Wilmington Transportation Company and left Boston for San Pedro in March 1920. Before leaving Boston, the ship was given a new paint job. However, as this was done in the winter months, some of the paint froze in place and did not dry completely. As the ship sailed into warmer water temperatures, the paint began to melt away. The vessel passed through the Panama Canal on March 18, 1920, and arrived in San Pedro where she was placed in dry dock for repairs and another coat of paint.

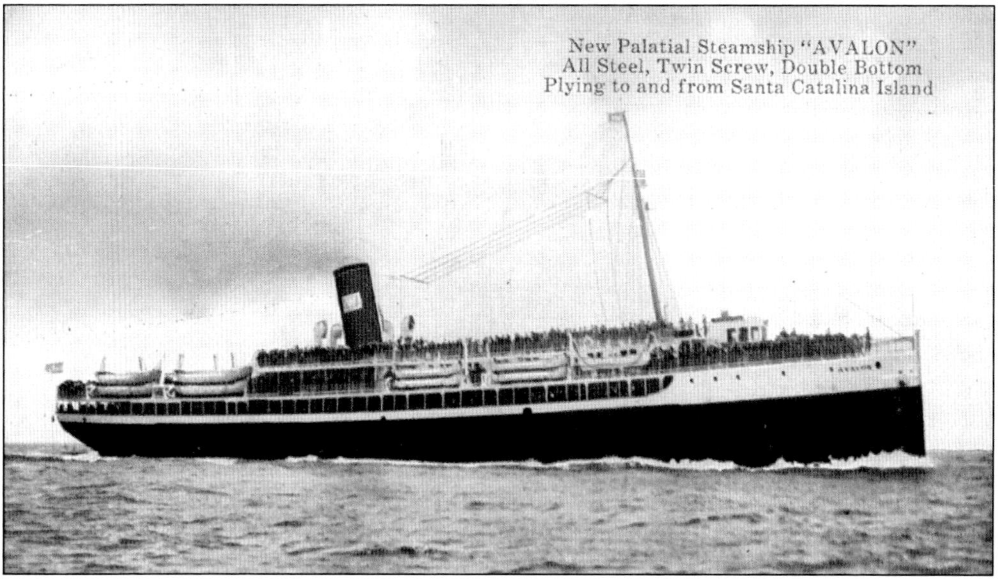

The *Avalon* was soon ready to start her career on the Catalina run and she made her maiden voyage across the San Pedro Channel on April 11, 1920. There was some initial hesitation among passengers regarding the safety of the vessel because in her former life as the *Virginia* her sister ship, the SS *Eastland*, met a tragic end on the Chicago River in 1915, killing hundreds of passengers. A rumor started that linked the *Avalon* to this incident, but it was quickly hushed once she arrived safely in Avalon Bay.

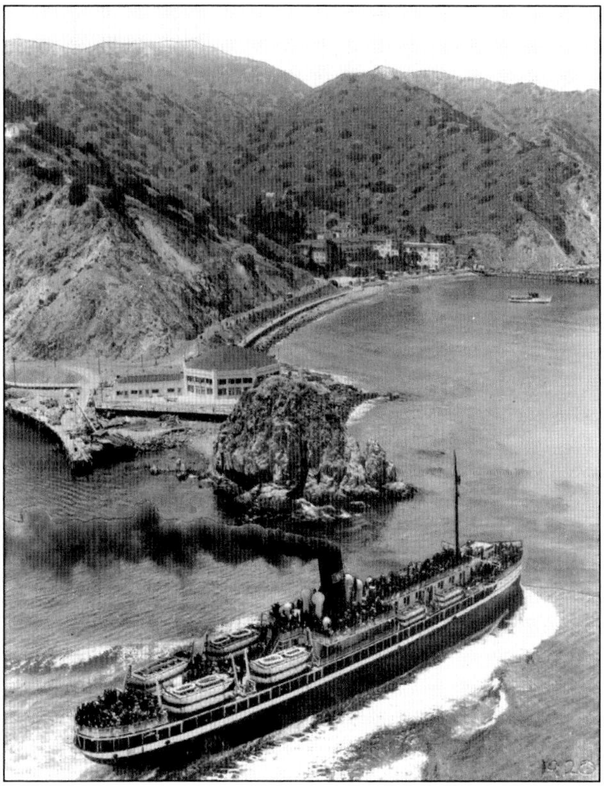

The *Avalon* became a quick favorite with travelers as she was elegantly appointed and was the largest passenger steamship to date plying the channel between the mainland and Catalina Island.

The *Avalon* soon became the flagship of the Wilmington Transportation Company fleet. This brochure from 1920 describes her as "a floating palace 300 feet in length, with a 42-foot beam. The staterooms for passengers are on the upper deck, aft of the bridge. Amidships are four deluxe cabins with private baths and hot and cold running water. Both forward and aft of the engine rooms are two magnificent ballrooms, finished in mahogany, with fancy glass windows and mirrors."

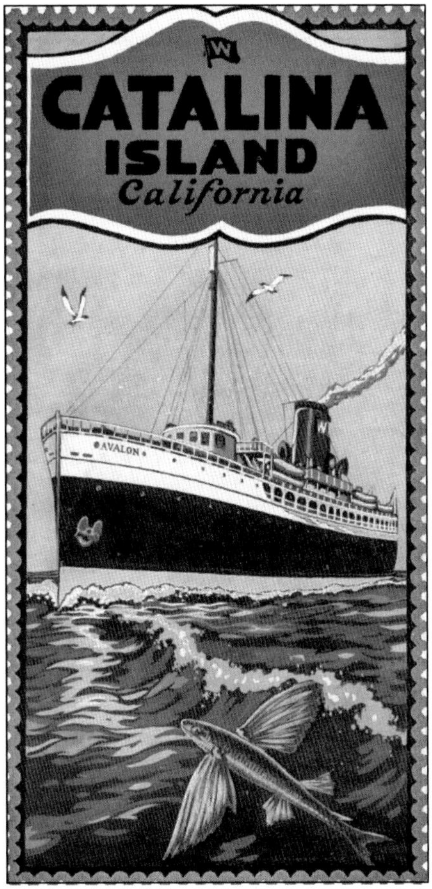

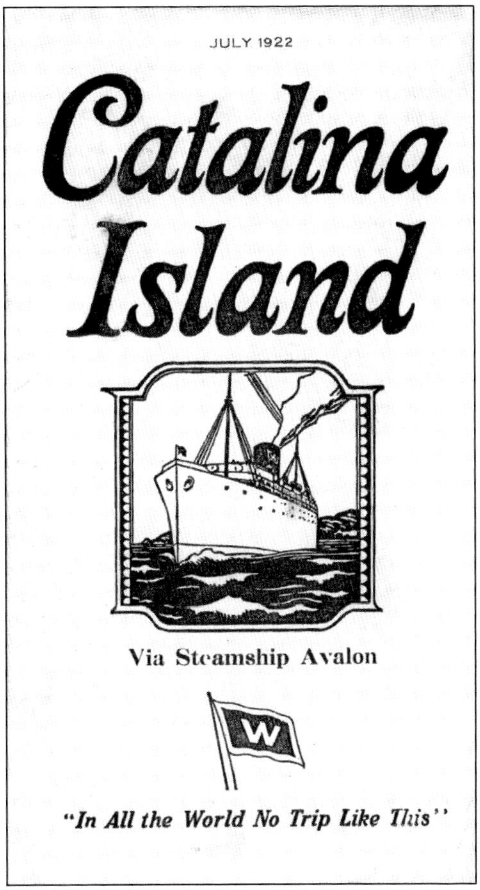

This brochure from 1922 advertises Catalina Island via Steamship *Avalon* as "In All The World No Trip Like This." This is one of the first known uses of this popular slogan used to advertise Catalina Island for many years.

CATALINA ISLAND LINE

★ LOS ANGELES TO AVALON ★

WILMINGTON TRANSPORTATION COMPANY

Effective May 1, 1923

SCHEDULE AND FARES

(Pacific Electric Through Trains Direct to Catalina Terminal at Wilmington Los Angeles Harbor)

Motorists should avail themselves of the fares from Wilmington—Tickets from Wilmington are on sale at all offices

From Los Angeles

Daily

Lv. Los Angeles, 6th & Main.... 9:00 a. m.
Lv. L. A. Harbor. Wilmington..10.00 a. m.
Ar. Avalon, Catalina Island......12:25 p. m.
Lv. Avalon........................ 4:00 p. m.
Ar. L. A. Harbor.................. 6:20 p. m.
Ar. Los Angeles.................. 7:15 p. m.

From Long Beach

Daily

Lv. Long Beach, Ocean Ave..... 9:15 a. m.
Lv. L. A. Harbor, Wilmington..10:00 a. m.
Ar. Avalon, Catalina Island......12:25 p. m.
Lv. Avalon .... 4:00 p. m.
Ar. L. A. Harbor.................. 6:20 p. m.
Ar. Long Beach.................. 6:45 p. m.

From Pasadena

Through Train Daily Except Sunday

Lv. Pasadena, P.E.Sta. Colo. St. 8:30 a. m.
Lv. L. A. Harbor, Wilmington..10:00 a. m.
Ar. Avalon, Catalina Island......12:25 p. m.
Lv. Avalon .... 4:00 p. m.
Ar. L. A. Harbor.................. 6:20 p. m.
Ar. Pasadena .... 8:00 p. m.

NOTE: AFTERNOON SERVICE TO THE ISLAND, AND MORNING RETURN FROM THE ISLAND EFFECTIVE JUNE 16, 1923.

From Los Angeles

(Daily except Sunday)

Lv. Los Angeles, 6th & Main.... 2:45 p. m.
Lv. L. A. Harbor, Wilmington.. 3:45 p. m.
Ar. Avalon, Catalina Island..... 6:15 p. m.
Lv. Avalon .... 8:00 a. m.
Ar. L. A. Harbor..................10:15 a. m.
Ar. Los Angeles..................11:15 a. m.

Pacific Electric trains leave from, and arrive at 6th and Main Station, Los Angeles.

From Long Beach

(Daily Except Sunday)

Lv. Long Beach, Ocean Ave..... 3:00 p. m.
Lv. L. A. Harbor, Wilmington.. 3:45 p. m.
Ar. Avalon, Catalina Island...... 6:15 p. m.
Lv. Avalon .... 8:00 a. m.
Ar. L. A. Harbor..................10:15 a. m.
Ar. Long Beach..................10:45 a. m.

Pacific Electric trains leave from and arrive at Pacific and Ocean Aves., Long Beach.

From Pasadena

(Daily except Sunday)
(Take Short Line, Colorado & Fair Oaks)

Lv. Pasadena .... 2:00 p.m.
Lv. Los Angeles, 6th & Main.... 2:45 p. m.
Lv. L. A. Harbor, Wilmington.. 3:45 p. m.
Ar. Avalon, Catalina Island..... 6:15 p. m.
Lv. Avalon .... 8:00 a. m.
Ar. L. A. Harbor..................10:15 a. m.
Ar. Los Angeles..................11:15 a. m.
Ar. Pasadena .... 12:30 p. m.

Pacific Electric trains for morning boat leave from S. P.—P. E. Station, Colorado and Broadway, Pasadena.

Catalina baggage cars leave P. E. Baggage Room, Sixth and Los Angeles Sts., Los Angeles at 8:20 a. m. daily
(Wilmington Trans. Co. reserves the right to change steamers and time of sailing without notice.)

FARES	From Los Angeles		From Long Beach		From Pasadena		From Wilmington	
	Full Fare	Half Fare	Full Fare	Half Fare	Full Fare	Half Fare	Full Fare	Half Fare
Round Trip to Catalina, 60 day return limit from Los Angeles, 10 day return limit from Long Beach and Pasadena	$ 3.10	$ 1.55	$ 2.45	$ 1.23	$ 3.55	$ 1.78	$ 2.25	$ 1 15
Round Trip to Catalina, including ride on Glass Bottom Boat over Submarine Gardens; same return limits as above	3.85	1.95	3.20	1:63	4.30	2.18	3.00	1.55
Complete One Day Trip. including round trip to Catalina, also ride on Glass Bottom Boat and luncheon at Hotel St. Catherine, same limits................	5.00	3.20	4.45	2.88	5.50	3.43	4.25	2.80

TICKETS

Main Entrance P. E. Bldg., 6th & Main, Los Angeles
Phone Pico 36 or 10864
6364 Hollywood Blvd. — Ph. Holly 4214
148 E. Colorado St., Pasadena. — Phone F. O. 46
126 W. Ocean Ave., Long Beach. — Phone 619-74

523 Beacon St., San Pedro. — Phone 1067
680 Main St., Riverside. — Phone 161
700 Main St., Riverside. — Phone 271
217 E. Broadway, San Diego. — Phone Main 1157
Catalina Terminal, foot of Canal St., Wilmington.
Phone Wilmington 127

Along with the introduction of the *Avalon*, the Wilmington Transportation Company opened a new terminal building in Los Angeles Harbor. Passengers could access the terminal from several points throughout Los Angeles via Pacific Electric trains. This brochure from 1923 includes the schedules for the trains originating from Los Angeles, Long Beach, and Pasadena, as well as the fares for cross-channel transportation. It was also possible to motor down to Wilmington, where one could park a car for 50¢ per day. A round-trip fare at this time was between $2.25 and $3.10, depending on the point of origin. The brochure also advertises a day trip package that included a round-trip to and from Catalina, a glass-bottom boat ride, and a luncheon at the Hotel St. Catherine for between $4.25 and $5.00.

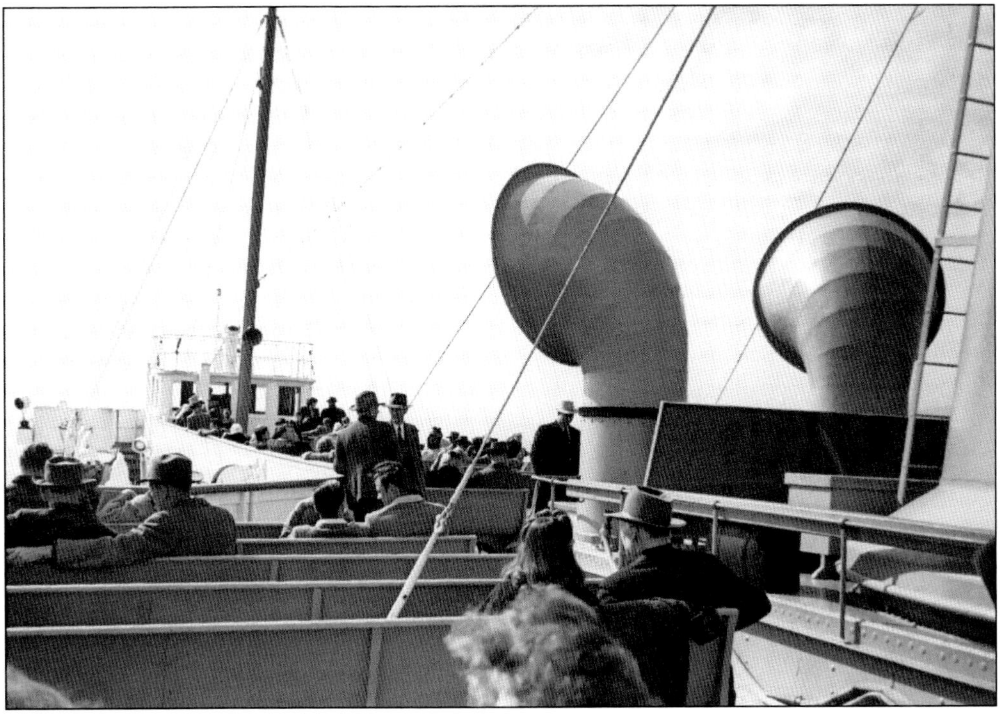

This is a view of the top deck of the *Avalon*. Passengers enjoyed tremendous views from there, spotting marine life and breathing in the salt air. At the beginning of her career on the Catalina run, the *Avalon* could carry up to 1,625 passengers with a crew of 60.

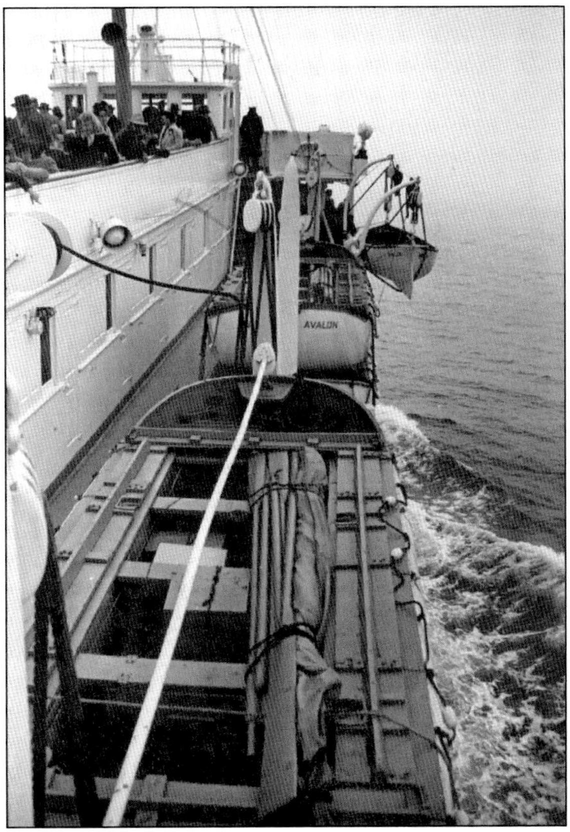

The *Avalon* was equipped with eight large lifeboats with a capacity for 76 passengers and eight smaller lifeboats with a capacity for 50 passengers each. According to an article about the *Avalon* in the *Los Angeles Times* in 1920, "every device possible for safety has been installed."

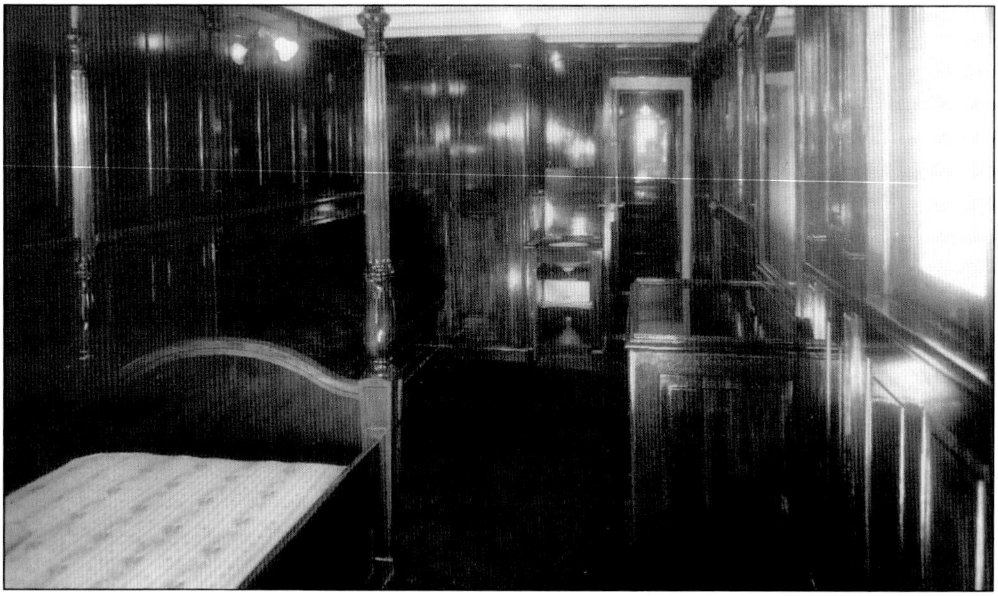

The *Avalon* had several staterooms, including four deluxe cabins with private baths. Ada Blanche Wrigley Schreiner, the granddaughter of William Wrigley Jr. remembers that her family was allowed to use the captain's quarters aboard the *Avalon* during the 1930s. She recalls that "these quarters were very sumptuous. The quarters were all dark, rich mahogany with everything possible built in. The bed was a large built-in with mahogany sides. The chests of drawers were also built in and very large. Even the walls were mahogany. It was very comfortable." (Courtesy of the Santa Catalina Island Company.)

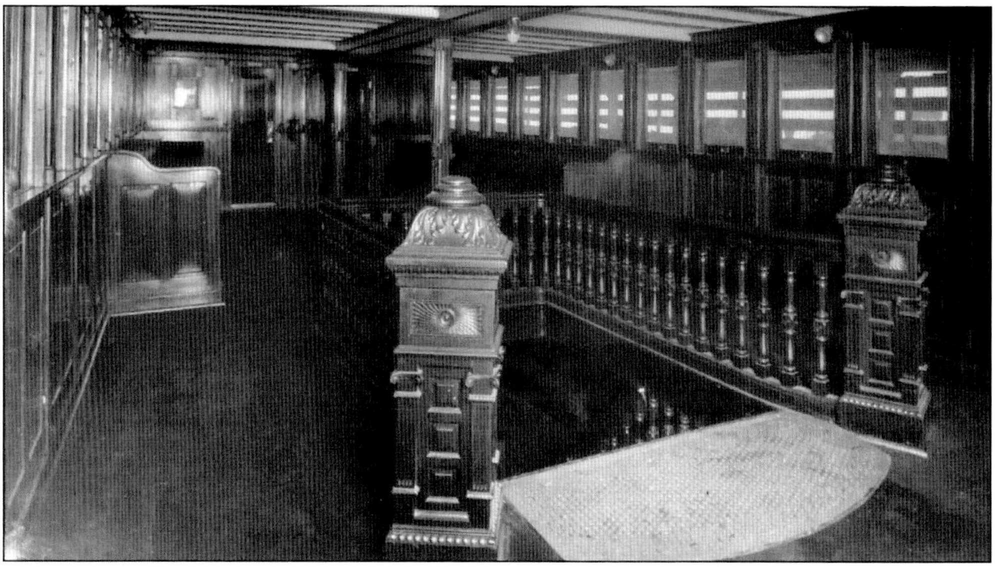

This is an interior view of the mahogany-rich *Avalon*. Ada Blanche "Blanny" Wrigley Schreiner recalled that she and her sister used to run about the ship, exploring every corner. Blanny and Deedee especially enjoyed trips across the channel when the seas were rough. They would go down to the ballroom and watch the passengers try to dance with the swells of the ocean. The *Avalon* had two ballrooms, and bands would to entertain passengers during the crossing. (Courtesy of the Santa Catalina Island Company.)

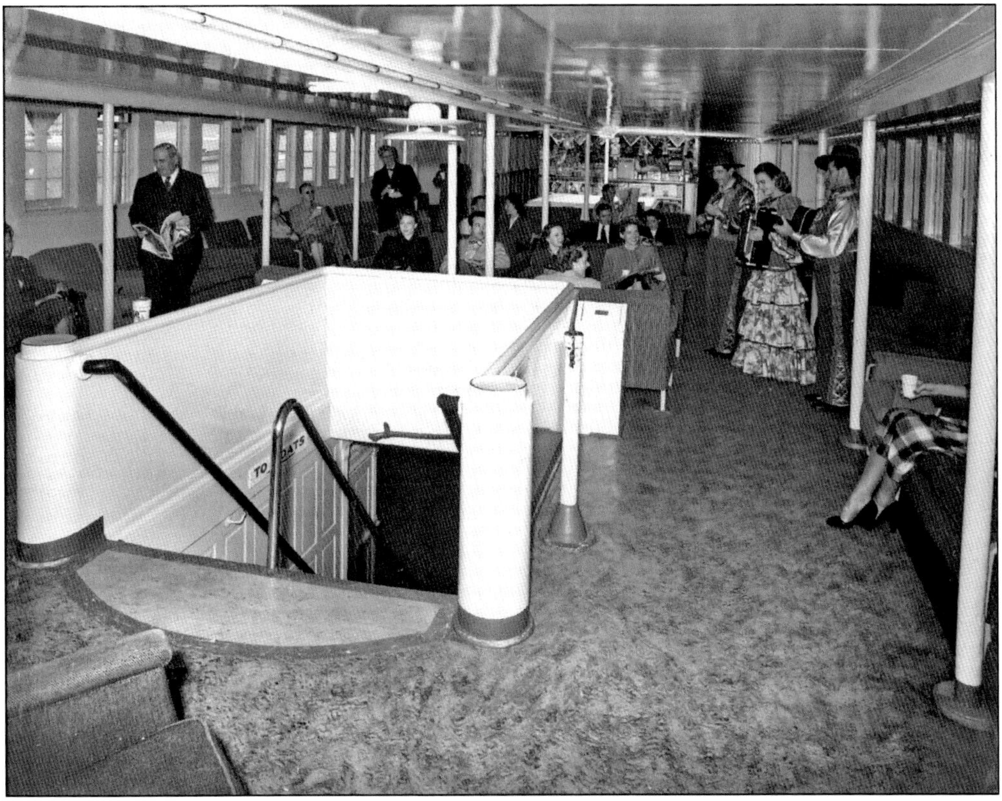

In the late 1940s, the *Avalon* was modernized and much of the dark mahogany woodwork was painted white. Passengers of the *Avalon* are pictured here relaxing in the salon while a Mexican band serenades them in 1948.

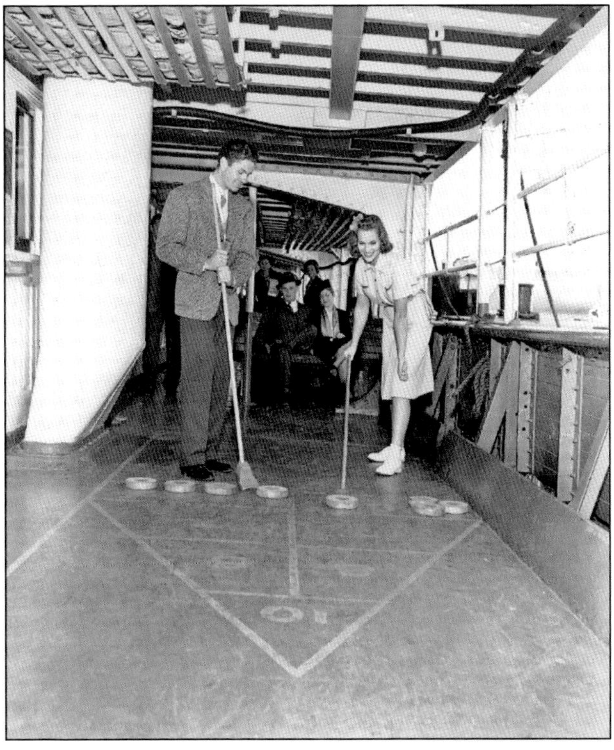

If passengers did not want to gaze out to sea or dance across the channel, they could play a game of shuffleboard. A variety of activities ensured that everyone would enjoy the voyage.

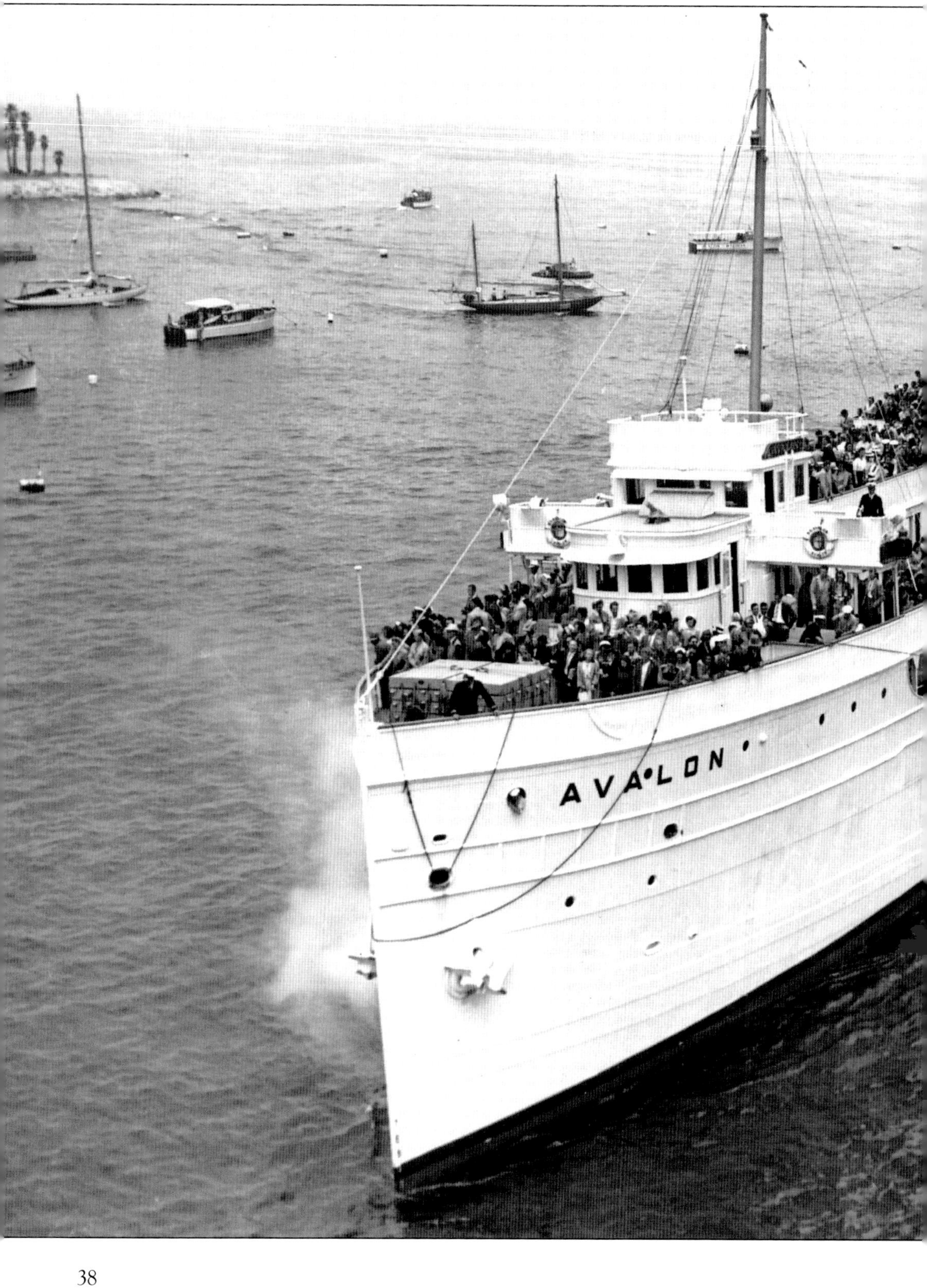
AVALON

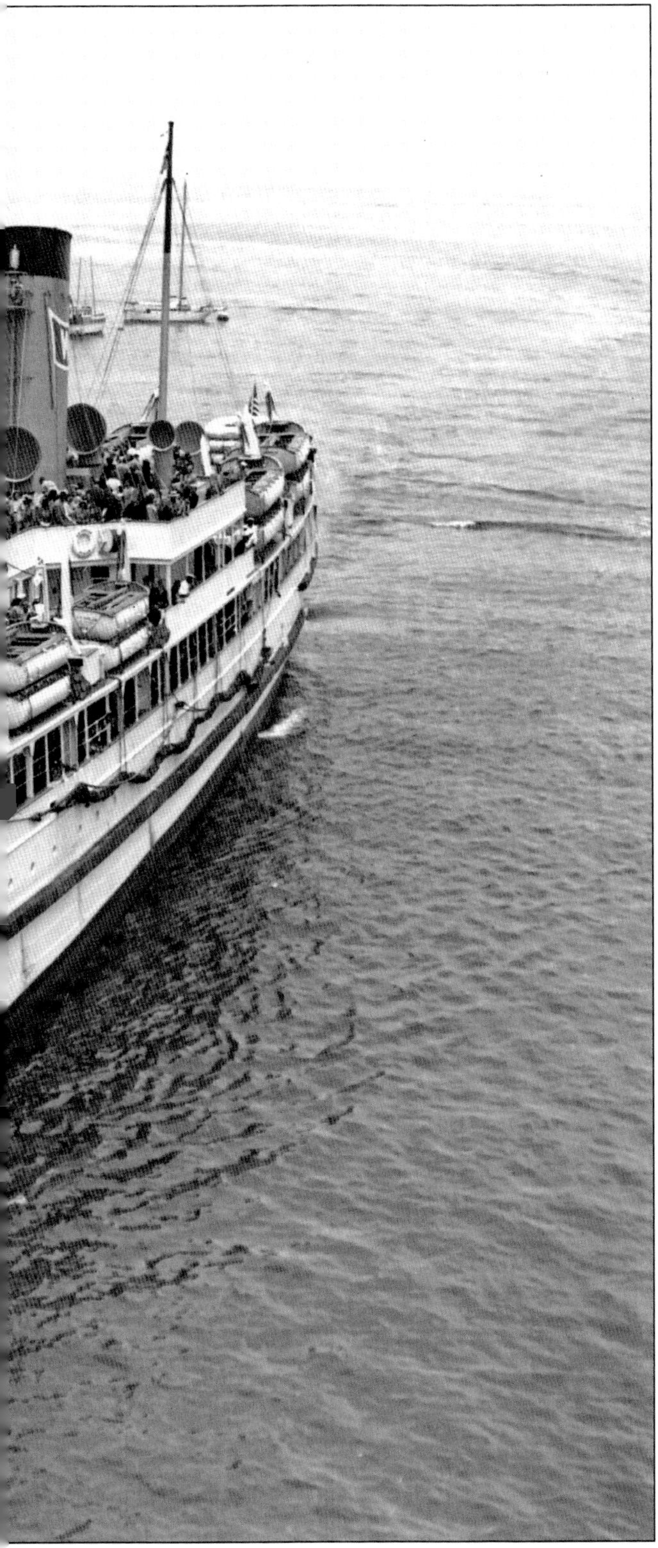

The *Avalon* was one of the largest passenger vessels to serve Catalina Island. She was 264.7 feet in length, and when was added to the Wilmington Transportation Company fleet, the steamer pier in Avalon had to be doubled to accommodate her. According to an article in the *Los Angeles Times* in 1920, "The steamer is driven with twin triple expansion steam engines each with 1500 horsepower each and two double-end Scotch boilers each with six furnaces to produce steam." The *Avalon* could do up to 16 knots and the journey across the channel took approximately 2 hours and 20 minutes.

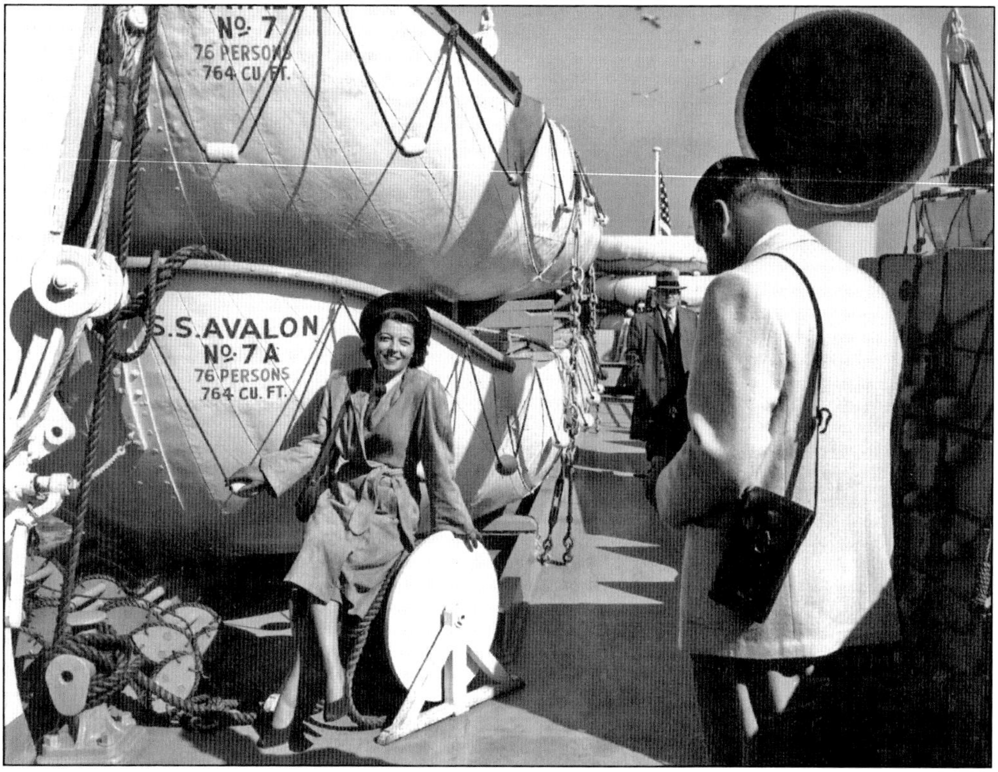

For many passengers, the *Avalon* was their first ocean-going experience. During the two-or-so-hour crossing they would explore the wonders of the steamship and enjoy the sights and sounds of the sea.

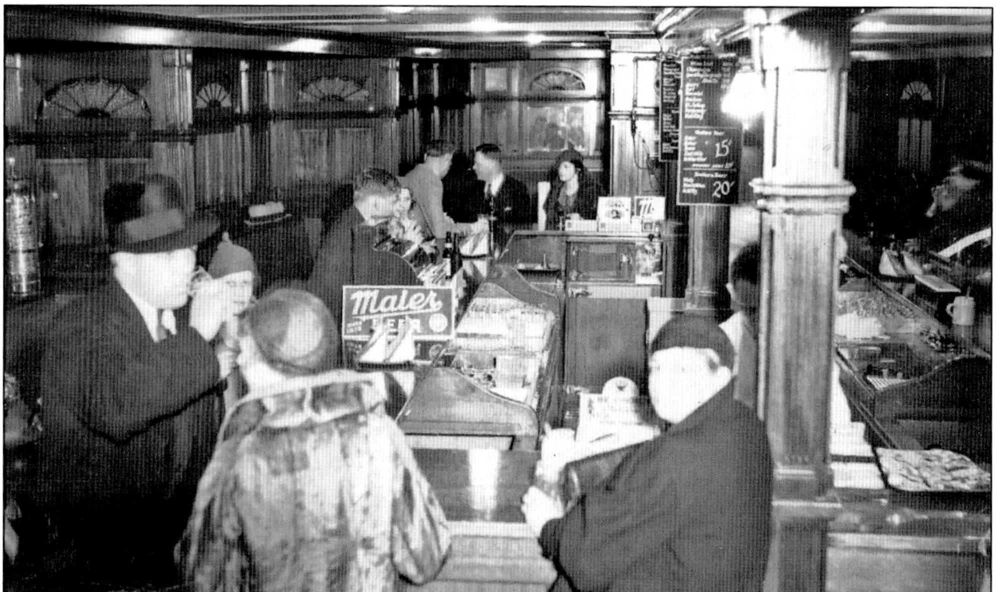

The *Avalon* featured a concession stand that kept passengers filled with food, beverages, and souvenirs as they crossed the channel.

Captain Alex Smith was born in Scotland in 1854. He arrived in San Pedro in the early 1880s and soon became employed by the Wilmington Transportation Company as a pilot for their tugboats. During the 1890s, Smith served as master for several ships that operated out of Los Angeles Harbor and later rejoined the Wilmington Transportation Company as captain of her ocean-going excursion vessels. He served as the captain of the SS *Warrior*, SS *Hermosa*, SS *Hermosa II*, SS *Cabrillo* and the SS *Avalon*.

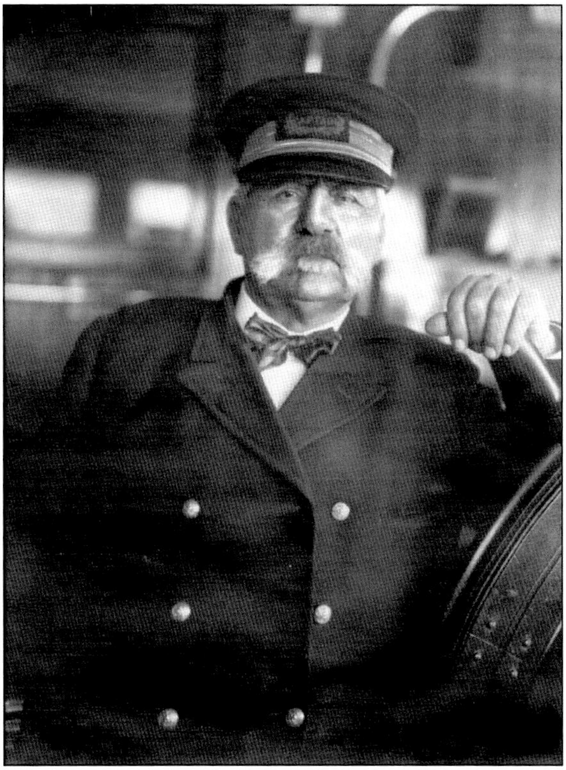

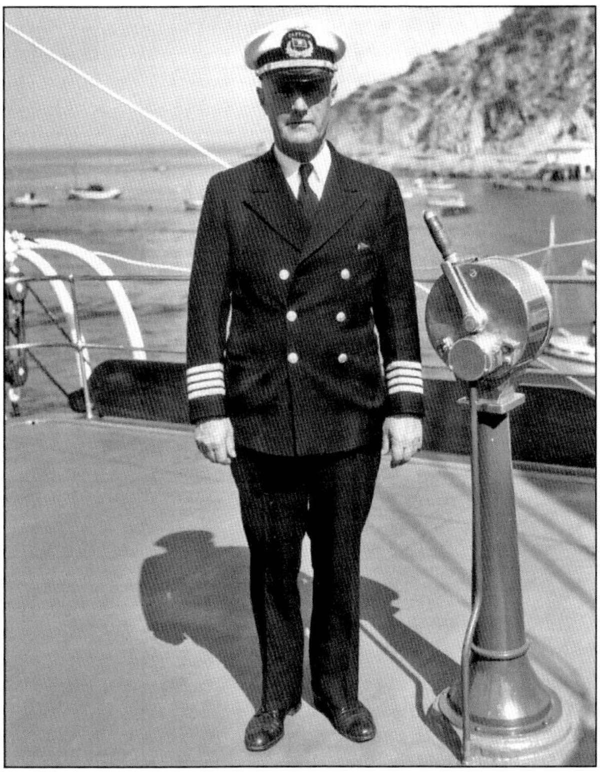

William Harrison Leisk was employed by the Wilmington Transportation Company for 30 years as a captain for the Catalina Island fleet. He retired as the captain of the *Catalina*, but also served as captain of the *Hermosa*, *Cabrillo*, and the *Avalon*. (Courtesy of the Santa Catalina Island Company.)

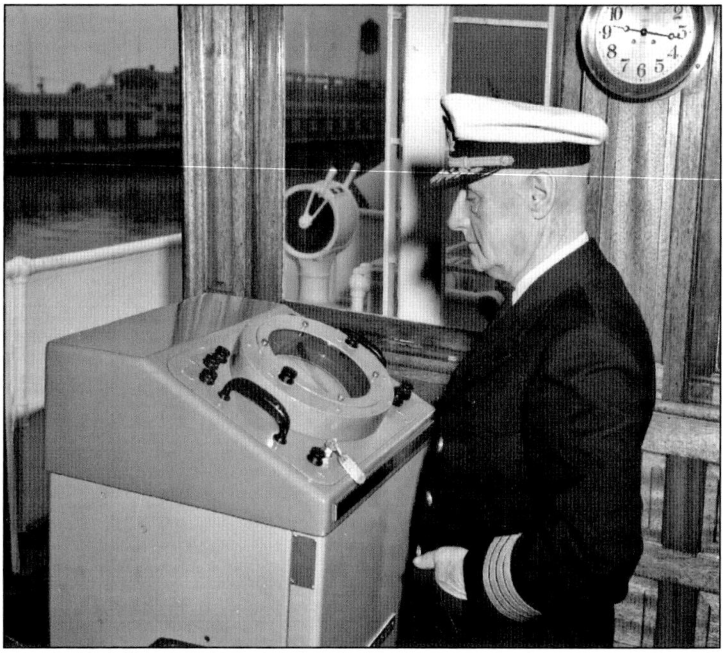

Pictured here is Captain William Leisk in the pilothouse of the *Avalon*. An article from the *Los Angeles Times* in 1952 describes Captain Leisk as being happy as the skipper of the *Avalon*. "He got to know the channel so well piloting the *Avalon* that he just used to put her in the groove and let her go." Captain Leisk was quoted as saying that "they don't build them like her [*Avalon*] anymore." (Courtesy of the Santa Catalina Island Company.)

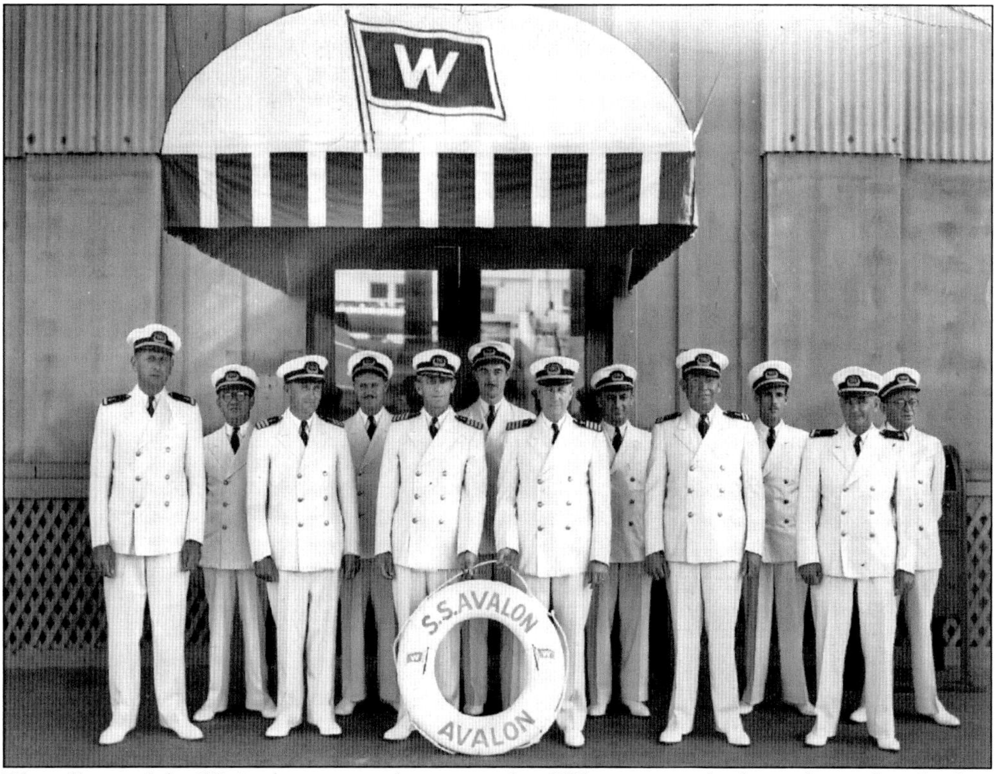

The officers of the SS *Avalon* pose at the terminal in Wilmington, which was located at the foot of Avalon Boulevard in Los Angeles Harbor. In fact, Avalon Boulevard was originally known as Canal Street and was renamed in honor of the *Avalon* upon the occasion of her first crossing to Catalina Island on April 11, 1920. (Courtesy of the Santa Catalina Island Company.)

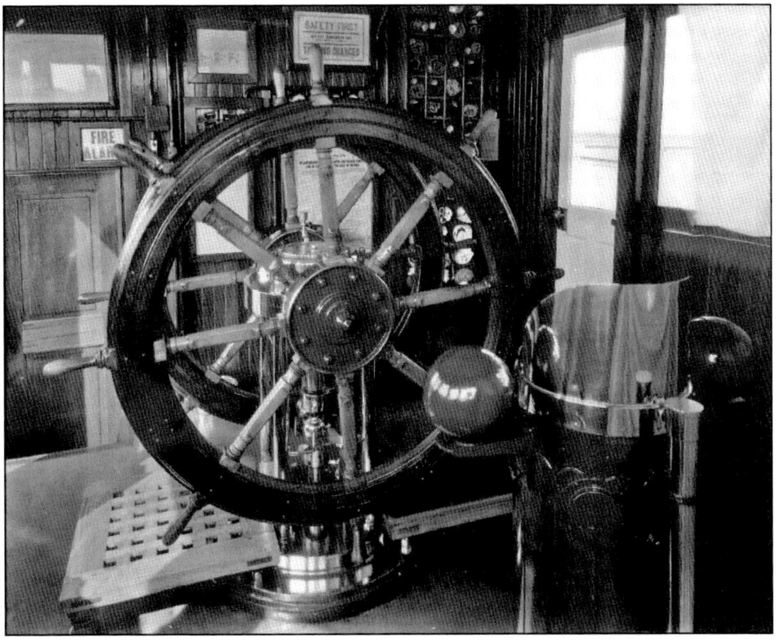

The wheelhouse of the SS *Avalon* is pictured here. A typical steamship wheelhouse included the ship's navigational equipment, a telegraph, and the ship's wheel. (Courtesy of the Santa Catalina Island Company.)

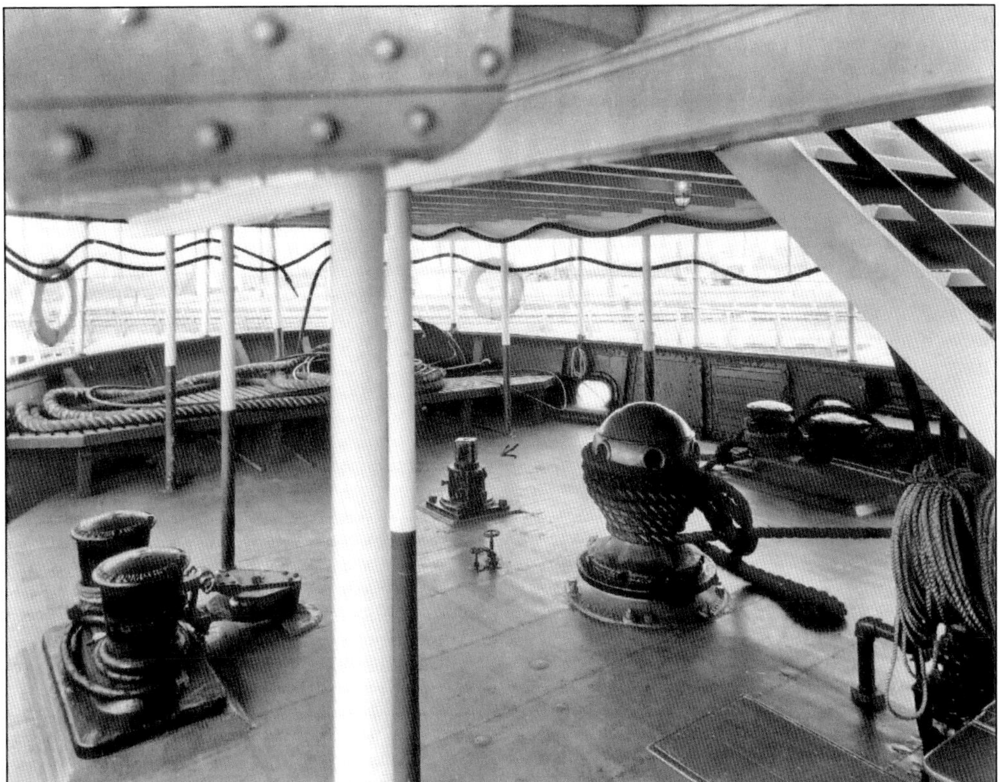

A view of the main deck of the *Avalon* shows the stern of the vessel. Island resident Hugh T. Smith remembers that the *Avalon* was a favorite boat among the islanders. "She ran throughout the winter months and rode the waves very well." (Courtesy of the Santa Catalina Island Company.)

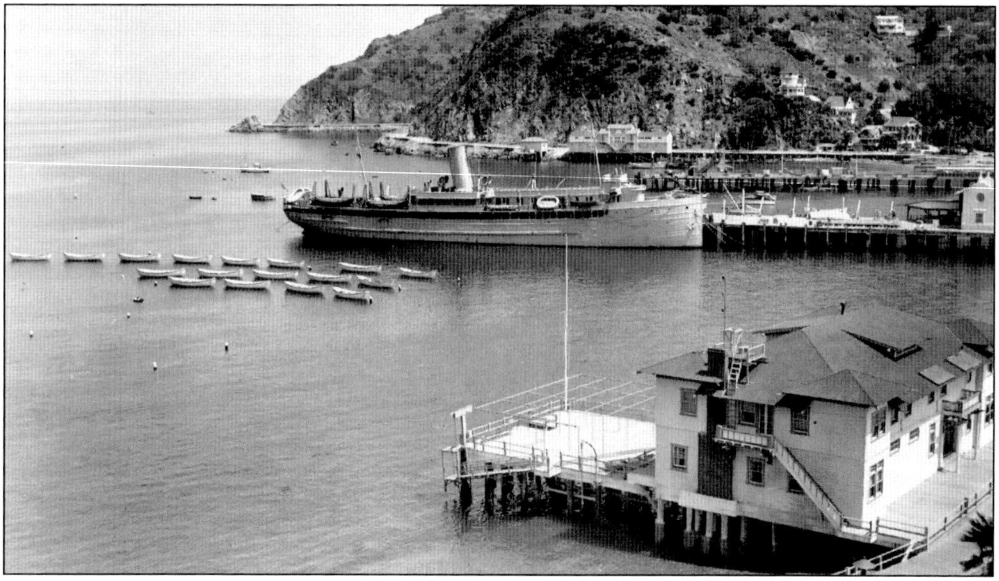

Two weeks after the bombing of Pearl Harbor, Catalina Island was declared a federal military zone and the San Pedro Channel was designated a controlled area for vessels. Shortly after this declaration, the SS *Avalon* was requisitioned by the United States War Shipping Administration along with the SS *Catalina* and SS *Cabrillo*. The *Catalina* and *Cabrillo* were sent to San Francisco Bay to be used as troop transports while the *Avalon* remained in service to the island.

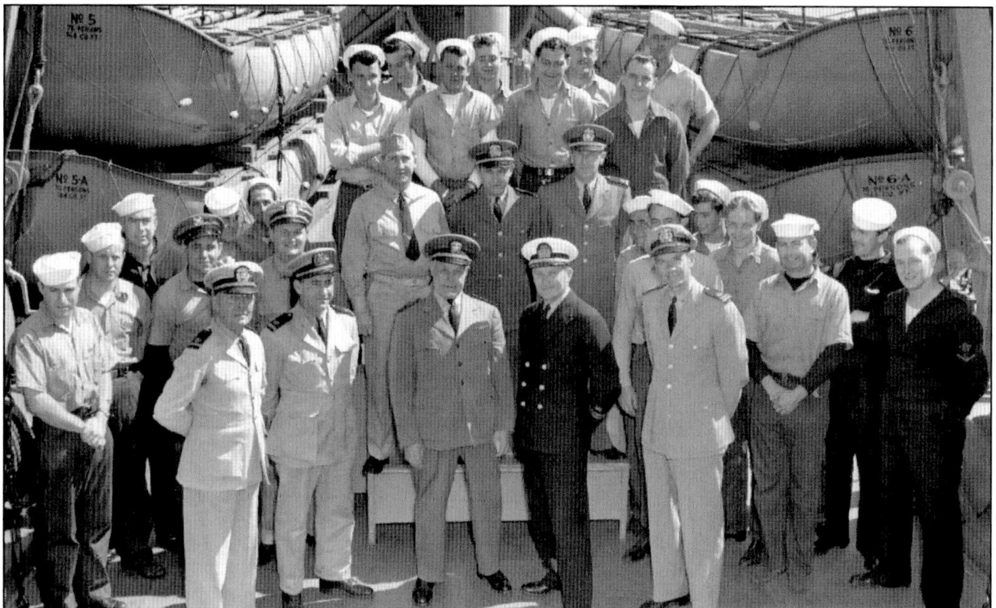

The cessation of regularly scheduled steamer service to the island meant that it would be shut down to tourism. In an effort to sustain his investment, Philip K. Wrigley, son of William Wrigley, Jr., began to actively pursue various branches of the military to use the island for the war effort. The military answered the call and soon the *Avalon* was carrying military personnel and supplies. During this time, the ship was crewed by United States Maritime Service personnel and recruits. (Courtesy of the Santa Catalina Island Company.)

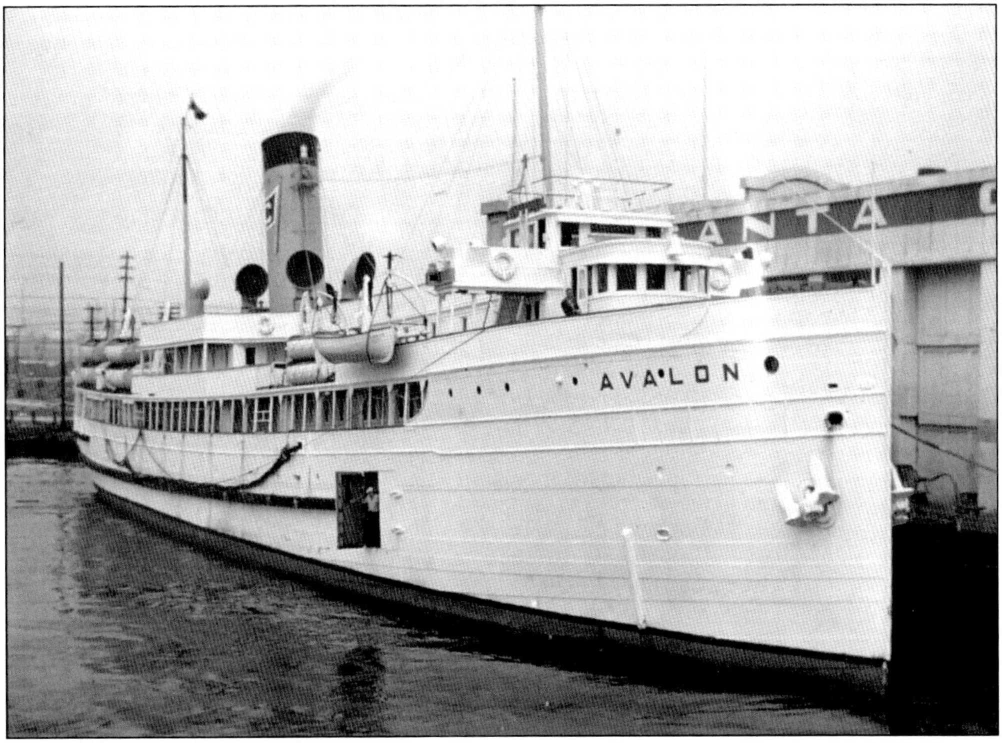

The *Avalon* was returned to the Wilmington Transportation Company on October 23, 1945. She was placed back on the Catalina run in March 1946. In 1948, the steamers began to run under the company name of Catalina Island Steamship Line. The traditional "W," for Wilmington Transportation Company that was painted on the steamer's smokestack, was replaced with a "C."

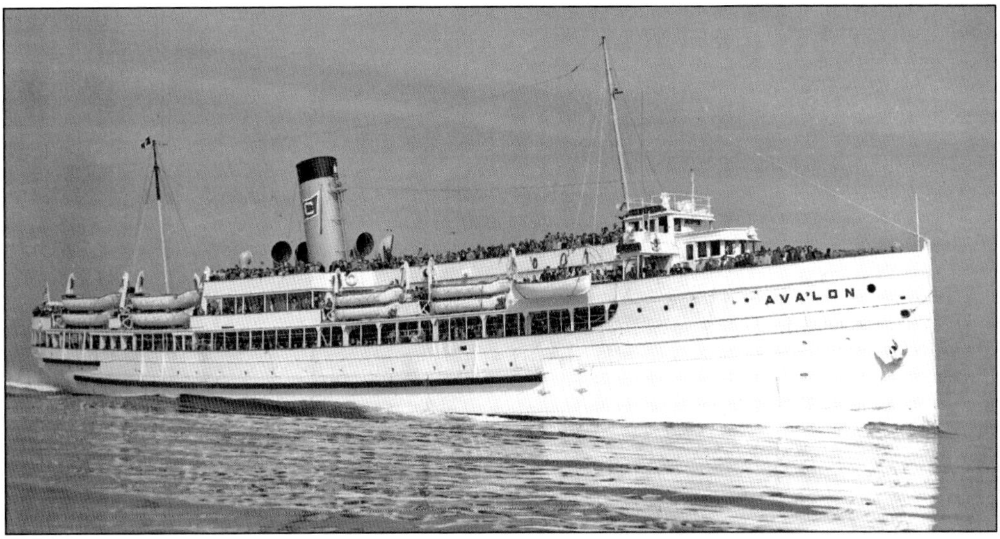

The *Avalon* continued on the Catalina run until 1951 when she was decommissioned from the fleet. For the next nine years, she would lay at the docks in Los Angeles Harbor awaiting the next chapter of her life. In 1960, she was sold to Everett J. Stotts of Artesia, California, for scrap. He began by shearing the ship of metal, furnishings, and equipment and continuing until the *Avalon* was stripped down to three feet above the water line.

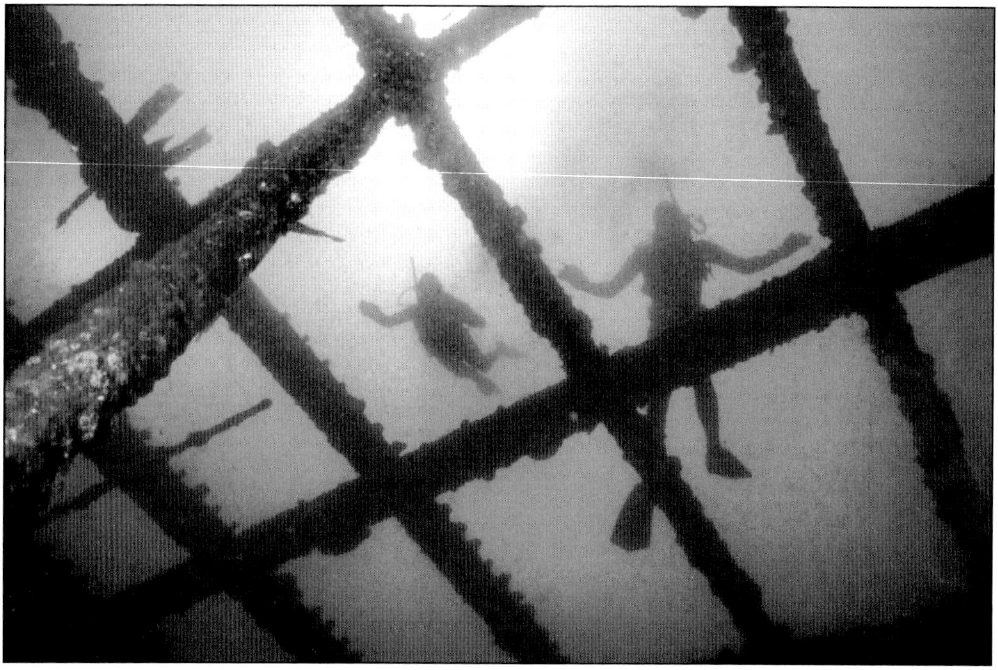

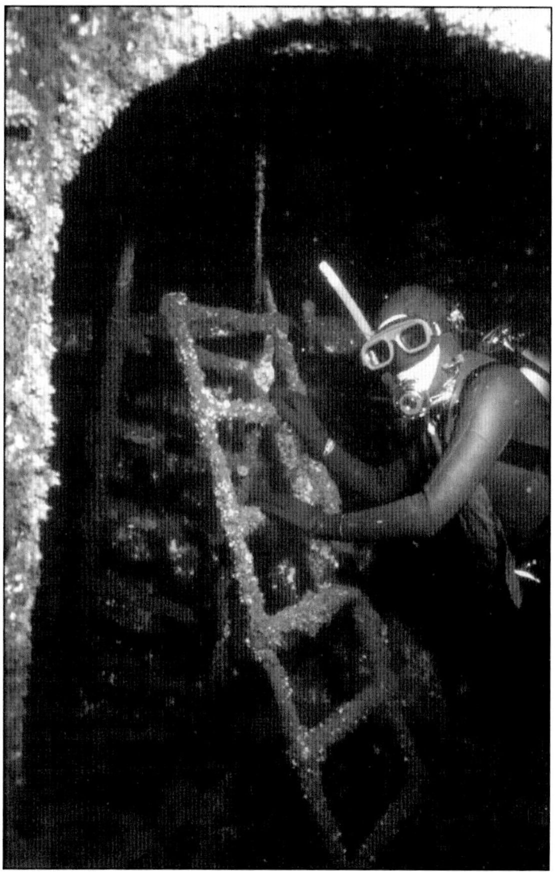

The *Avalon* managed to survive two fires that occurred during the scrapping process and was later towed out of Los Angeles Harbor in July 1961 and anchored off of Point Vincente. Soon after being towed there her anchor chain snapped during a storm and what remained of the ship sunk to the ocean floor. (Photograph by Jack McKinney; courtesy of the Patrick Smith Collection.)

The *Avalon* now lies at the bottom of the sea in approximately 80 feet of water. The remains of the ship are accessible to seasoned scuba divers. This photograph was taken during a dive to the wreck site. (Photograph by Jack McKinney; courtesy of the Patrick Smith Collection.)

Three

SS CATALINA

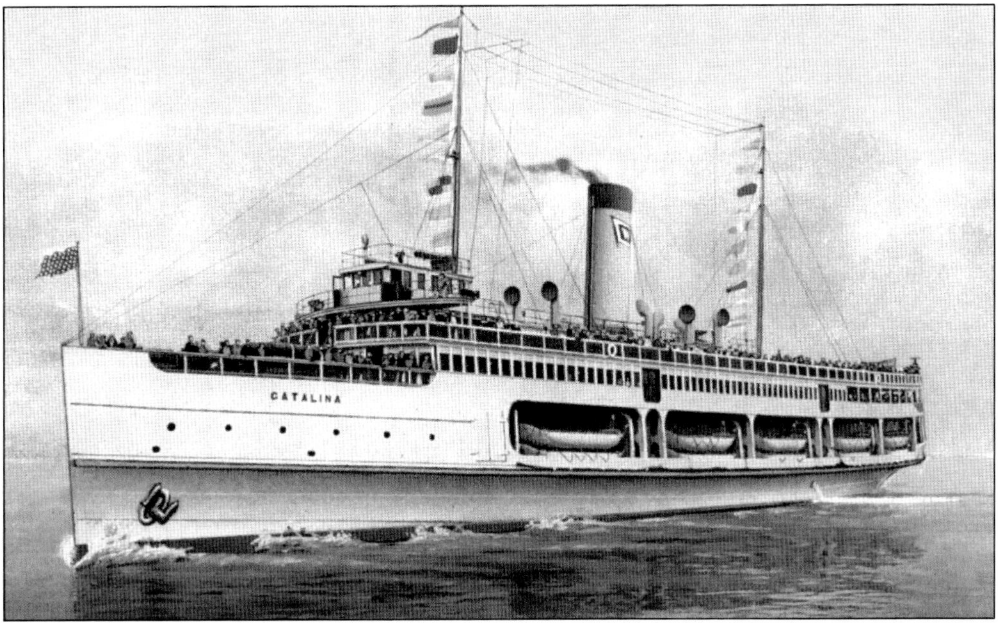

The beautiful SS *Catalina*, largest of all the steamships that transported passengers to and from Catalina Island, was fondly known as the Great White Steamer. William Wrigley Jr.'s Wilmington Transportation Company commissioned the *Catalina* to be built at the Los Angeles Shipbuilding and Dry Dock Company (now Todd Pacific Shipyards) in 1923. Construction costs for the ship exceeded $1 million and she was the biggest, fastest, and most luxurious vessel to date. The ship was very well appointed and as she was built specifically as a deluxe passenger vessel, every attention was given to passenger comforts. The Great White Steamer was added to the Catalina run in the summer of 1924 and she served the island for 50 years. She carried over 22 million passengers across the San Pedro Channel to Catalina Island and still has a fond place in many a heart.

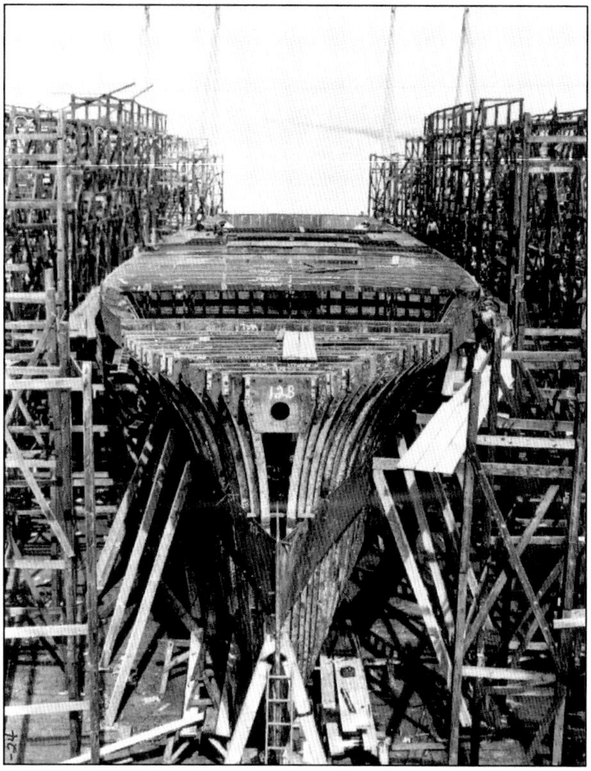

The *Catalina* is pictured here under construction in Los Angeles Harbor in 1923. Her keel was laid on December 26, 1923, and the first rivet was driven by William Wrigley Jr. himself. Wrigley was quoted in the *Los Angeles Times*, "The *Catalina*'s work is going to be between Los Angeles Harbor and Avalon and I want to see her built in Los Angeles by Los Angeles Shipbuilders." The Los Angeles Shipbuilding and Dry dock Company obtained the construction contract for the *Catalina* after competing with every yard on both the Atlantic and Pacific Coasts.

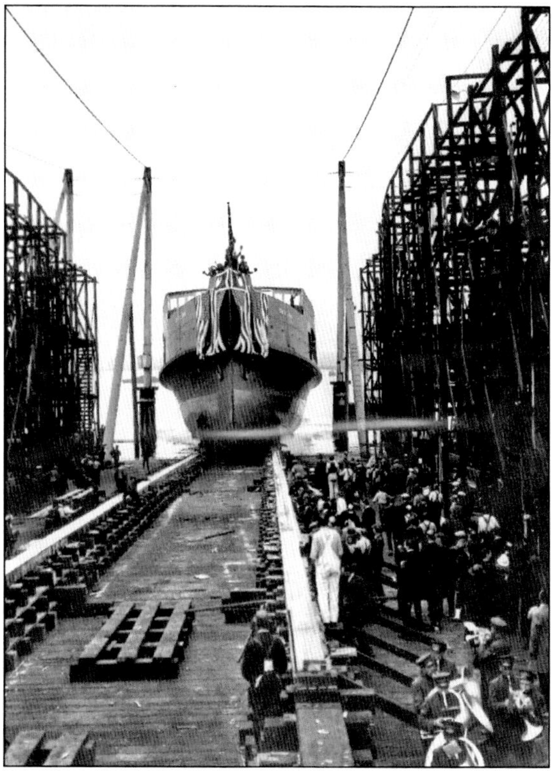

The *Catalina* was launched on the morning of May 3, 1924. According to a feature in the *Catalina Islander* on May 7, 1924, from the docks in San Pedro, "Mayor Cryer of Los Angeles yelled 'Bon Voyage, *Catalina*!' and three thousand more voices took up the cry, and the band played the "Star Spangled Banner." It was some "send-off" for the palatial passenger steamship."

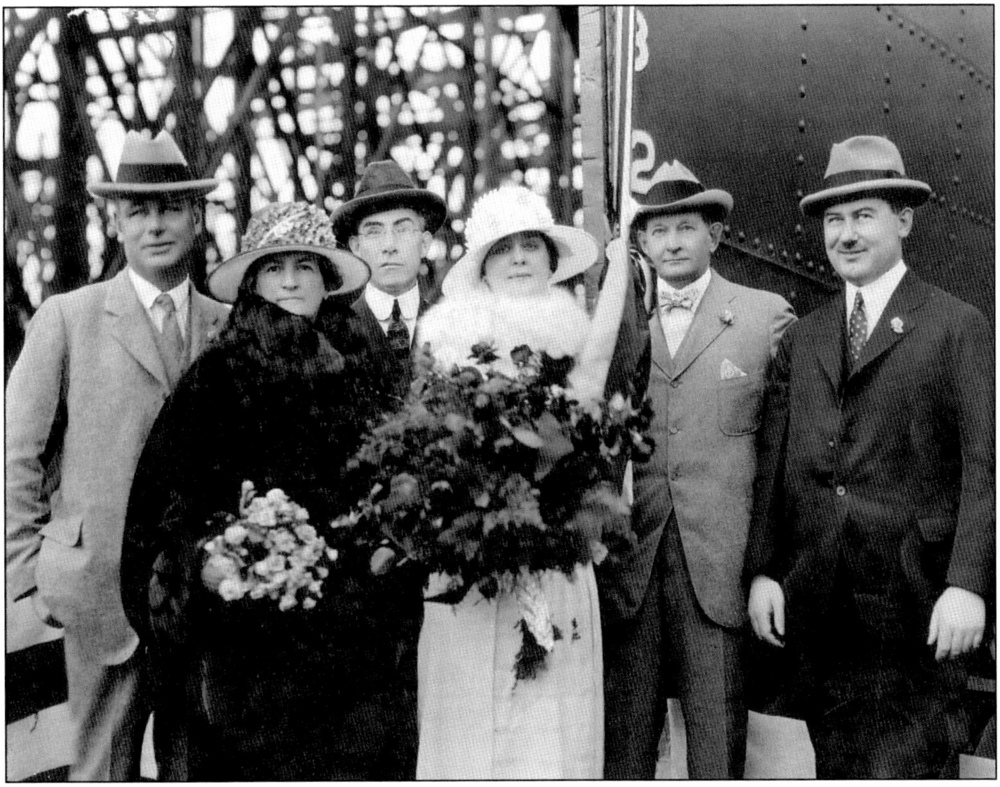

The *Catalina* was christened by Dr. Marcia A. Patrick (in white) of Los Angeles. She was the sister of Joseph H. Patrick, the then president of the Wilmington Transportation Company. Also pictured at far left are David M. Renton, Manager of Construction and Improvement Projects for the Santa Catalina Island Company, and his wife Elizabeth.

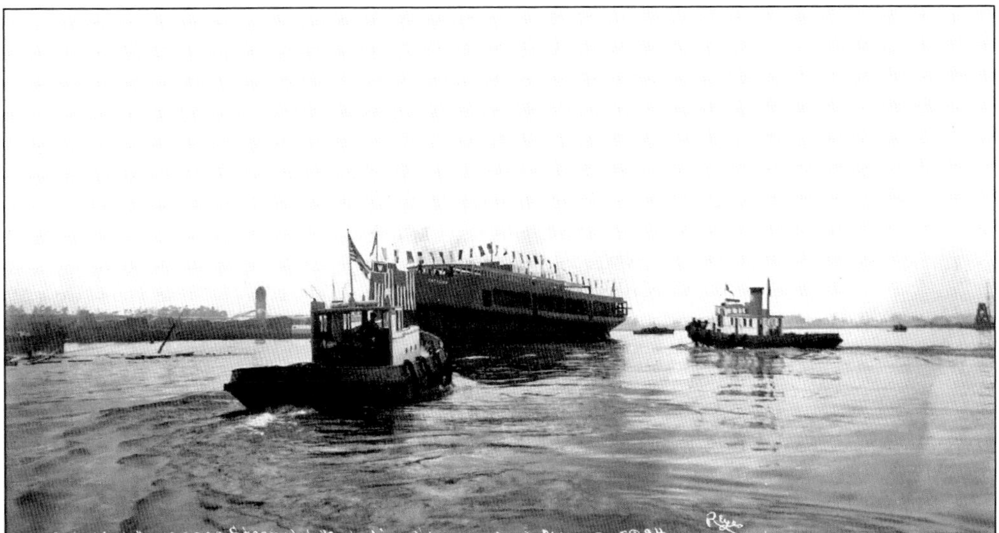

Upon the successful launching of the *Catalina*, the tugboats *Captain William*, *David P. Fleming*, and *D. M. Renton* led the new vessel into dry dock for completion. The tugs were named after officials of the Wilmington Transportation Company and the Santa Catalina Island Company.

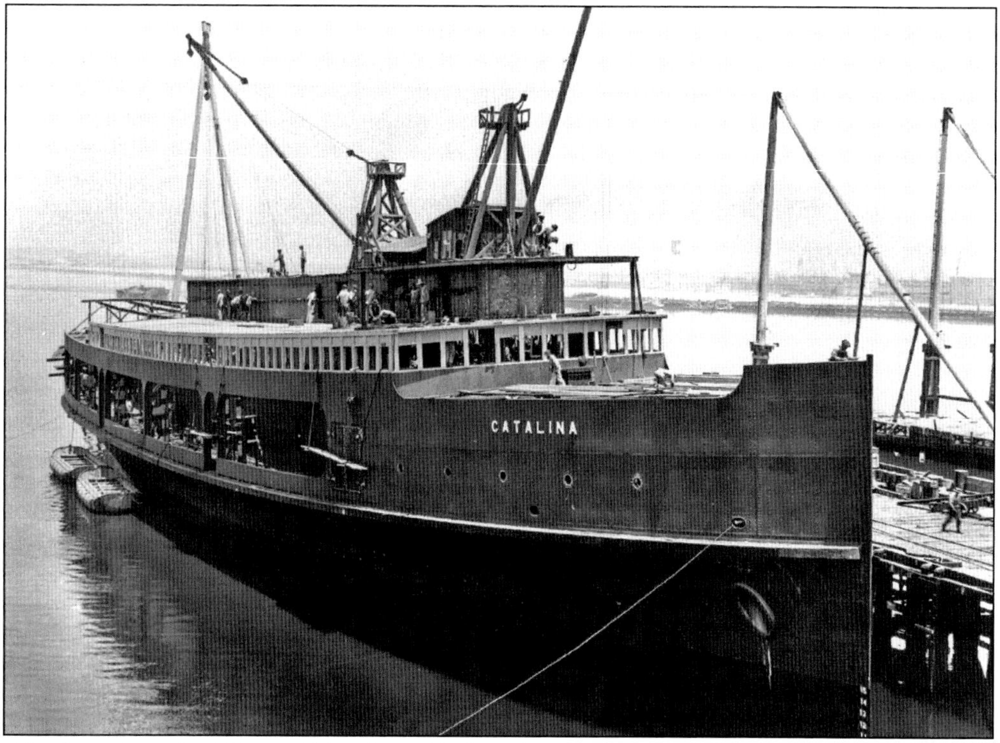

After launching the 301-foot, 7½-inch steel hull of the *Catalina*, crews went to work on completing the superstructure of the ship designed by L. E. Caverly, chief engineer of the Los Angeles Shipbuilders and Dry Dock Company. The *Catalina* had a total of five decks, three of which were accessible to passengers. She was luxuriously appointed with 14 staterooms, a large ballroom, and a glass-enclosed saloon deck.

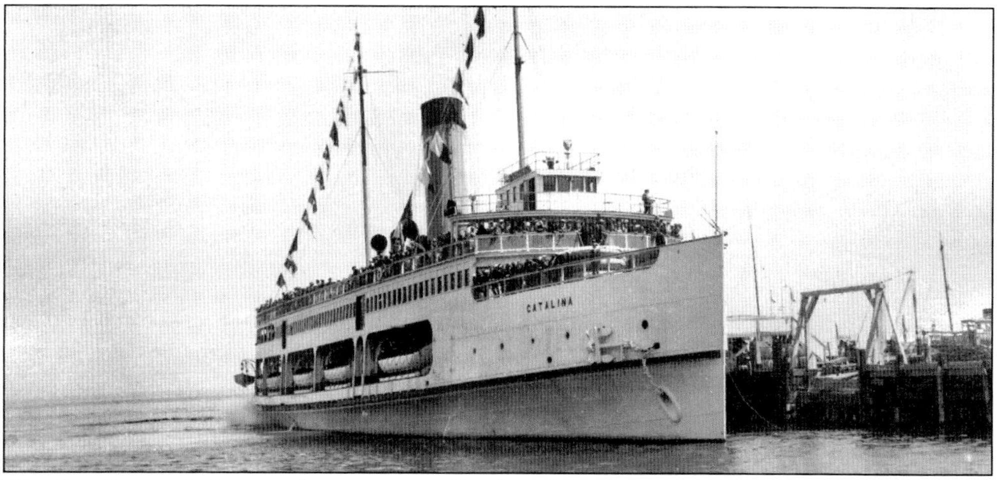

The *Catalina* made her maiden voyage to Catalina Island on June 30, 1924. This photograph shows the ship during her inaugural season. Originally, the anchor, seen on the bow, sat lower on the ship and it was soon discovered that once at sea the ship would take on water through the anchor hawser. For the 1924 season, the anchor was strapped to the fender of the ship. At the end of the season, the *Catalina* was placed in dry dock and the anchor hawser was permanently moved. (Courtesy of Roy Rose.)

The *Catalina* immediately began to appear on brochures and promotions for Catalina Island. She was a beautiful ship, and the largest and fastest vessel in the Wilmington Transportation Company fleet. She was equipped with twin-screw propellers and two triple-expansion steam engines. The *Catalina* could do up to 17 knots and cross the channel in two hours with over 1,900 passengers.

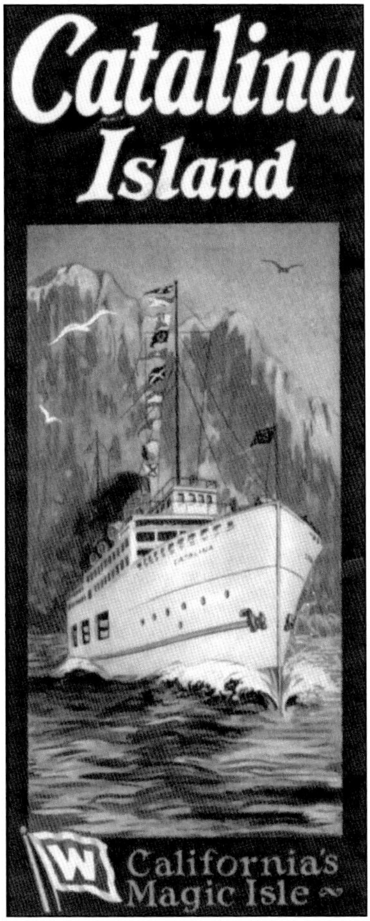

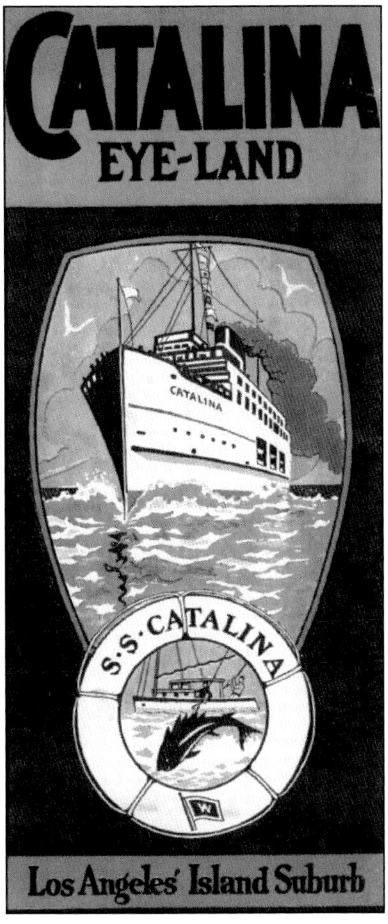

This 1926 brochure for "Catalina Eye-land" highlights the steamships. They are advertised as "The steamships 'Catalina' and 'Avalon' ply between the island and mainland: Million dollar Ferryships to Fairyland, with orchestra for dancing."

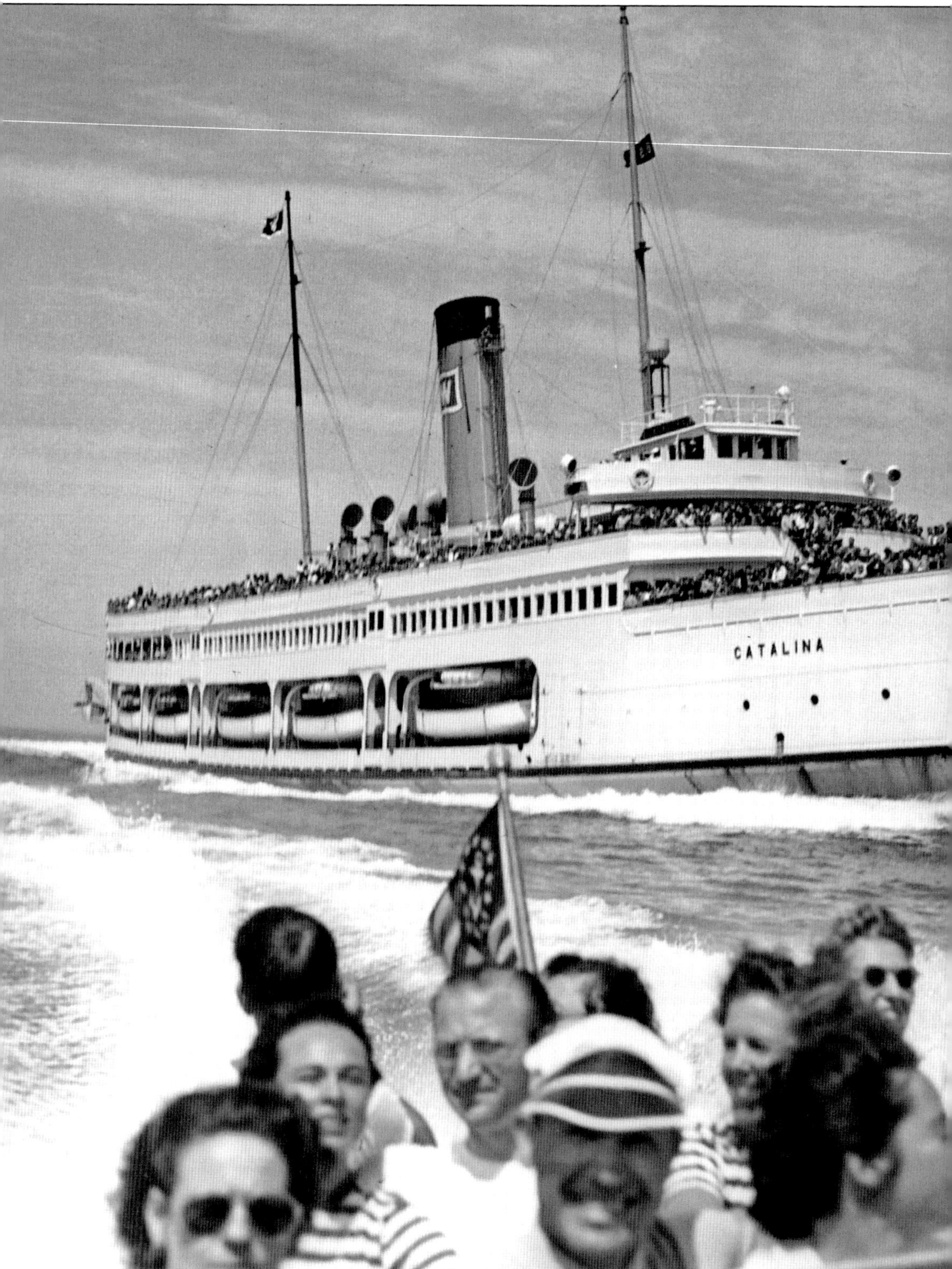
CATALINA

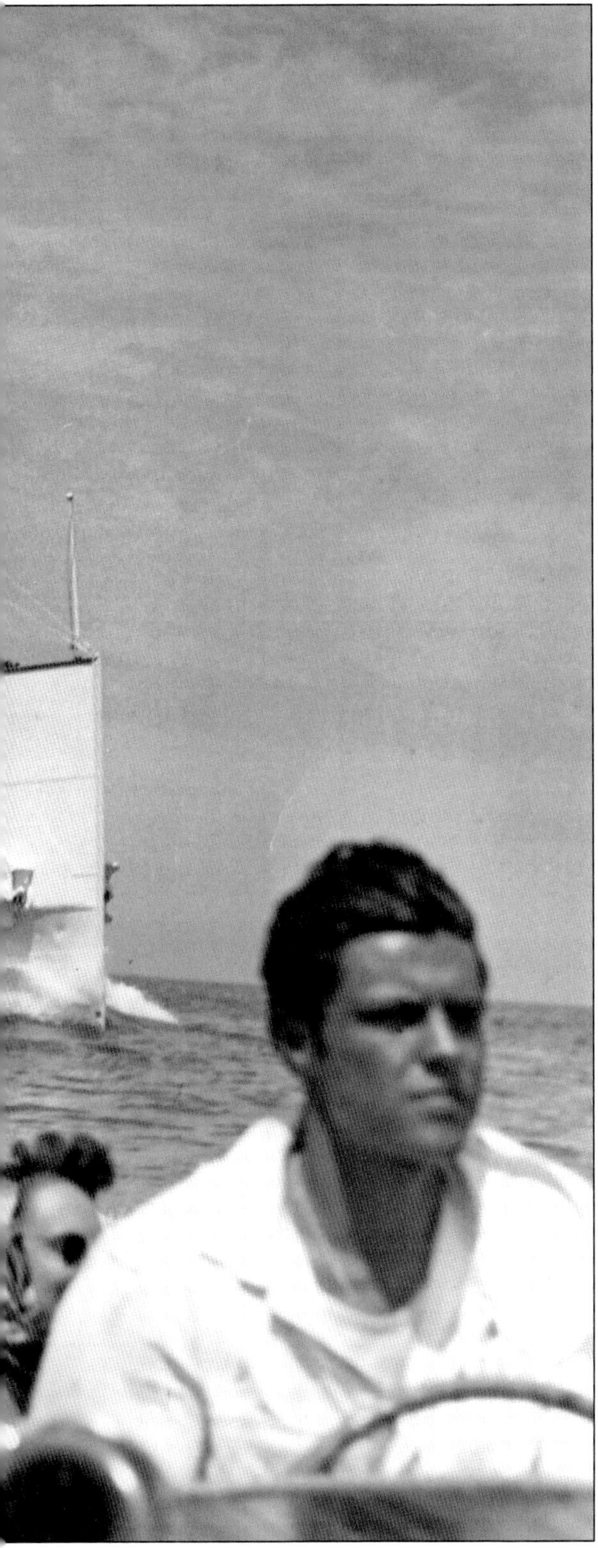

The *Catalina* quickly became a favorite among visitors and residents. During her years of service to the island she made over 9,000 trips and carried over 22 million passengers, which is more than any other passenger steamer in history. The *Catalina* is pictured here being led into Avalon Bay by a *Miss Catalina* speedboat, piloted by Doug Bombard. Doug's father Al Bombard developed the *Miss Catalina* speedboats in 1921, and they served as official greeters of the steamships for many years. Doug Bombard later founded Catalina Express, which plays a crucial role in today's water transportation to the island.

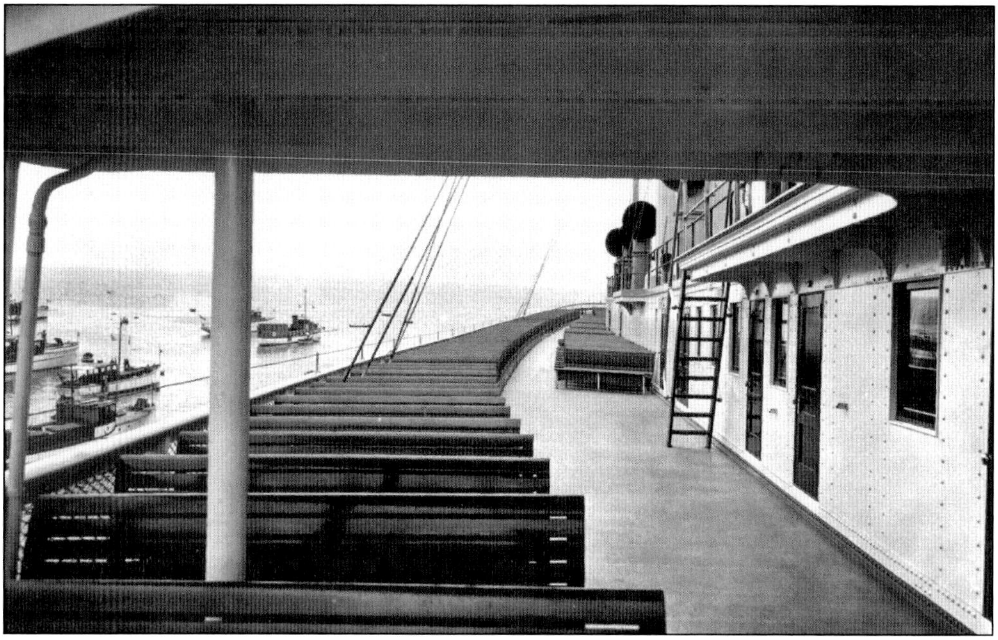

Since the *Catalina* had been built expressly for passenger service, she was designed for capacity and comfort. The ship had five decks that were accessible to passengers. The uppermost deck was the bridge deck, which included the pilothouse and captain's cabin. The promenade deck, pictured here, provided open-air seating for passengers.

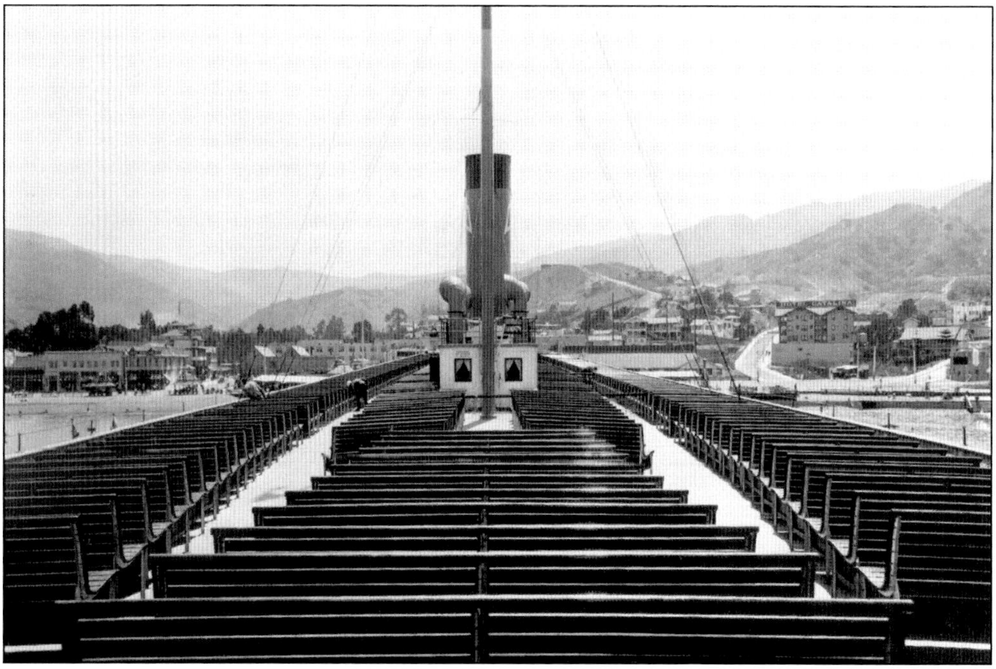

The promenade deck had hundreds of oak benches where passengers could relax in the sun during the two-hour crossing. Common sights along the way were freight ships, sailboats, seaplanes, and marine life, such as dolphins and seals. There was also an incredible view of Avalon as the steamer docked at the pier.

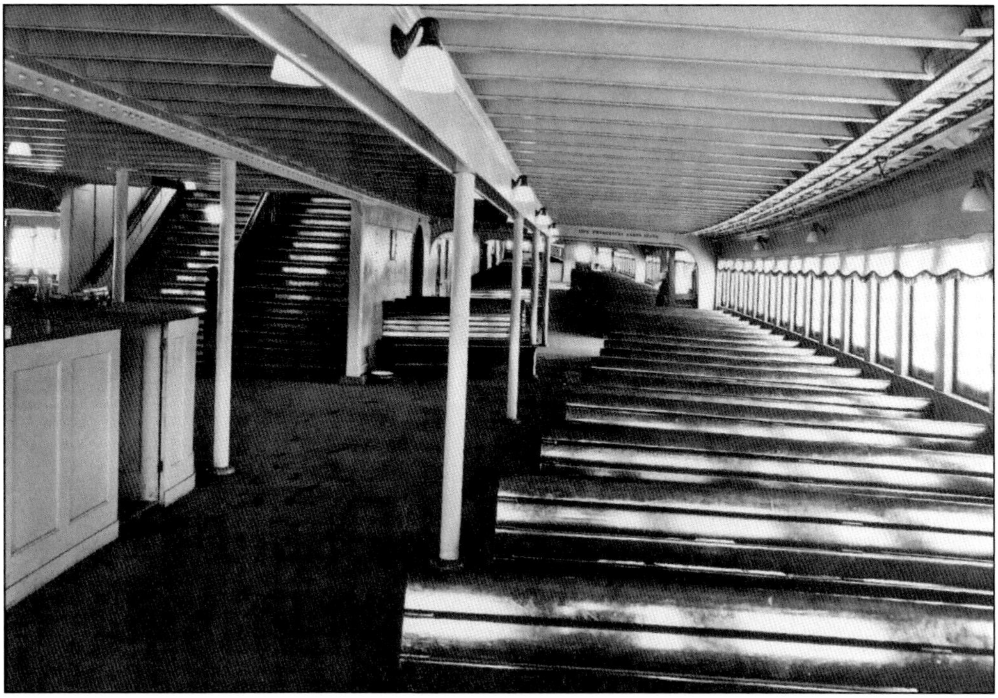

The saloon deck was entirely enclosed by glass (except for two small sections on the stern and bow) and the windows could be opened during the warm summer months. It included a refreshment counter, cushioned bench seating, and a ballroom.

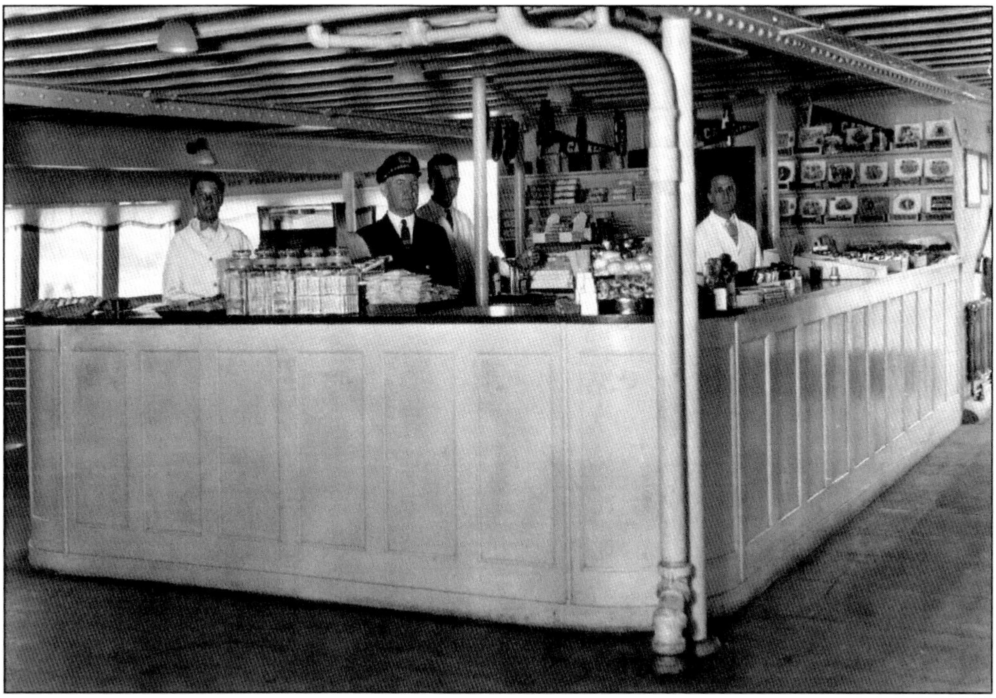

A variety of items were sold at the refreshment counter on the *Catalina*, including souvenirs, food, beverages, and, of course, Wrigley's gum.

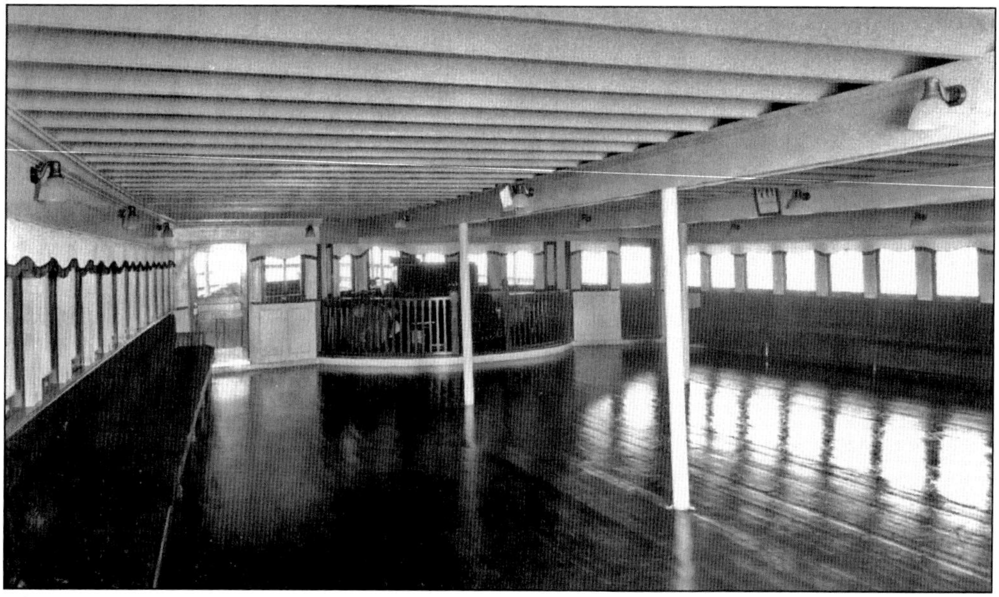

The empty ballroom of the *Catalina* is pictured here. Dancing on the steamship was quite pleasant when the channel was smooth, but it could get quite interesting on days when the sea picked up. Ada Blanche Wrigley Schreiner, daughter of Philip K. Wrigley, fondly remembers going to the ballroom with her sister to watch the dancers during the crossing. They particularly enjoyed trips when the ocean was rough because "it was hysterical to watch the people try to dance with the swell."

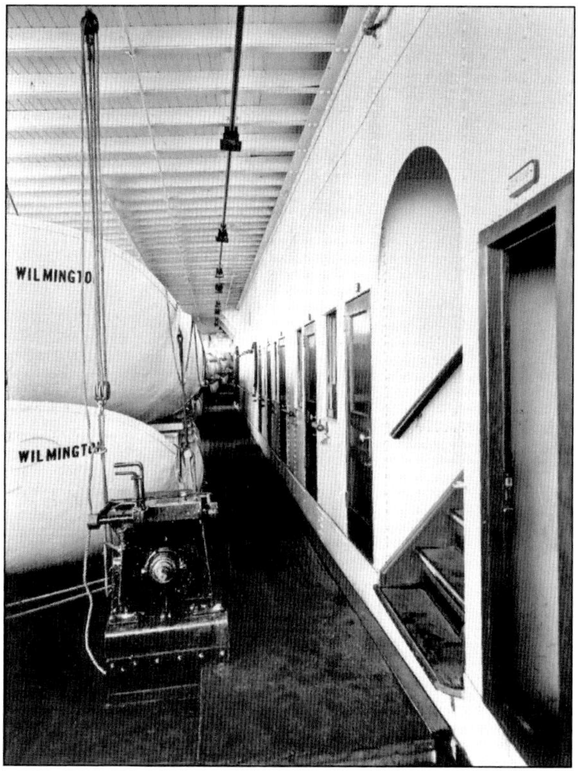

The lowest passenger level was known as the lower deck. The lower deck included ship machinery, a baggage room, and the chief engineer's cabin. The decks were narrow because the ship's lifeboats were also stored on this deck. The passenger area of the lower deck included the purser's office, a mail room, restrooms, and 10 staterooms. This photograph shows the lifeboats and doors to the staterooms. From this deck, passengers could also view the ship's engines through port holes.

The below decks of the *Catalina* are what kept the ship in operation. A steamship is so called because it employs a steam engine, which transfers energy through the expansion and cooling of steam in a cylinder equipped with a moveable piston. Early marine steamers employed single-expansion steam engines with the boiler introducing steam into the cylinders where it expanded and then exhausted. The next development was double-expansion engines, where the exhausted steam was then used to power another low-pressure cylinder.

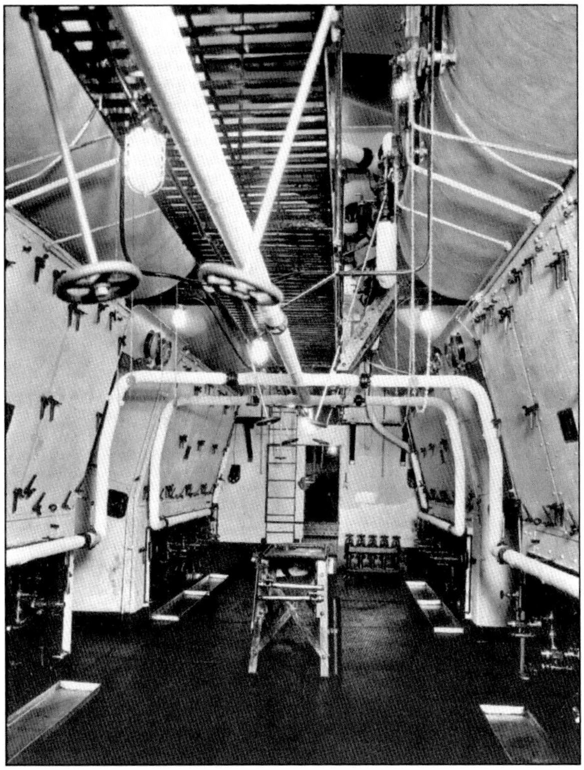

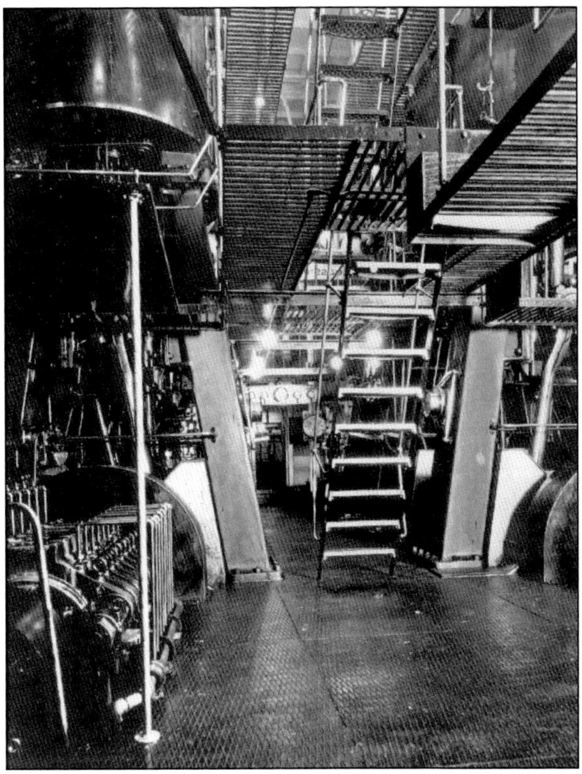

Triple-expansion engines, like those used in the *Catalina*, were introduced in 1873. The Hooven, Owens, Renthschler Company of Hamilton, Ohio, built the Catalina's triple-expansion engines. The engine room of the *Catalina* included two large triple-expansion steam engines, telegraphs, gauges, steam pumps, pipes, and a skilled crew ensuring a safe crossing for the hundreds of passengers on the decks above.

Time Table

Effective February 16, 1928

Pacific Electric Through Trains Direct to Catalina Terminal at Wilmington (Los Angeles Harbor)

From Los Angeles

Pacific Electric "Catalina Special" trains leave from, and arrive at 6th and Main St. Station, Los Angeles.

	Daily
Lv. Los Angeles, 6th & Main	9:00 a. m.
Lv. L. A. Harbor, Wilmington	10:00 a. m.
Ar. Avalon, Catalina Island	12:05 noon
Lv. Avalon	3:30 p. m.
Ar. L. A. Harbor	5:30 p. m.
Ar. Los Angeles	6:40 p. m.

From Long Beach

Pacific Electric "Catalina Special" trains leave from, and arrive at Pacific and Ocean Aves., Long Beach.

	Daily
Lv. Long Beach, Ocean Ave.	9:25 a. m.
Lv. L. A. Harbor, Wilmington	10:00 a. m.
Ar. Avalon, Catalina Island	12:05 noon
Lv. Avalon	3:30 p. m.
Ar. L. A. Harbor	5:30 p. m.
Ar. Long Beach	6:00 p. m.

From Pasadena

Take 8:18 A. M. Pacific Electric Short Line to 6th and Main Sts., Los Angeles, and change to "Catalina Special"

	Daily
Lv. Los Angeles, 6th & Main	9:00 a. m.
Lv. L. A. Harbor, Wilmington	10:00 a. m.
Ar. Avalon, Catalina Island	12:05 noon
Lv. Avalon	3:30 p. m.
Ar. L. A. Harbor	5:30 p. m.
Ar. Pasadena (via Short Line)	7:30 p. m.

Catalina baggage cars leave P. E. Baggage Room, Sixth and Los Angeles Sts., Los Angeles, at 8:20 a. m. daily

FARES	From Los Angeles		From Long Beach		From Pasadena		From Wilmington	
	Full Fare	Half Fare	Full Fare	Half Fare	Full Fare	Half Fare	Full Fare	Half Fare
Round Trip to Catalina, 60-day return limit from Los Angeles, 10-day return limit from Long Beach and Pasadena	$ 3.10	$ 1.55	$ 2.45*	$ 1.23*	$ 3.55*	$ 1.78*	$ 2.25	$ 1.15
Round Trip to Catalina, including ride on Glass Bottom Boat over Submarine Gardens; same return limits as above	3.85	1.95	3.20	1.63	4.30	2.18	3.00	1.55
Complete One-Day Trip, including round trip to Catalina, also ride on Glass Bottom Boat, and luncheon at Hotel St. Catherine; same limits	5.00	3.20	4.45	2.88	5.50	3.43	4.25	2.80
Two-Day Trip, including round trip, one night and four meals at Hotel St. Catherine, with Glass Bottom Boat ride, **per person**	10.00	7.00	9.45	6.73	10.50	7.25	9.25	6.65
Three-Day Trip, including round trip, two nights and seven meals at Hotel St. Catherine, with Glass Bottom Boat ride, **per person**	15.00	11.00	14.45	10.73	15.50	11.25	14.25	10.65

*60-day limit ticket from Long Beach, full fare, $2.85; half fare, $1.43. From Pasadena, full fare, $3.80; half fare, $1.90.

CATALINA ISLAND TICKET OFFICES

Ticket offices of this Company are located at the following addresses:

6th & Main Sts., Los Angeles............Phone TRinity 2961
Gardner Pharmacy, Gardner Jct..........Phone GRanite 3278
La Brea Pharmacy, La Brea Ave...........Phone HOlly 1394
Ever Ready Drug Store, Hollywood & Highland.....HE. 1136
Duffin's Travel Service, 6733 Hollywood Blvd........GL. 5505
Parker's Pharmacy, Hollywood & Vermont....OLympia 1312
Fair Oaks, Cor. Union, Pasadena (P.E. Station).Terrace 6407
156 W. Ocean Ave., Long Beach (P. E. Sta.)...Phone 619-74
Venetian Square, Long Beach..................Phone 640-59
Seaside Cottages, Long Beach.................Phone 626-298
106 N. Brand, P. E. Ticket Office, Glendale.......Glendale 21
5607 Pasadena Ave., Highland Park.....Phone GArfield 0179
110 W. Seventh St., San Pedro.................Phone 1067
318 N. Sycamore St., Santa Ana.................Phone 393
217 E. Broadway, San Diego...............Phone Main 6348
117 N. Central Ave., Phoenix, Ariz..............Phone 24575
Catalina Terminal, foot of Avalon Blvd.......Wilmington 127

And at leading hotels in Los Angeles and Pacific Electric Agencies at outlying points.

SERVICE FROM SANTA MONICA BAY DISTRICT

Motor Coach Company "Sunset Stages" operate daily from Santa Monica, Ocean Park, Venice, Del Rey, El Segundo, Manhattan, Hermosa, Redondo, Torrance and Lomita to Wilmington.

Ticket offices of this Company are located at the following addresses:

Santa Monica, 717 Santa Monica Blvd..........Phone 218-71
Santa Monica, 1509 Ocean Blvd...............Phone 456-74
Ocean Park, 120 Pier Ave.....................Phone 610-70
Venice Speedway and 17th Ave., Owl Auto Park, Opposite Firehouse ....Phone 615-47
El Segundo, Converse Pharmacy..................Phone 60
Redondo Beach, 116 N. Pacific Ave., Stage Depot.Phone 5571
Torrance, Torrance Pharmacy.....................Phone 3-J
Lomita, Post Office Bldg.........................Phone 13-J
San Pedro, 132 W. Fifth St......................Phone 2677

ATTENTION—MOTORISTS—if you motor down, follow the red fists from Los Angeles out South Main Street and Harbor Boulevard to Anaheim Street, Wilmington; thence east to Fries Street; thence south to Catalina Terminal, at foot of street. Garage in Terminal; storage 50c per day. Motorists should avail themselves of the fares from Wilmington. Tickets from Wilmington are on sale at all offices.

The Wilmington Transportation Co. reserves the right to change steamers and time of sailing without notice.

0M—0 7 28

78.9.22 5:1

Both the *Catalina* and the SS *Avalon* made daily trips to Catalina Island during the summer season. The *Catalina* would load passengers and sail from Wilmington first, followed shortly thereafter by the *Avalon*. The *Catalina* would dock on the north side of the steamer pier and glass-bottom boats would be docked on the south side waiting for passengers. Many people traveled to Catalina Island on packages, which often included a glass-bottom boat ride. These people would often get off the steamship and step right onto a glass-bottom boat.

The officers of the *Catalina* pose aboard their vessel in 1938. The dedicated crew of the *Catalina* ensured passenger safety on hundreds of voyages each summer. The crew was all highly qualified as skilled sailors and technicians. The ship originally had 43 crewmembers, each with a specific job that kept the ship running smoothly and efficiently. The number of crew aboard the *Catalina* eventually grew to over 70.

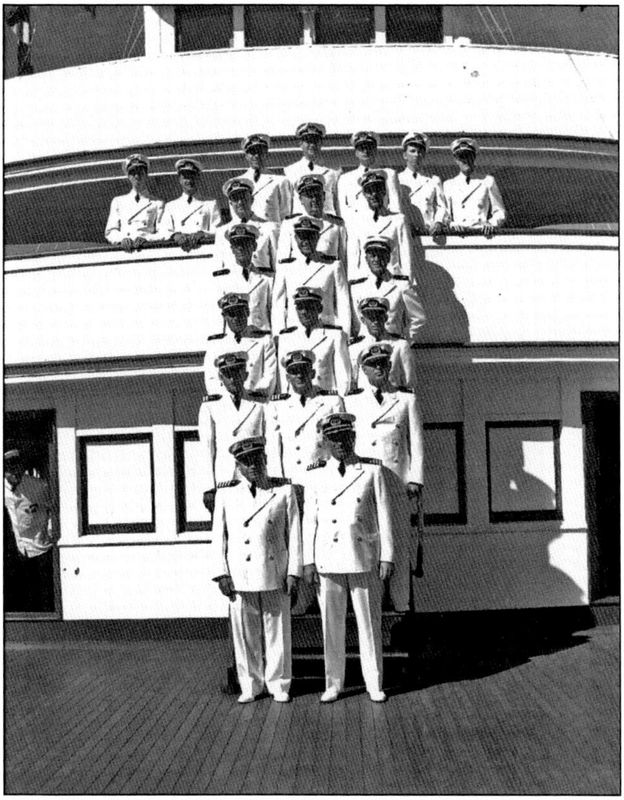

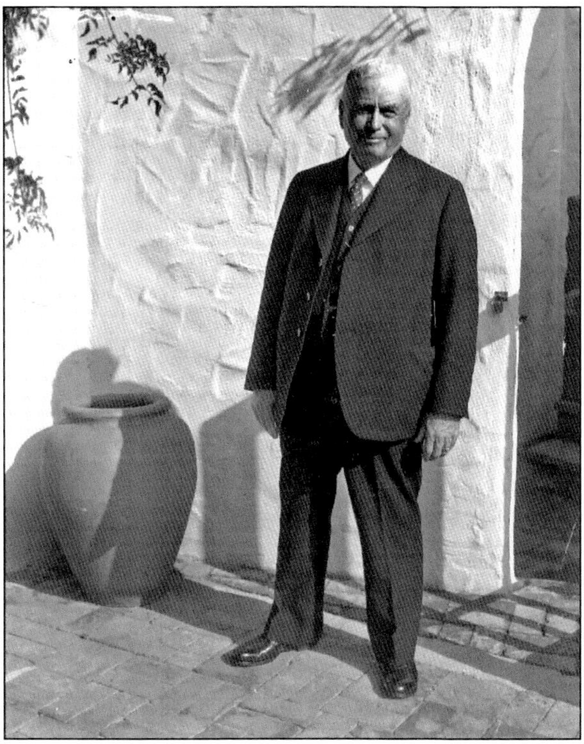

Capt. Arthur A. Morris joined the Wilmington Transportation Company in 1917. He served as the commodore of the company's fleet of vessels and was the first captain of the *Catalina*. Morris is remembered fondly, along with other captains of the SS *Catalina* such as Hans Christensen and Lee Mussetter.

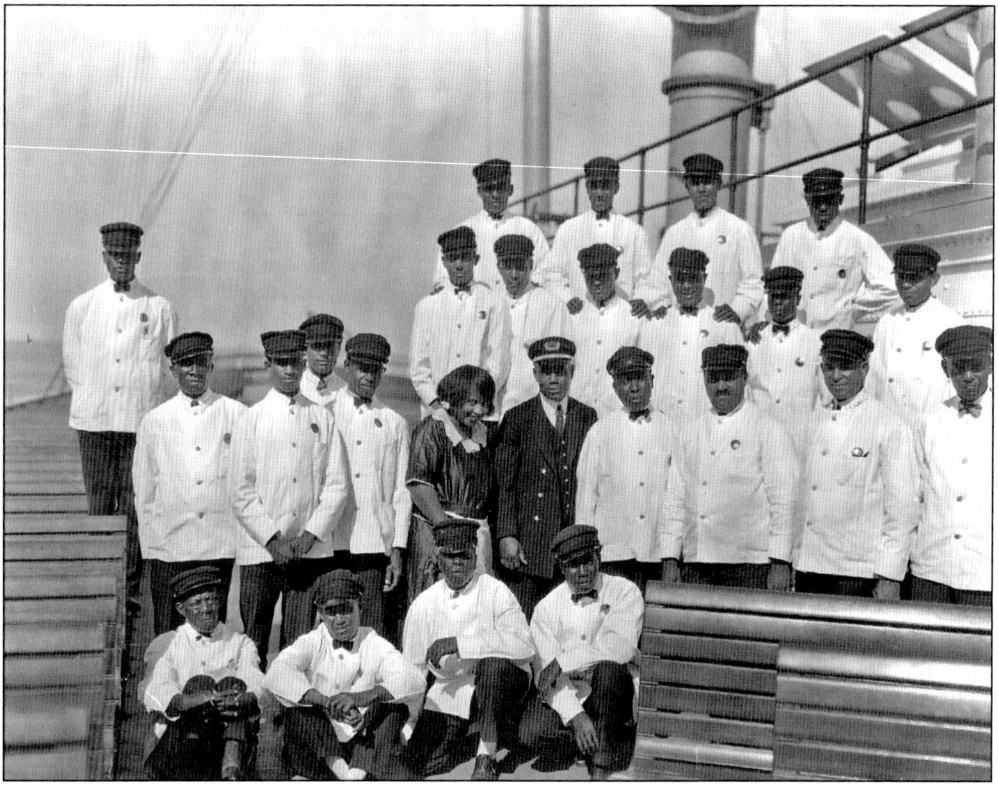

A 1920s photograph depicts some of the men and women who faithfully served on the *Catalina*. The photograph features concessionaires, porters, and stevedores. The concessionaires served food and drinks to passengers, the porters assisted passengers with a variety of needs, and the stevedores handled the luggage.

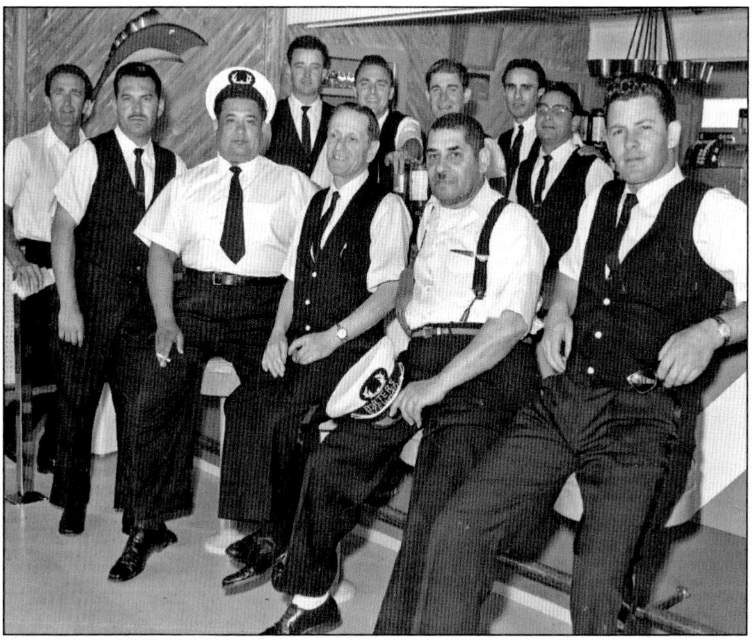

The proud steward department of the *Catalina* takes time for a photograph in 1960. The stewards provided information for passengers and sold tickets for Catalina's tours and attractions on board the steamship.

Stevedores would greet the steamships at the pier and prepare to unload the passengers' luggage. Originally, luggage and freight were passed hand-to-hand, but a conveyor was later developed. The baggage and freight were put in carts and rolled to the freight shed by tractors. Everything would be sorted in the freight shed and then delivered to island visitors, residents, and businesses.

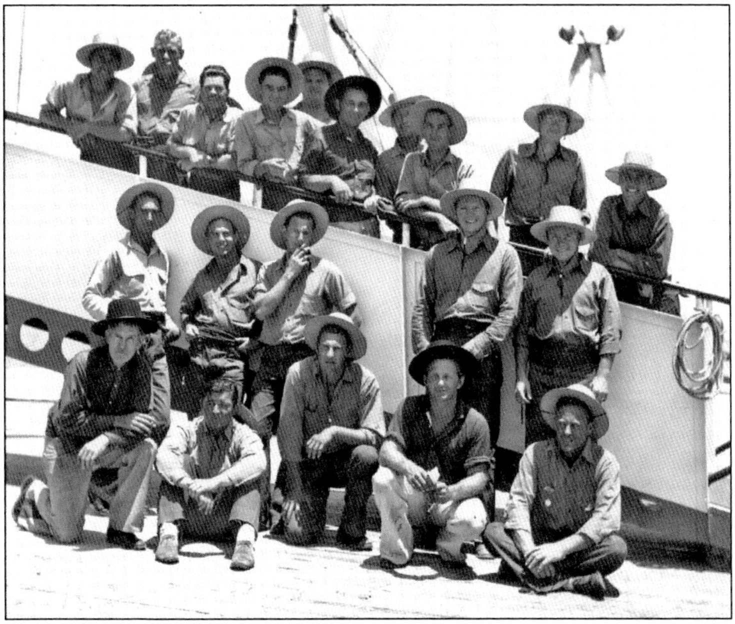

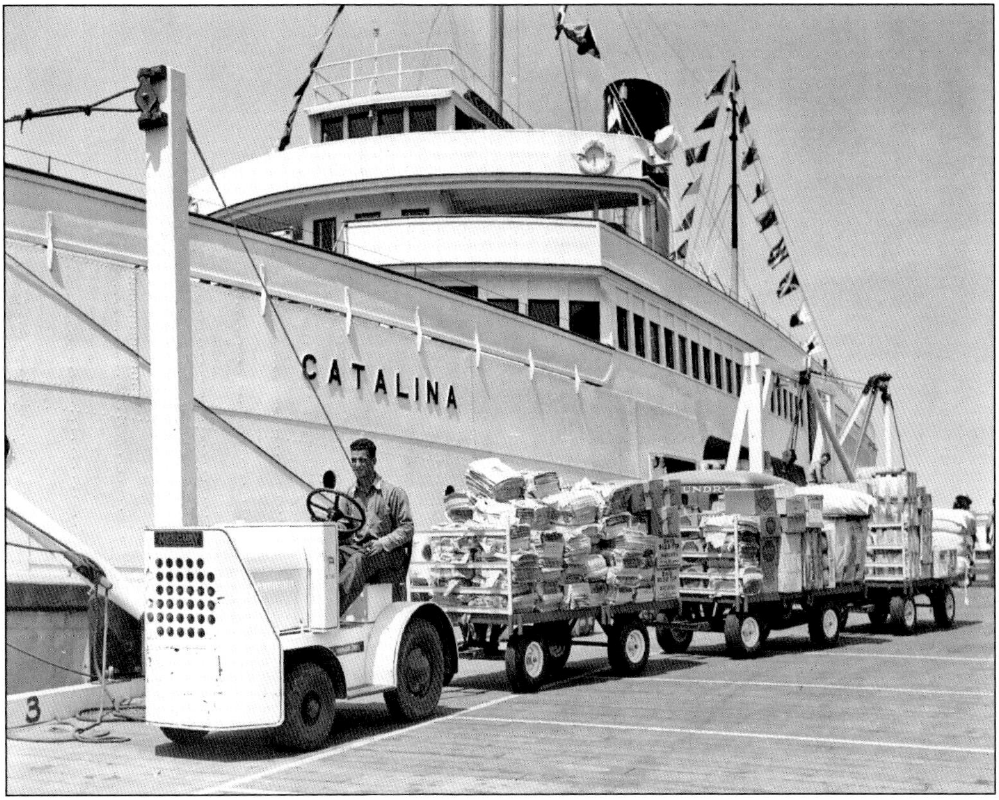

This photograph shows newspapers and supplies being unloaded from the *Catalina*. Throughout Catalina's steamship history, the vessels were used to transport much needed supplies for residents and visitors. A variety of provisions, vehicles, and even horses were carried across the channel by steamship. Early ships also carried fresh water and the mail.

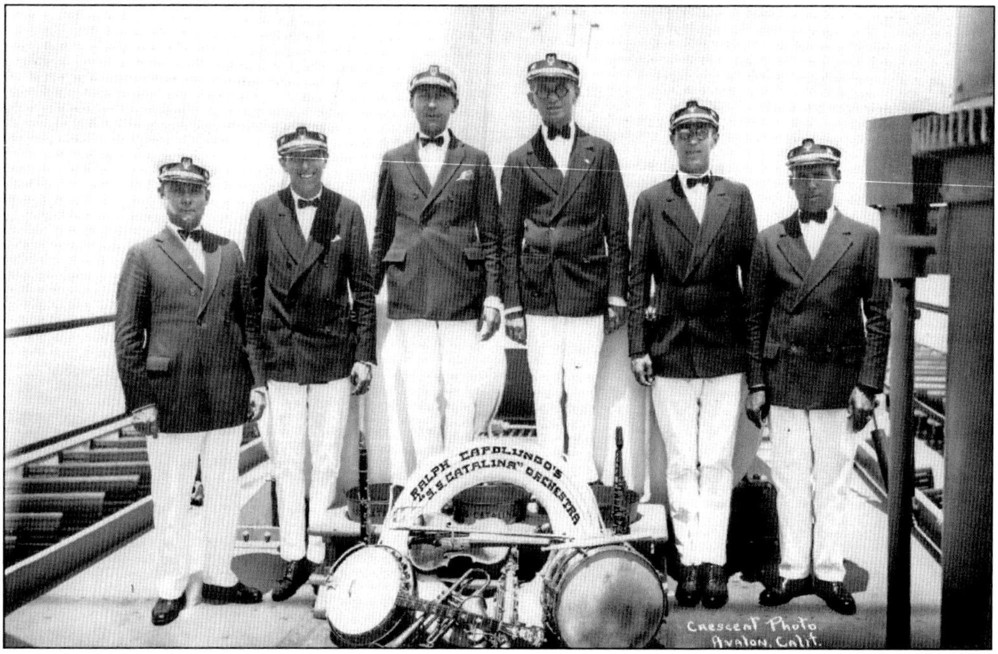

The *Catalina* had an official orchestra or band throughout her history. In the early years, the orchestra would greet passengers as they arrived at the Wilmington terminal. Once the passengers boarded, the orchestra would head to the ballroom and entertain visitors as they danced across the channel. This photograph depicts the Ralph Capolundo's *Catalina* Orchestra. (Courtesy of the Santa Catalina Island Company.)

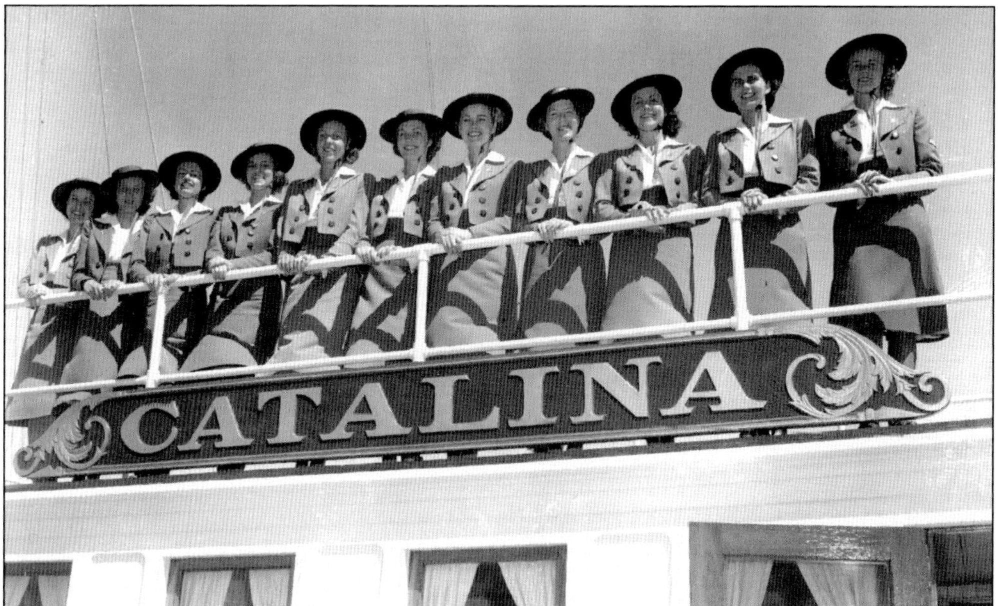

Couriers were employed by the Santa Catalina Island Company to accompany passengers on the steamships and relay information about the island to those who were interested. As hospitality ambassadors for Catalina Island, couriers offered directions to hotels and attractions, suggested interesting tours, and photographed visitors.

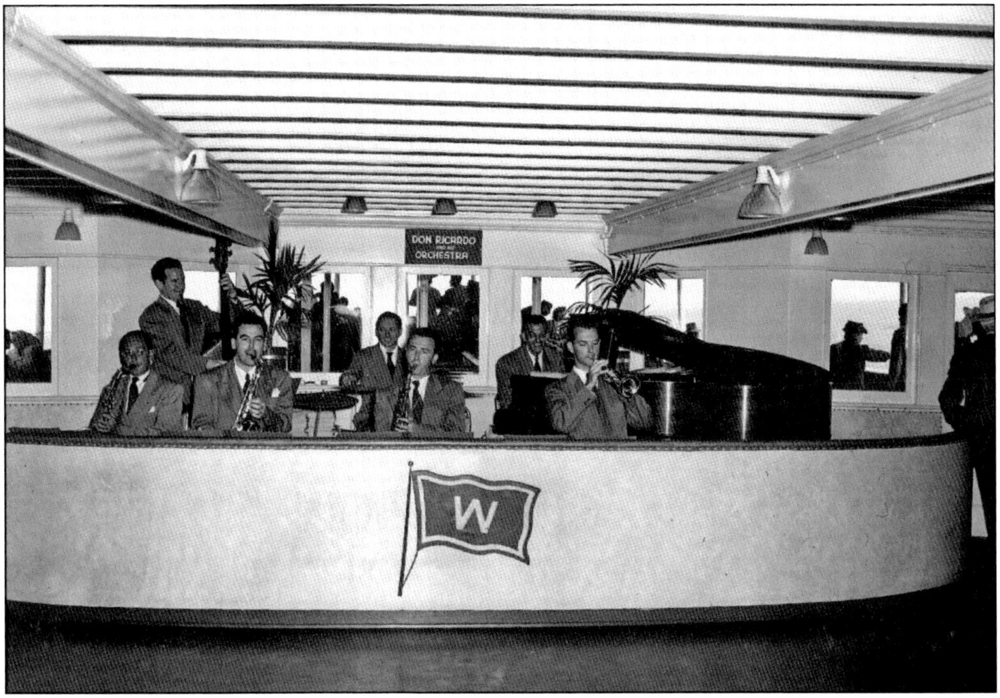

The Don Ricardo Orchestra was a Catalina favorite. They delighted visitors in the Casino ballroom and accompanied the Great White Steamer for many years.

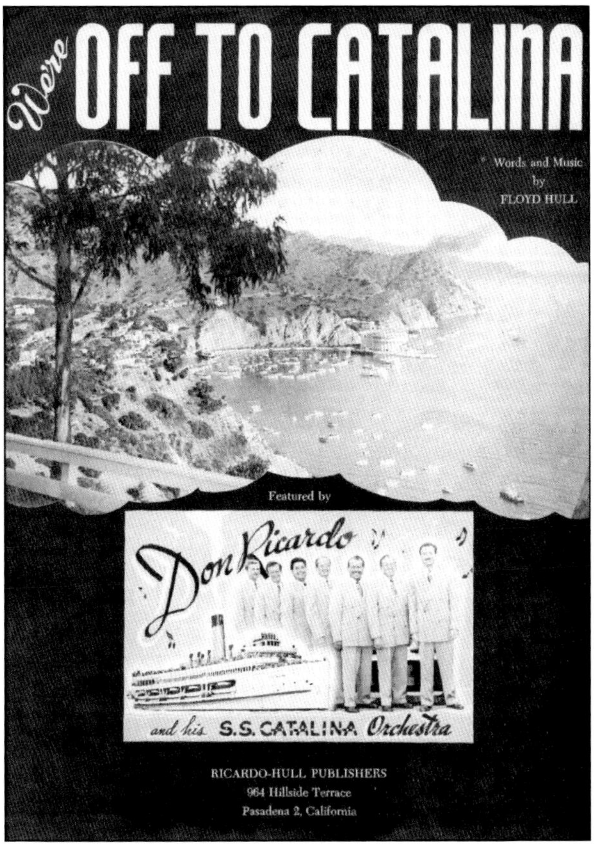

Don Ricardo and his *Catalina* Orchestra often performed the song "We're Off to Catalina," which was written and arranged by Floyd Hull in 1948. Catalina Island has been the inspiration for many songs over the years. Two Catalina favorites are "Avalon," written by Al Jolson, and "26 Miles," written by Bruce Belland and Glenn Larson of the Four Preps. (Sheet music courtesy of Roy Rose Collection.)

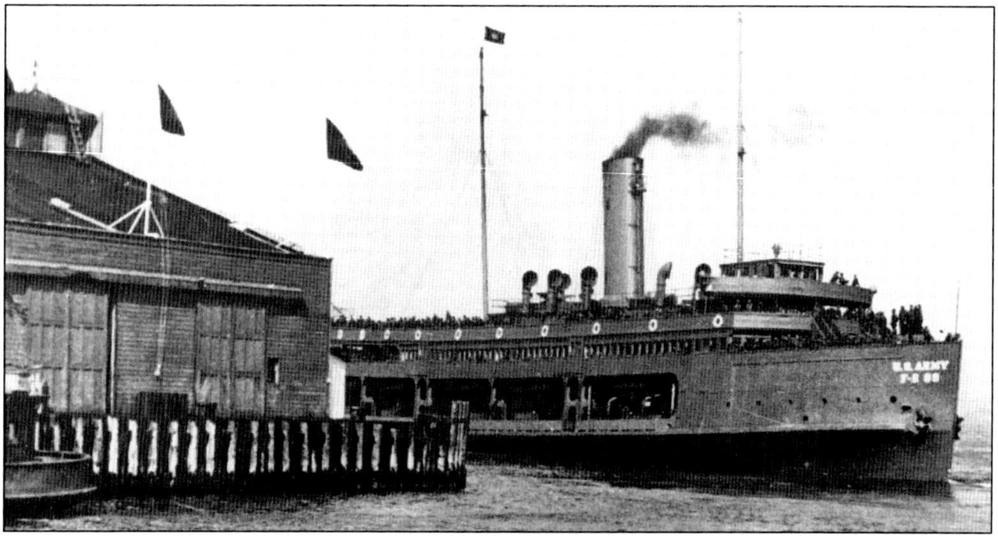

Shortly after the outbreak of World War II, the *Catalina* was requisitioned by the United States War Shipping Administration, along with the SS *Avalon* and the SS *Cabrillo.* The *Catalina* was painted gray and taken to San Francisco Bay, which was the main port of embarkation for troops bound for the Pacific theatre. She was designated *FS 99* and would be used as a troop transport throughout the bay. The *Catalina* proudly served her country and carried a total of 820,199 men, more than any other army troop transport during the war.

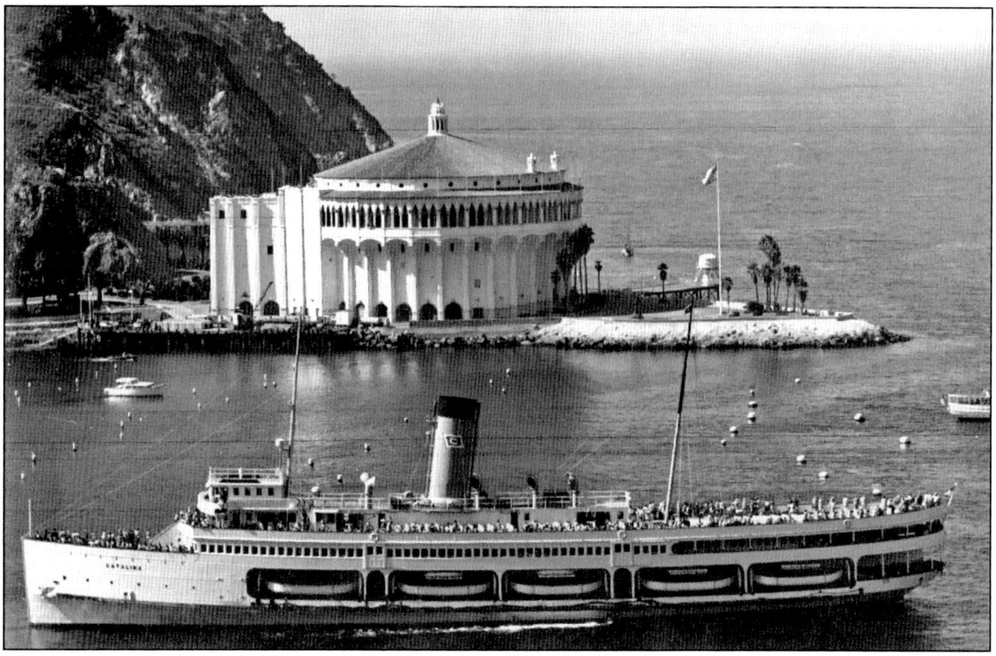

The *Catalina* was decommissioned in April 1946 and returned to the Wilmington Transportation Company. She was refurbished and placed back on the Catalina run in July 1946. Shortly thereafter, the steamers began running under the name Catalina Island Steamship Line and the traditional "W" on the smokestack was replaced with a "C." The company's name was changed again to the Catalina Island Sightseeing Line before being later dissolved when the *Catalina* was sold to M.G.R.S., a Los Angeles Harbor sightseeing company, in 1959.

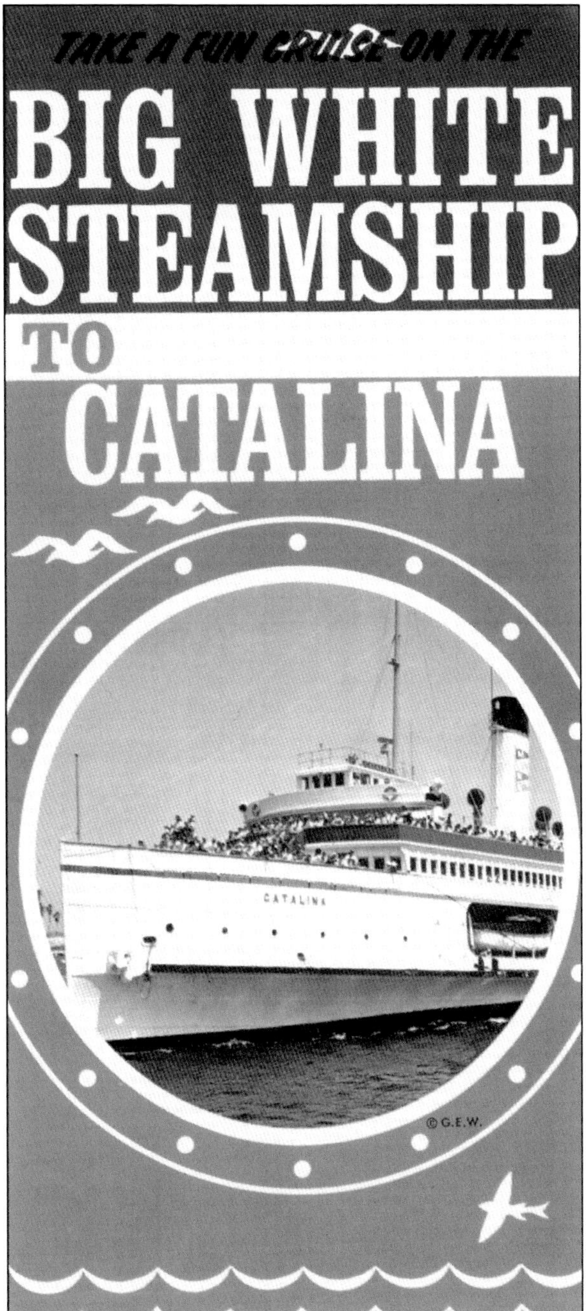

Catalina Island Sightseeing Line experienced difficulties with the labor unions governing the steamship crews and the high cost of operating the ships. As a cost-saving measure, the steamships were taken off the Catalina run during the winter months. Ultimately, the *Catalina* was sold to M.G.R.S., which made some significant alterations to the ship. The promenade deck was painted turquoise and trimmed with a yellow railing and a pink strip was added below the saloon deck. The ventilators were painted pink and the funnel was repainted with the letters M.G.R.S. in four flags. This brochure is from the first season that the *Catalina* ran under M.G.R.S. operation.

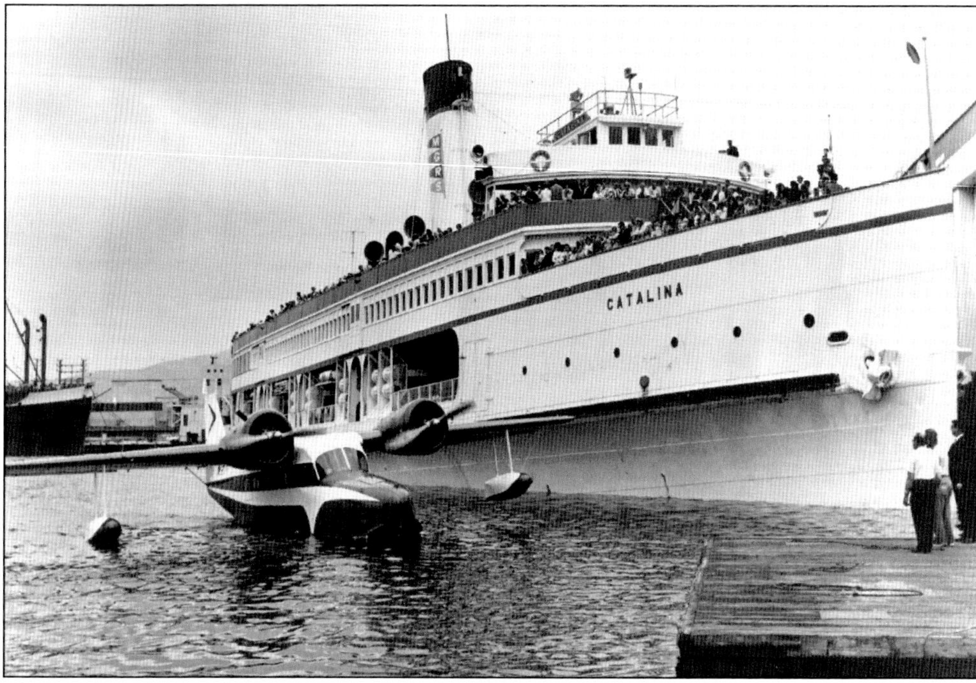

The masts of the *Catalina* were later removed, as well as the lifeboats and their davits. The wooden lifeboats were replaced with inflatable rafts, which opened up more deck space for additional passenger seating and increased the ship's capacity. These modifications left the ship very top heavy, so needing to add weight, they poured concrete on the deck. It was a specific kind of concrete that could withstand the vibration of the ship.

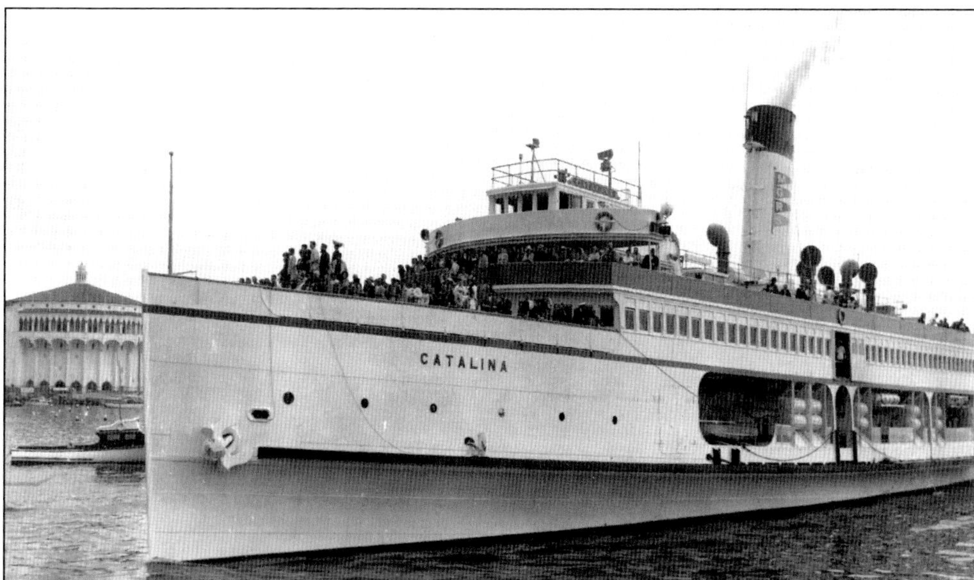

The *Catalina* ran under the operation of M.G.R.S. for 10 years. Charles Stilwell, owner of M.G.R.S., made a passionate attempt to maintain a successful operation, but continued labor disputes forced him to sell in 1970. Carolyn Stanalan of Bellflower, California, and her investors purchased the M.G.R.S. line and changed the name of the company to Catalina Transportation Company.

"Catalina Cappy the Clown" was added to the hospitality crew of the *Catalina* during this time. He would greet passengers with a smile and a handshake as they boarded the vessel and entertain youngsters during the crossing. Many island visitors and residents fondly remember him.

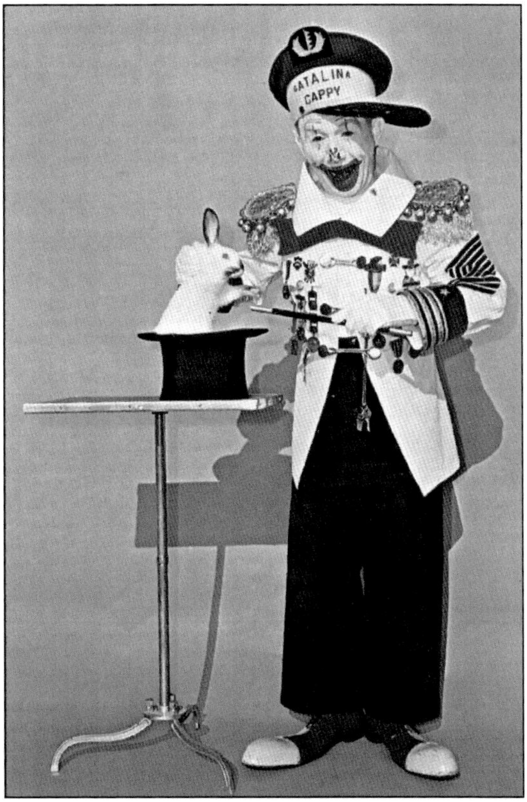

Pictured here is the concession stand on the *Catalina* in the 1970s. The stand was filled with visitor necessities such as hats, sunglasses, and many Catalina Island souvenirs in case a visitor didn't have time to shop in Avalon. (Courtesy of the Santa Catalina Island Company.)

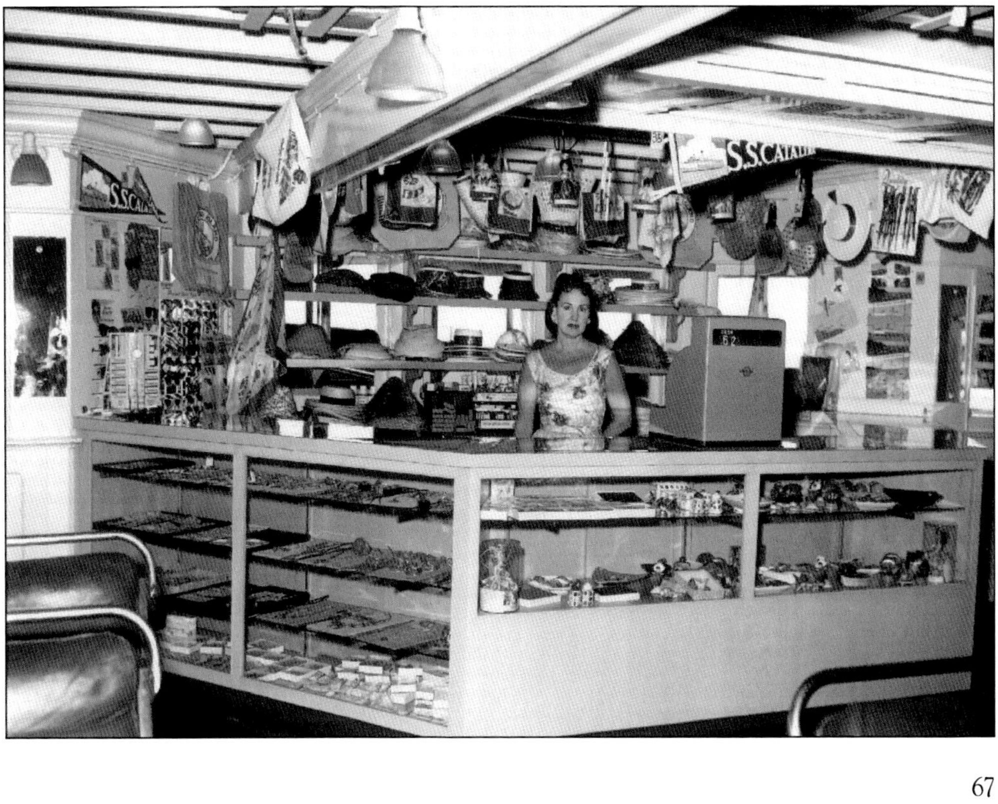

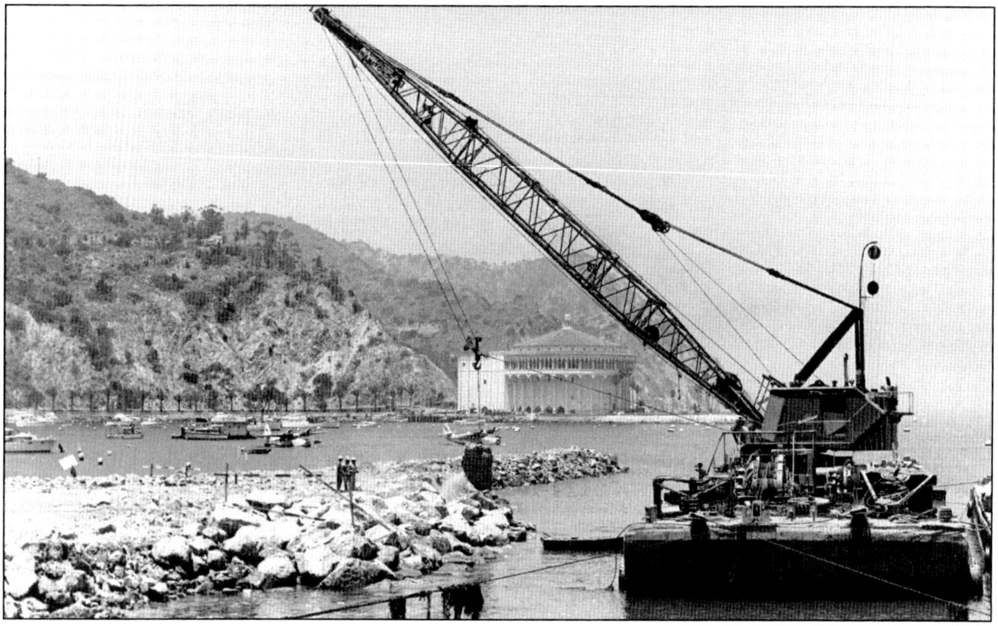

The long-standing steamer pier in Avalon was dismantled in the late 1960s and the Cabrillo Mole was built. The mole was part of an overall plan for harbor improvement by the City of Avalon and was designed as a docking facility for several ships. The seaward side was designed to accommodate larger ships such as the *Catalina*. The Cabrillo Mole was finished in time for the 1969 season and has since served as Avalon's primary dock.

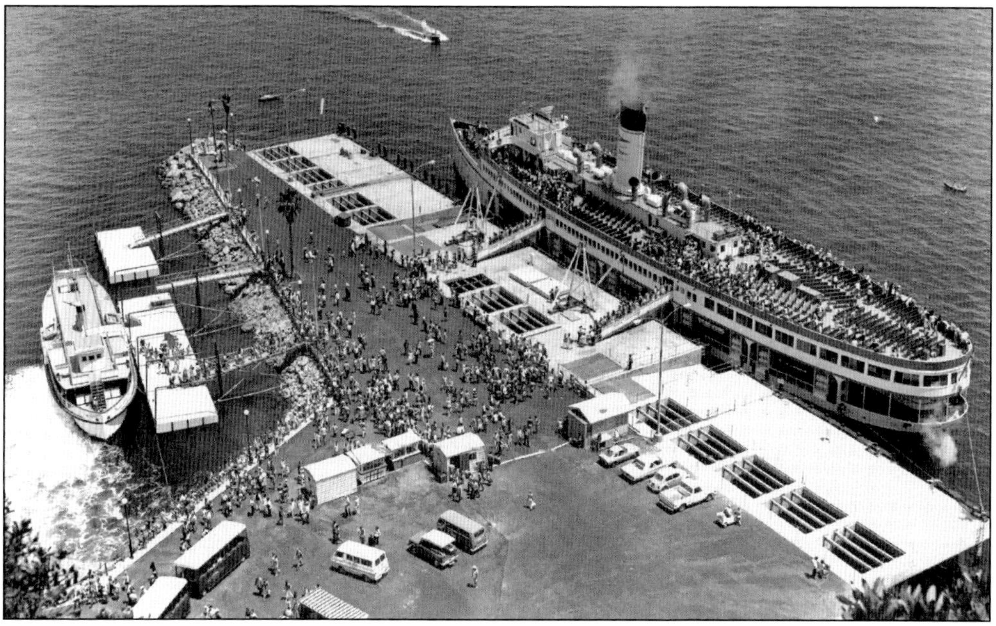

The *Catalina* continued to run during the summer seasons until 1975. Labor disputes continued to plague her regularly scheduled service, but when she did run, the vessel docked on the mainland at a new Catalina terminal at Berth 95 in San Pedro and landed in Avalon at the Cabrillo Mole. Once the landing was complete, it was discovered that the *Catalina* did not dock well against the straight surface of the mole. Flexible fenders were then added to better accommodate the *Catalina*.

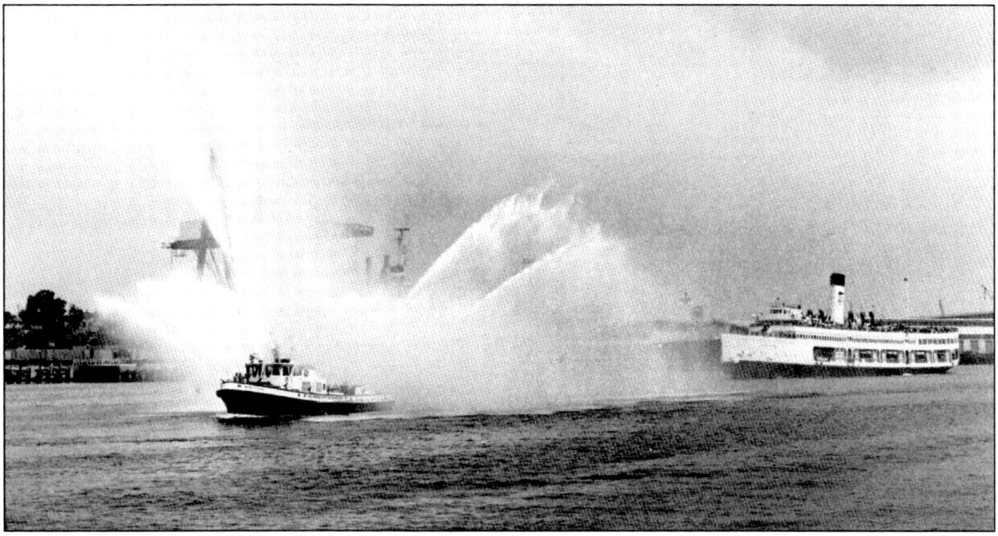

The *Catalina* made her final voyage on September 14, 1975. She was retired from the Catalina run after several years of labor disputes and financial difficulties. In 1976, she was placed on the National Register of Historic Places and was registered as a California State Historical Landmark. Officials at Catalina Transportation Company sought to resolve her financial difficulties, but she could find no permanent home.

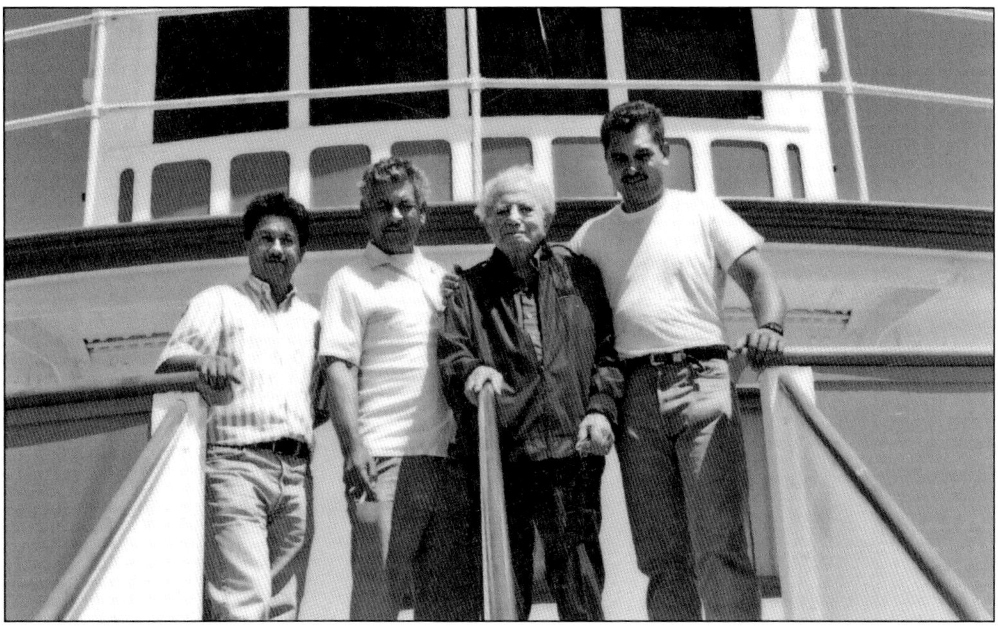

The *Catalina* was offered at auction in 1977 and purchased by real estate agent Hymie Singer (pictured second from the right), who bought the ship as a Valentine's Day present for his wife. Singer had good intentions for the ship, but no real plan. Suggested uses were a restaurant, an entertainment complex, or a ferry ship in the Bahamas. While the use of the ship was being decided, the *Catalina* was moved around several times to different locations in Los Angeles Harbor and along the southern California coast. In late July 1978, the *Catalina* was moved to an anchorage off the coast of Santa Monica. The ship was left there to avoid the expense of docking fees and the unguarded ship was extensively vandalized during this time.

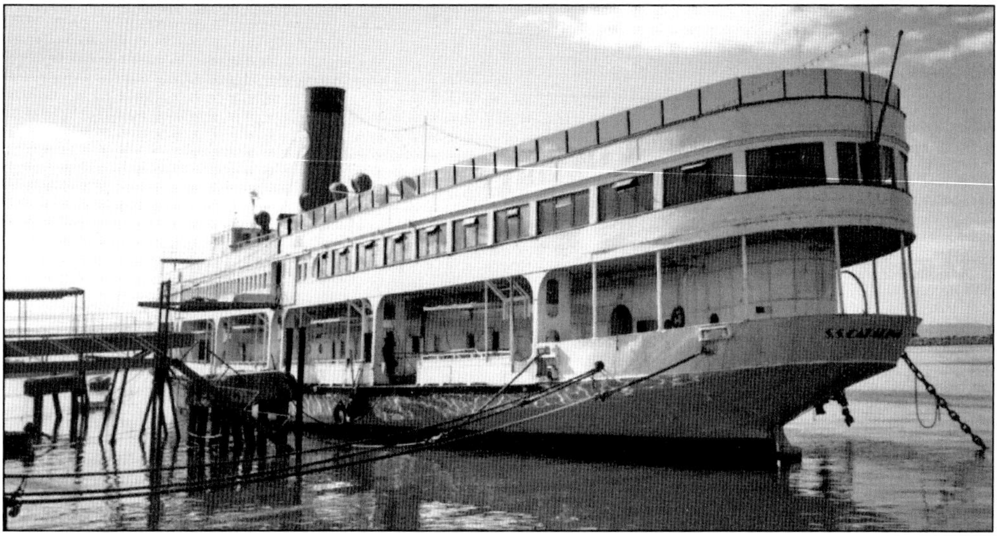

The *Catalina* was eventually declared a hazard to other boaters by the coast guard and a Los Angeles superior court judge ordered her removal from the Santa Monica anchorage. She was towed to Long Beach and ideas and proposals for the use of the ship swirled around for several years, but no plan ever came to fruition. After being moved around several times within Los Angeles Harbor, she broke free of her anchor and had a near miss with a loaded oil tanker. As a result, the Coast Guard and Department of Justice planned to levy fines and seize the ship. Before the papers could be served, the *Catalina* was hooked to a tugboat and towed out of the harbor and the country. On March 4, 1985, the *Catalina* dropped anchor in Ensenada, Mexico, where she remains today.

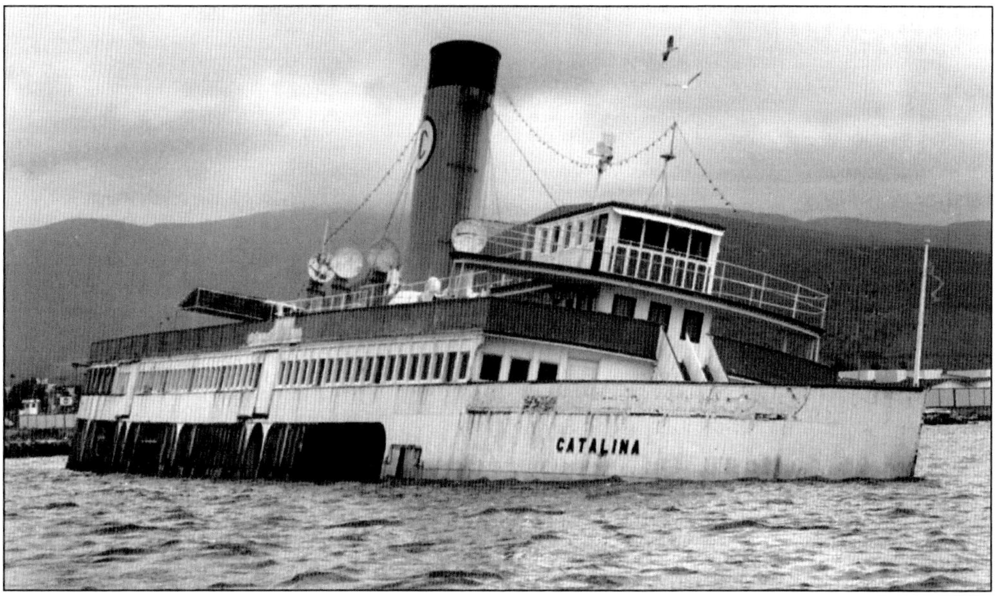

Initial plans to convert the *Catalina* into a floating entertainment center with disco, shops, and restaurants met with marginal success, but were ultimately abandoned by 1988. Since then, the Great White Steamer has languished in Ensenada Harbor. In 1997, she began to take on water during a bad storm and the following year began to sink into the mud. Several American-based groups have been trying long and hard to save the once glorious ship, but their efforts have met with resistance. Today the last ship of Catalina's romantic steamer era remains half-sunk in the Mexican harbor.

Four

An Ocean Voyage

The adventure of Catalina Island began not when visitors arrived at the island, but when they boarded the steamer in Wilmington or San Pedro. Early postcards from the 1900s show the voyage across the channel as an important and memorable part of the entire Catalina experience. In the first half of the 20th century, the Catalina steamers were often the first introduction to ocean travel for many passengers. To encourage travelers, the Bannings, and later the Wrigleys, added ships to the fleet that were efficient and comfortable and some were quite luxuriously appointed with electric lights and exotic wood finishes. The Wrigley's first steamer, the *Avalon*, was hailed in papers and postcards as "palatial" and the *Catalina* cost a cool $1 million to build in 1923. A "day-tripper" would have only four hours on shore to explore the pleasures of Avalon and the island, so the two hours spent crossing the channel each way was an integral part of the Catalina experience. The many activities, sights, and sounds enjoyed by the passengers insured that it was as advertised, "In all the world, no trip like this!"

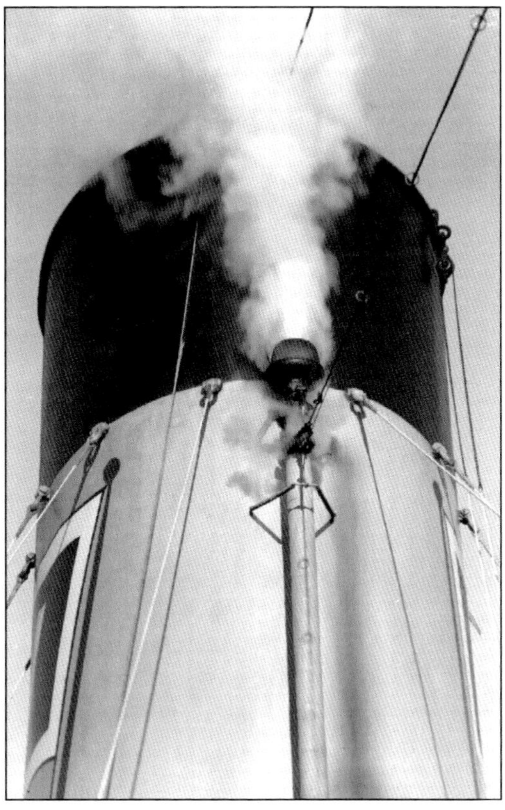

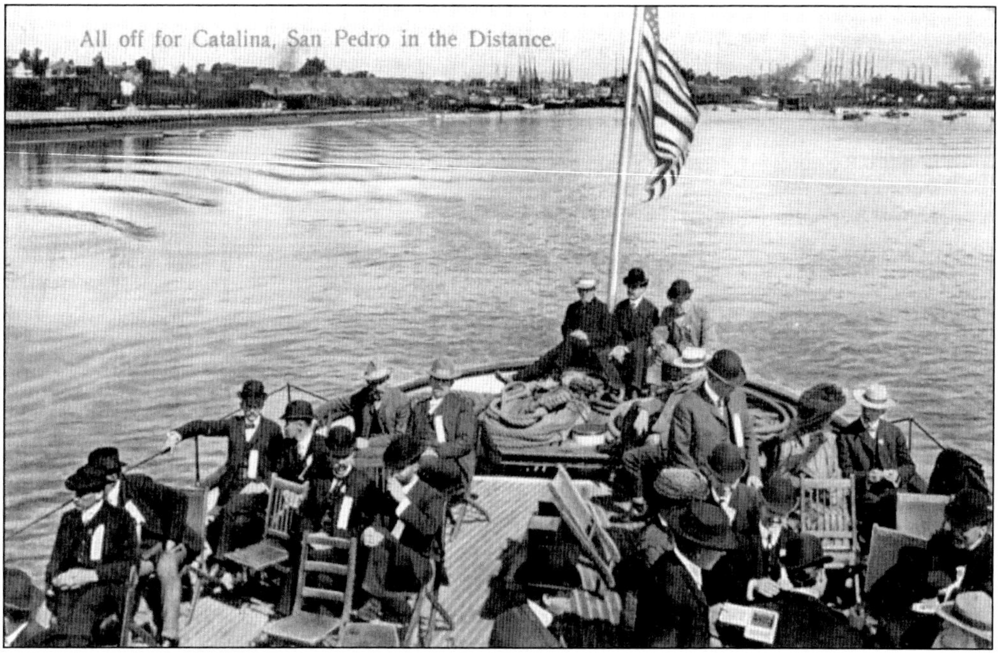

Early steamship technology, along with advances in the railroad and electricity, ushered in a period of tremendous growth for California. During the 1880s, thousands of people flocked to Southern California. Small towns sprang up in the Los Angeles area and they were soon linked by electric trolley cars. These trolley cars carried thousands of travelers from several points in the Los Angeles area directly to Los Angeles Harbor.

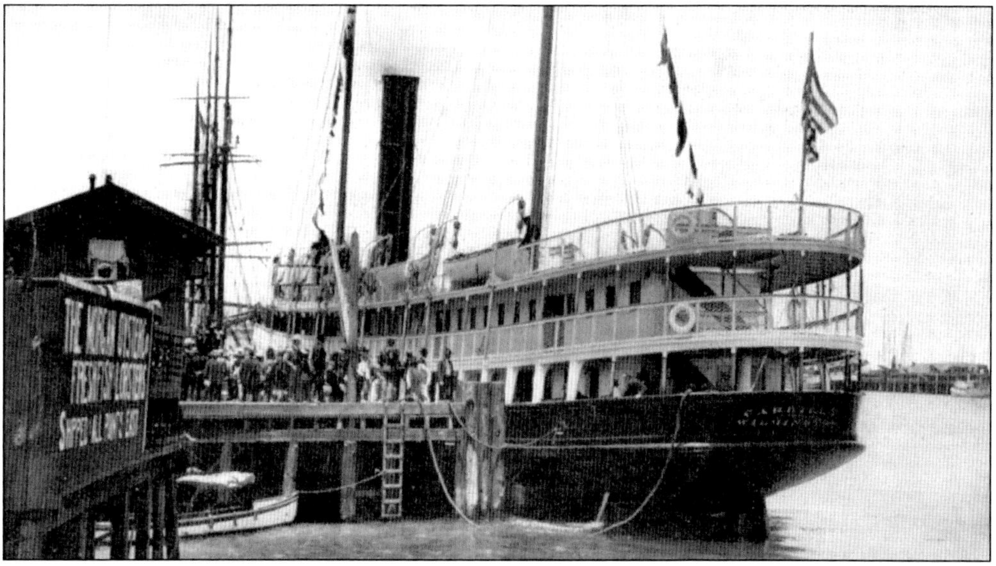

Phinneas Banning, who founded the Wilmington Transportation Company, was also a pioneer in the development of Los Angeles Harbor. He promoted the building of a railroad from Los Angeles to Wilmington and creating a harbor in San Pedro. With the railroad and electric trolley cars, the trip from downtown Los Angeles to the Banning's wharf in Wilmington took only 45 minutes. From there, passengers could board one of the Wilmington Transportation Company's excursion ships and venture out to sea. Passengers are pictured here loading the SS *Cabrillo*.

Many of the people who settled in California or traveled to the western state had crossed hundreds or thousands of miles in order to set their eyes on the Pacific Ocean. Catalina Island would have been an enticing trip, allowing passengers to experience their first ocean voyage and visit a Pacific island. It was an exciting time for adventurous travelers. This rare photograph, taken on the top deck of the *Cabrillo*, shows passengers enjoying the crossing in the 1900s.

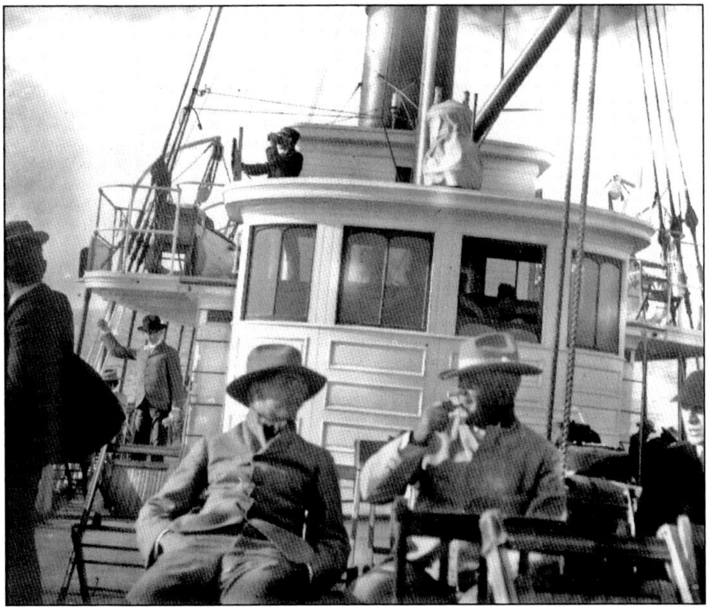

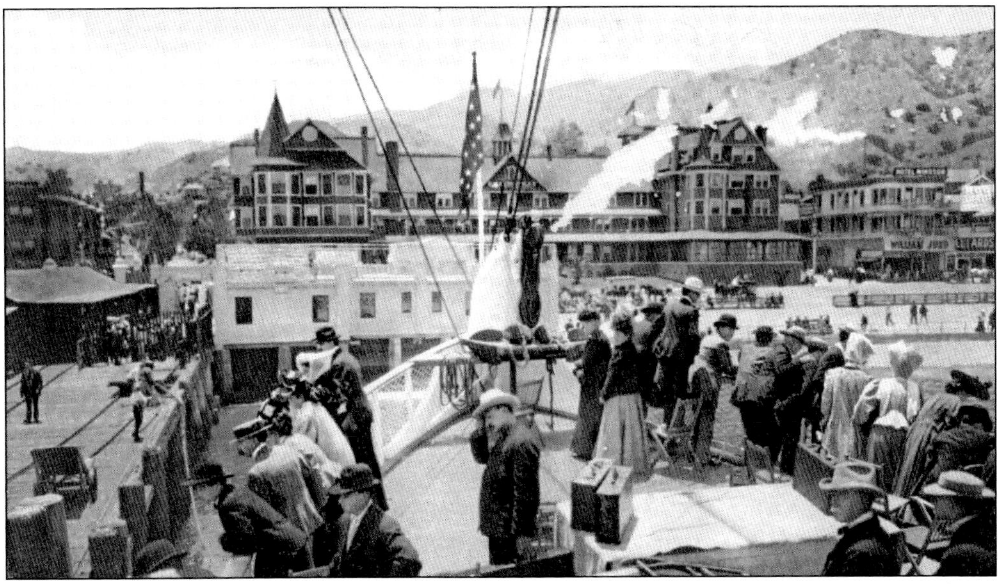

During these early days of ocean travel to Catalina Island, crossing the San Pedro Channel was an exciting and significant part of the adventure. The trip across the channel could take up to four hours and in many cases passengers spent more time at sea than visiting the island. For this reason, the channel crossing was an important aspect of the Catalina experience for many years. In fact, for many people, the trip to Catalina began long before they reached the ocean.

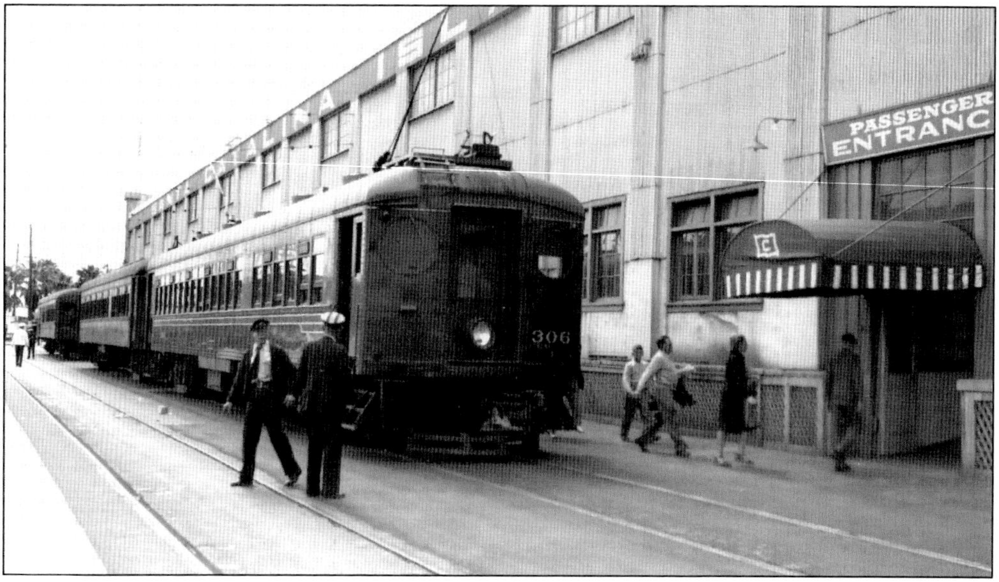

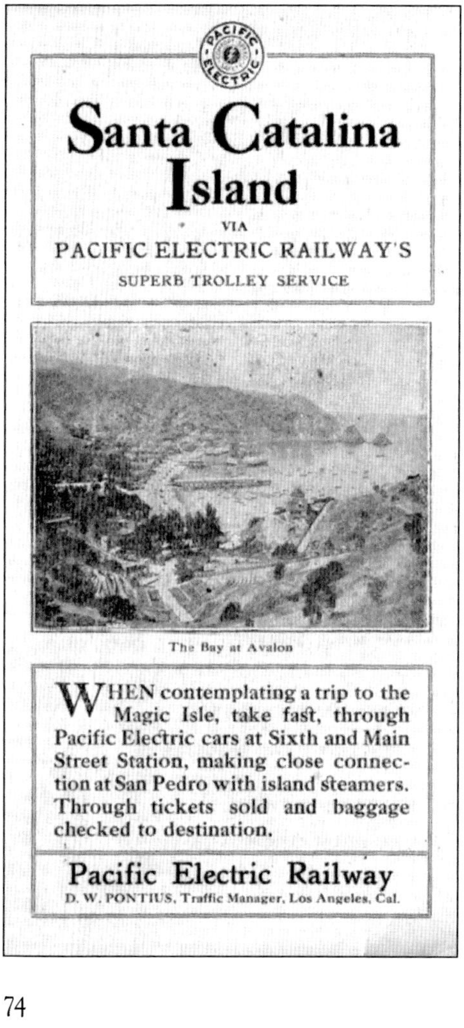

Often visitors bound for Catalina Island began their trip aboard a Pacific Electric Trolley Car or "Red Car." The electric trolley car service played a crucial role in the development of Los Angeles as it provided a link to towns and points of interest throughout the Los Angeles area. The red cars made the mountains, beaches, and suburbs accessible at a time when many people did not have independent modes of transportation. Pacific Electric Railway offered trips to Mount Lowe, San Gabriel Mission, Rubio Canyon, Santa Ana, and the beaches of Southern California, and took passengers directly to the Catalina terminal in Wilmington.

Trains for the Catalina terminal left the Pacific Electric Station at Sixth and Main Streets in downtown Los Angeles at 9:00 a.m. everyday. Trains also left from Pacific and Ocean Avenues in Long Beach at 9:15 a.m. daily, and several per week ran from Pasadena, leaving Colorado Boulevard and Broadway at 8:30 a.m. Returning passengers would arrive in Los Angeles, Long Beach, or Pasadena in the early evening.

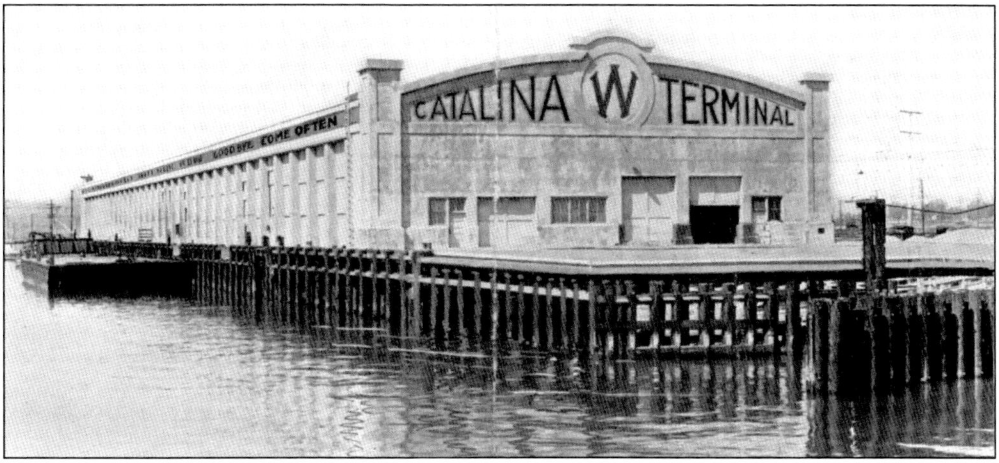

The new terminal in Wilmington opened in 1920, the same season that the SS *Avalon* was introduced to the Wilmington Transportation Company fleet. The Catalina terminal at Wilmington was easily accessible by train or automobile. For passengers motoring down to the terminal, there were several well-defined routes from Los Angeles and neighboring points, each leading the way directly to the terminal with red metal "fist" signs pointing the way.

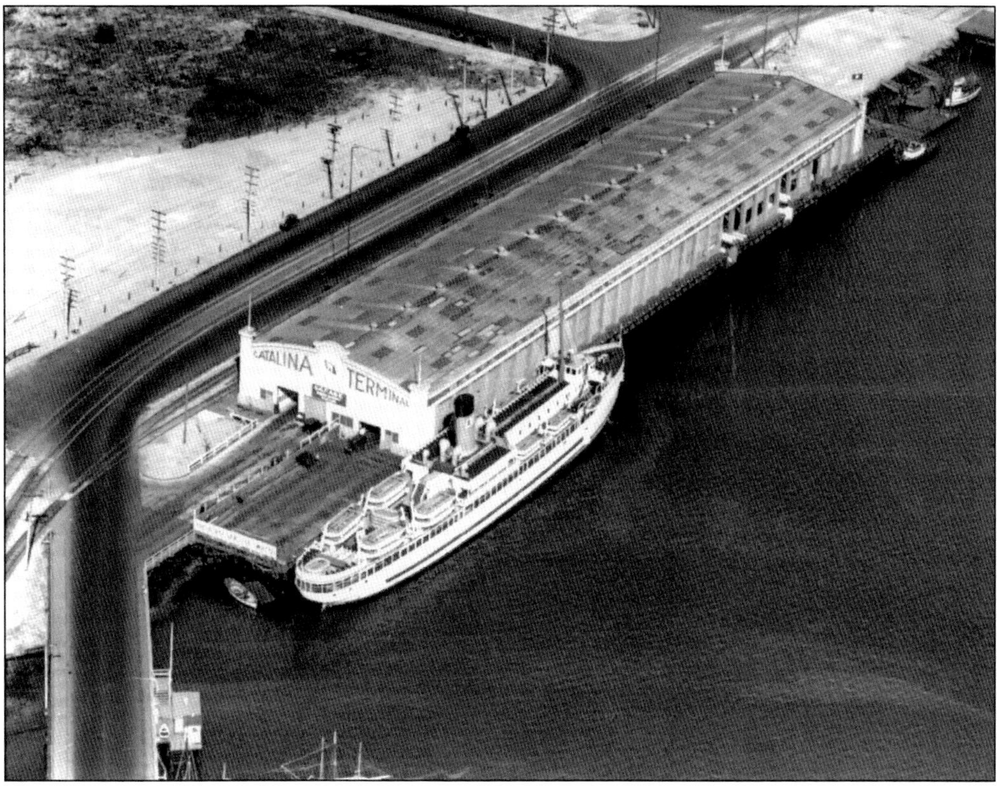

A brochure from the 1920 season describes the "new" Catalina terminal as affording every convenience to island-bound travelers. It included an "excellently appointed restaurant, news stand, waiting rooms and rest rooms. Commodious interior parking space to accommodate 250 automobiles and complete facilities for business arrangements and information." The Wilmington terminal served as the primary embarkation for ocean travel to Catalina Island for 48 years.

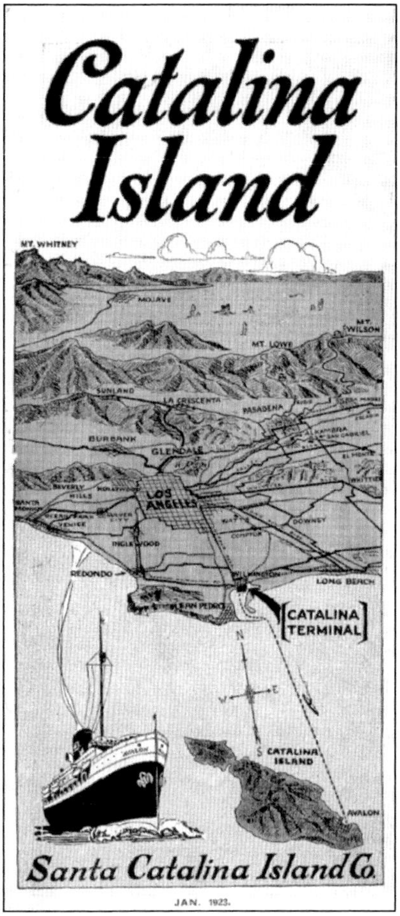

This brochure from 1923 includes a wonderful drawing that depicts the location of the Wilmington terminal within the Los Angeles area and the route taken by the steamships to Catalina Island. The brochure describes Catalina Island as being "twenty five miles off the Harbor of Los Angeles. It is reached from Los Angeles in about three hours. The Pacific Electric Railway connects at Wilmington with the Wilmington Transportation Company—Wrigley Line steamships. Auto boulevards also lead directly to the pier."

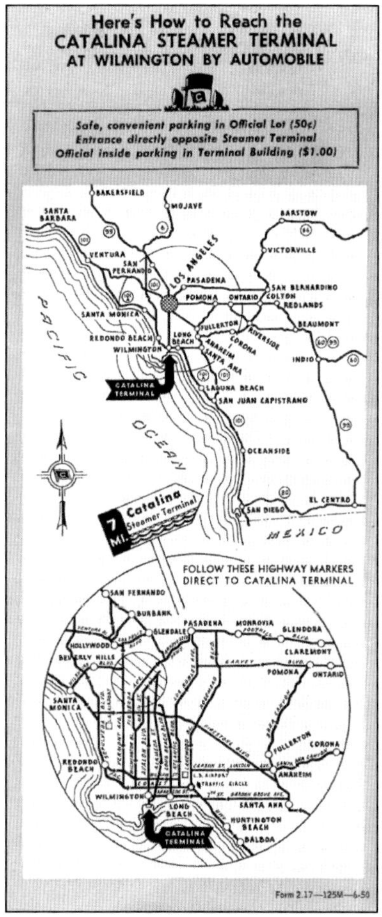

This later brochure from 1950 includes a similar map with a more detailed drawing of the location of the Catalina terminal within Los Angeles Harbor. The steamships' summer schedule remained the same for many years. The SS *Catalina* would leave Wilmington at 9:30 a.m., followed by the SS *Avalon* at 10:00 a.m. The *Catalina* would arrive in Avalon 11:40 a.m., and the *Avalon* would arrive at 12:20 p.m. Both steamers would leave *Avalon* at 4:30 p.m.

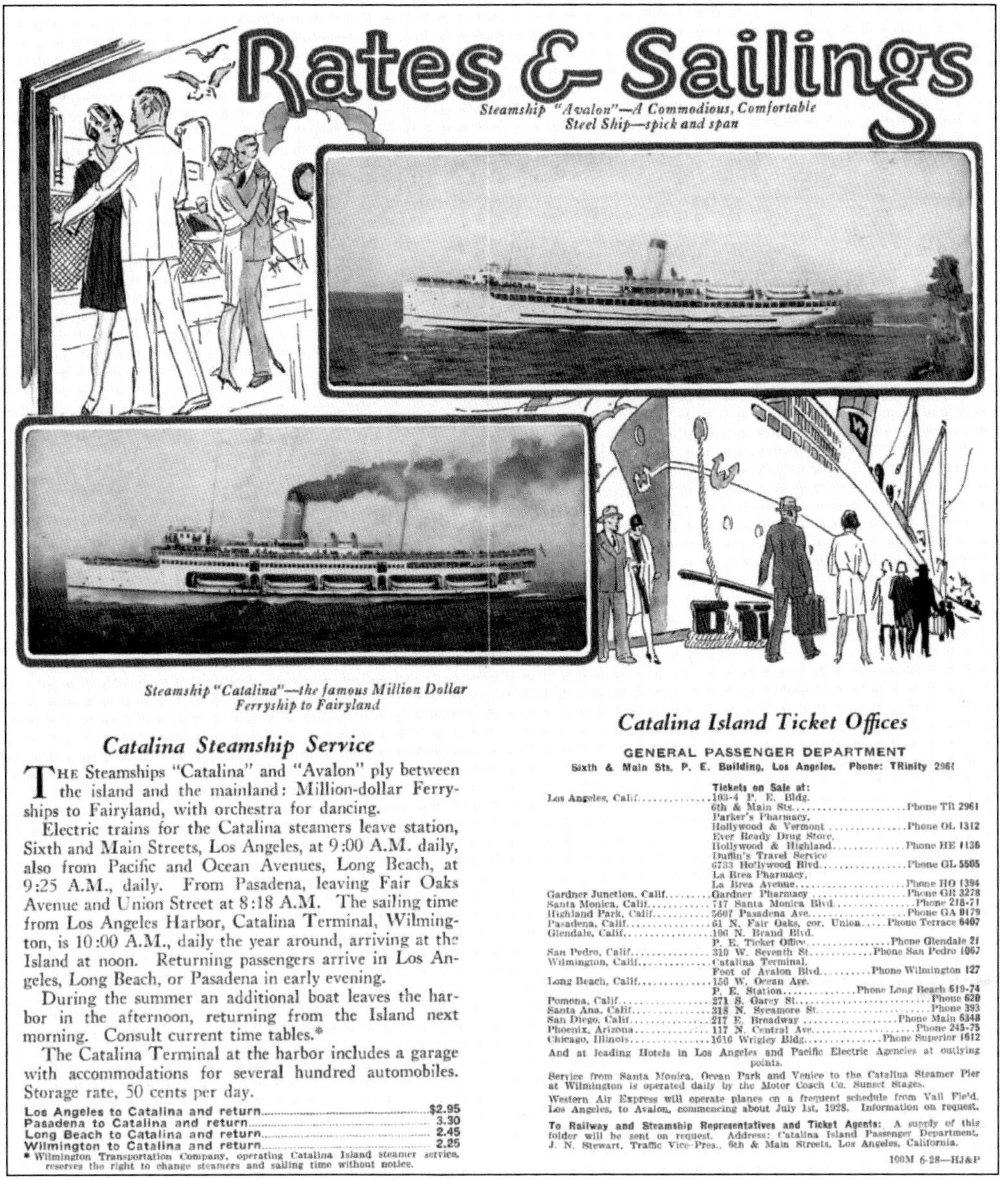

Rates & Sailings

Steamship "Avalon"—A Commodious, Comfortable Steel Ship—spick and span

Steamship "Catalina"—the famous Million Dollar Ferryship to Fairyland

Catalina Steamship Service

THE Steamships "Catalina" and "Avalon" ply between the island and the mainland: Million-dollar Ferryships to Fairyland, with orchestra for dancing.

Electric trains for the Catalina steamers leave station, Sixth and Main Streets, Los Angeles, at 9:00 A.M. daily, also from Pacific and Ocean Avenues, Long Beach, at 9:25 A.M., daily. From Pasadena, leaving Fair Oaks Avenue and Union Street at 8:18 A.M. The sailing time from Los Angeles Harbor, Catalina Terminal, Wilmington, is 10:00 A.M., daily the year around, arriving at the Island at noon. Returning passengers arrive in Los Angeles, Long Beach, or Pasadena in early evening.

During the summer an additional boat leaves the harbor in the afternoon, returning from the Island next morning. Consult current time tables.*

The Catalina Terminal at the harbor includes a garage with accommodations for several hundred automobiles. Storage rate, 50 cents per day.

Los Angeles to Catalina and return	$2.95
Pasadena to Catalina and return	3.30
Long Beach to Catalina and return	2.45
Wilmington to Catalina and return	2.25

* Wilmington Transportation Company, operating Catalina Island steamer service, reserves the right to change steamers and sailing time without notice.

Catalina Island Ticket Offices

GENERAL PASSENGER DEPARTMENT

Sixth & Main Sts, P. E. Building, Los Angeles. Phone: TRinity 2961

	Tickets on Sale at:	
Los Angeles, Calif.	103-4 P. E. Bldg. 6th & Main Sts.	Phone TR 2961
	Parker's Pharmacy, Hollywood & Vermont	Phone OL 1312
	Ever Ready Drug Store, Hollywood & Highland	Phone HE 1136
	Duffin's Travel Service 6733 Hollywood Blvd.	Phone GL 5505
	La Brea Pharmacy, La Brea Avenue	Phone HO 1394
Gardner Junction, Calif.	Gardner Pharmacy	Phone GR 3278
Santa Monica, Calif.	717 Santa Monica Blvd.	Phone 218-71
Highland Park, Calif.	5607 Pasadena Ave.	Phone GA 0179
Pasadena, Calif.	61 N. Fair Oaks, cor. Union	Phone Terrace 6407
Glendale, Calif.	106 N. Brand Blvd. P. E. Ticket Office	Phone Glendale 21
San Pedro, Calif.	310 W. Seventh St.	Phone San Pedro 1067
Wilmington, Calif.	Catalina Terminal, Foot of Avalon Blvd.	Phone Wilmington 127
Long Beach, Calif.	150 W. Ocean Ave. P. E. Station	Phone Long Beach 619-74
Pomona, Calif.	271 S. Garey St.	Phone 620
Santa Ana, Calif.	318 N. Sycamore St.	Phone 393
San Diego, Calif.	217 E. Broadway	Phone Main 6348
Phoenix, Arizona	117 N. Central Ave.	Phone 245-75
Chicago, Illinois	1616 Wrigley Bldg.	Phone Superior 1612

And at leading Hotels in Los Angeles and Pacific Electric Agencies at outlying points.

Service from Santa Monica, Ocean Park and Venice to the Catalina Steamer Pier at Wilmington is operated daily by the Motor Coach Co. Sunset Stages.

Western Air Express will operate planes on a frequent schedule from Vail Field, Los Angeles, to Avalon, commencing about July 1st, 1928. Information on request.

To Railway and Steamship Representatives and Ticket Agents: A supply of this folder will be sent on request. Address: Catalina Island Passenger Department, J. N. Stewart, Traffic Vice-Pres., 6th & Main Streets, Los Angeles, California.

100M 6-28—HJ&P

This wonderful brochure provides the Rates and Sailings for 1928. The photographs of the *Avalon* and the *Catalina*, along with the drawings of couples dancing and passengers boarding one of the steamers, offered potential visitors a glimpse of the channel-crossing experience. This interesting brochure was printed at a time of great growth for Avalon and Catalina Island. It shares that "the palatial new Casino, under construction, will have a seating capacity of 2,000 persons in its auditorium on the main floor and a ballroom on the second floor large enough to accommodate 1,800 couples at one time." The brochure also mentions the opening of the "new" Catalina Bird Park and the "new" Catalina Country Club House. The Casino, Bird Park, and Country Club were all improvement projects launched by William Wrigley Jr. to enhance Catalina's visitor experience.

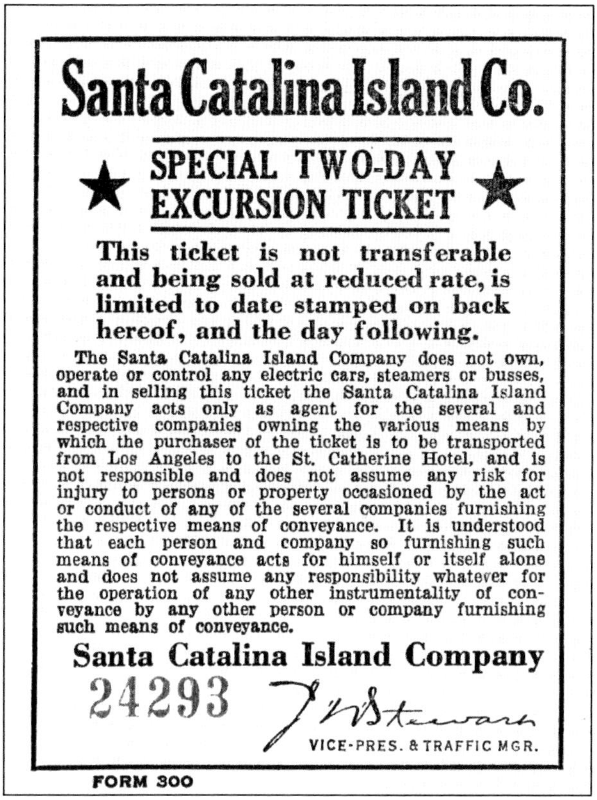

Santa Catalina Island Co.

SPECIAL TWO-DAY EXCURSION TICKET

This ticket is not transferable and being sold at reduced rate, is limited to date stamped on back hereof, and the day following.

The Santa Catalina Island Company does not own, operate or control any electric cars, steamers or busses, and in selling this ticket the Santa Catalina Island Company acts only as agent for the several and respective companies owning the various means by which the purchaser of the ticket is to be transported from Los Angeles to the St. Catherine Hotel, and is not responsible and does not assume any risk for injury to persons or property occasioned by the act or conduct of any of the several companies furnishing the respective means of conveyance. It is understood that each person and company so furnishing such means of conveyance acts for himself or itself alone and does not assume any responsibility whatever for the operation of any other instrumentality of conveyance by any other person or company furnishing such means of conveyance.

Santa Catalina Island Company

24293 J. W. Stewart

VICE-PRES. & TRAFFIC MGR.

FORM 300

This passenger ticket was a "Special Two-Day Excursion Ticket" from 1929. The Santa Catalina Island Company, which owned the Wilmington Transportation Company as well as several hotels and attractions on the island, sold vacation packages to visitors. An excursion package included round-trip fare on one of the Catalina steamers, a glass-bottom boat ride, and a luncheon at the Hotel St. Catherine. Overnight packages would include accommodations at the Hotel Atwater, Hotel St. Catherine, or the Island Villas.

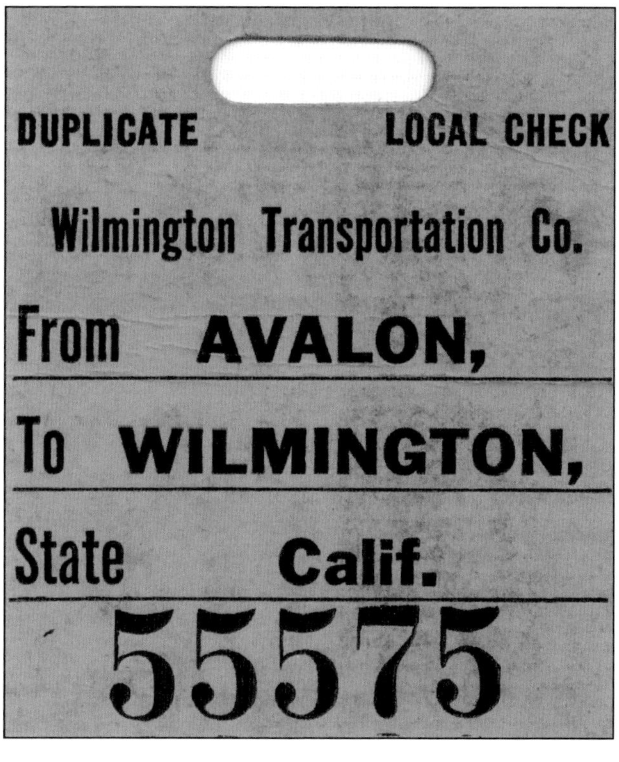

Passengers were encouraged to check all of their baggage upon arrival at the Wilmington terminal. The baggage was placed in trolley cars and rolled into the hull of the ship. Once passengers reached the island, their luggage could be picked up at the baggage terminal on the steamer pier or, more likely, taken directly to the passenger's hotel.

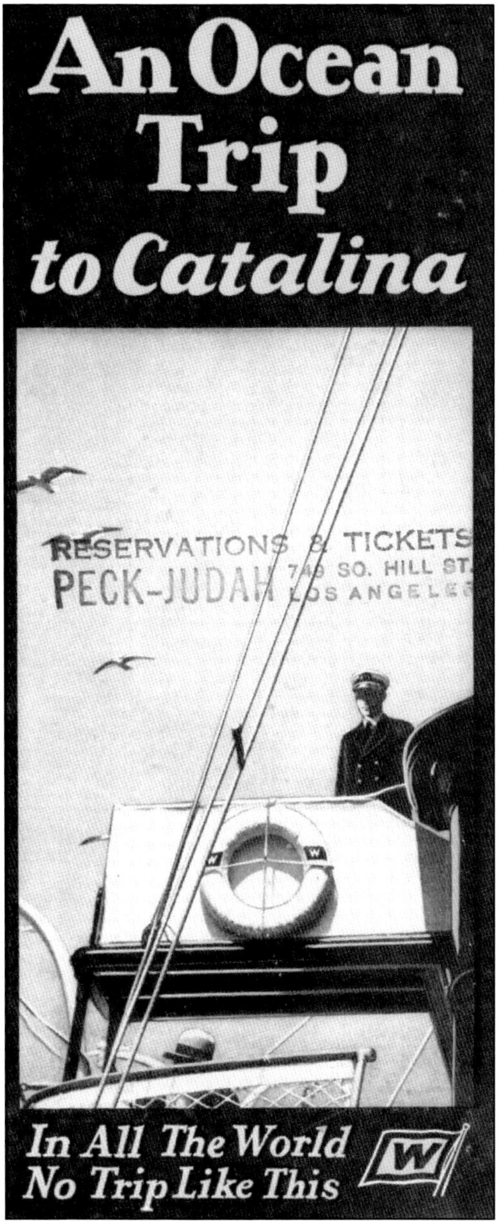

Crossing the San Pedro Channel was such an important aspect of the Catalina experience that the Santa Catalina Island Company produced a brochure documenting the exciting voyage. The brochure reads "Don't say, 'I've never been to sea', when this historic voyage takes but a day. . . . In all the world there are few more far-famed strips of water which separates California and Catalina. Only twenty five miles across, this channel has been the scene of more important discoveries, more glorious adventures, than probably any other waters of this western world. Today, this beautiful channel lures us moderns as it did the mariners of old. The crossing remains a voyage of delight. Historically, it covers a span of four centuries. Actually, the trip to Catalina may be made in two hours on the Catalina steamers, and a wonderful, never to be forgotten trip it is. Let's go. Let's leave the mainland and its bustle, and go a-sailing on the Spanish Main. Let's go to Catalina—the Magic Isle of the Pacific—where our cares are far behind and our joy is unconfined!"

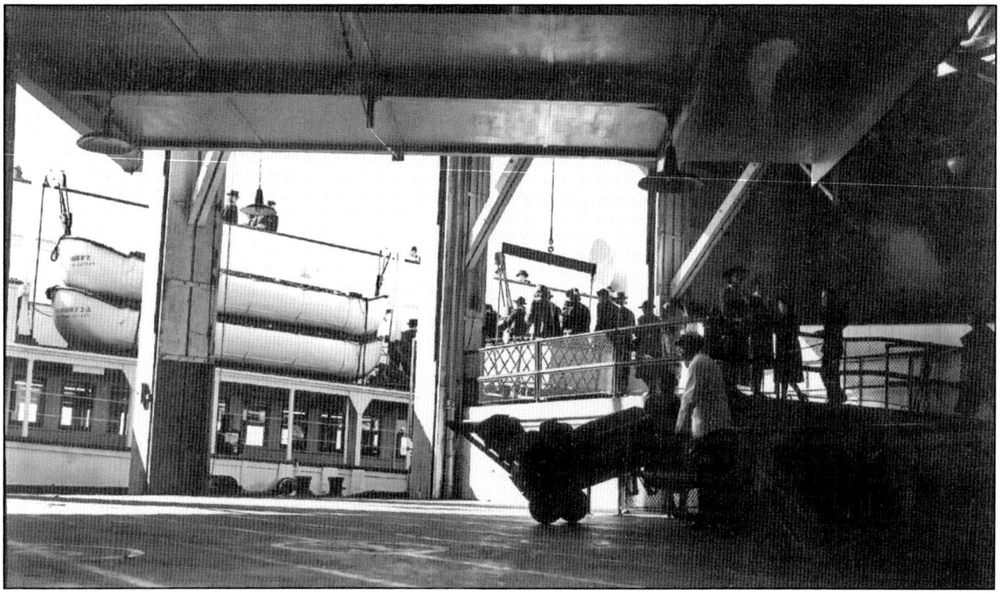

Once passengers arrived at the Catalina terminal in Wilmington, they would line up to board the steamer and the ship's orchestra would play until the last passenger stepped aboard. This photograph shows the interior of the Catalina terminal, with passengers stepping across the gangplank onto the *Avalon* to begin their ocean adventure.

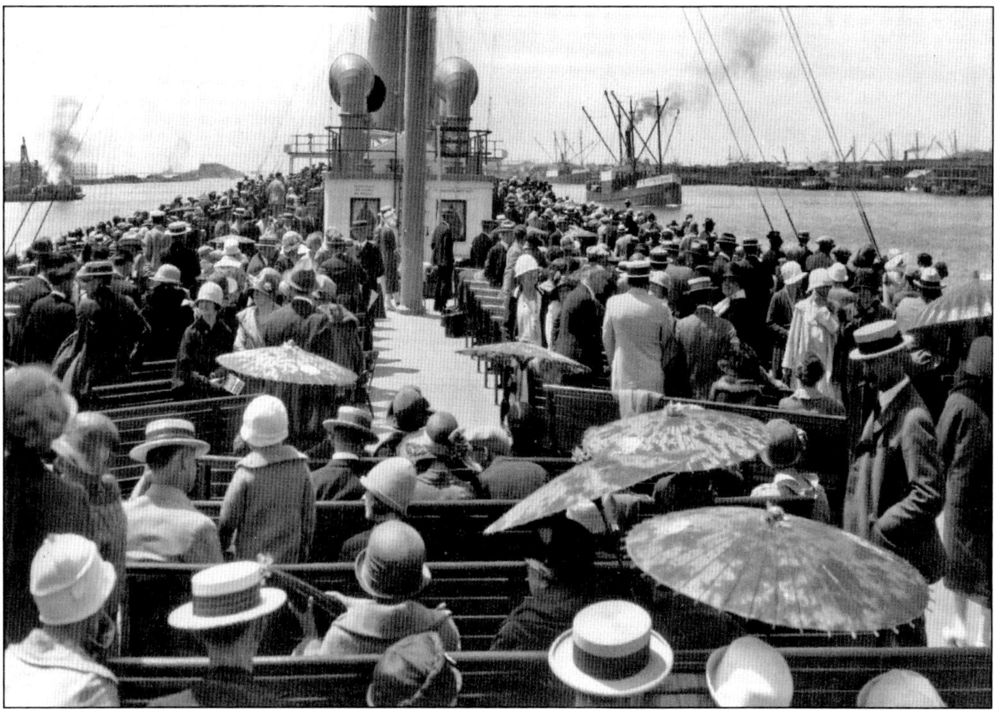

As the ship slowly steamed out of Los Angeles Harbor, a "spieler" would give passengers information about the points of interest along the way. It could take up to 20 minutes to pass through the harbor's many interesting sights, including the ferry terminal, shipyards, fireboats, canneries, and ocean liners.

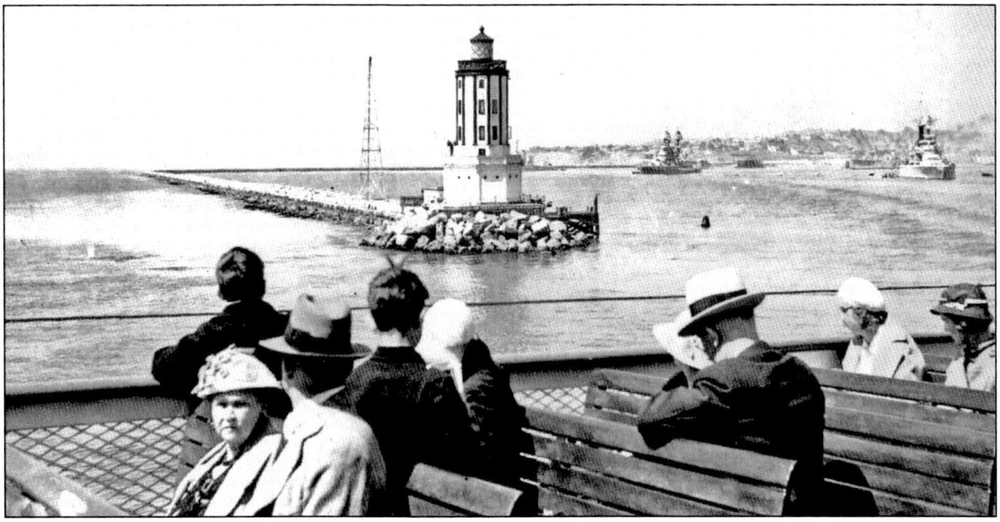

A brochure from 1923 describes the trip through the harbor as being of "especial interest" and "the Catalina steamer passes along the entire length of the United States Naval Training Station. It also passes through the Battleship Fleet, affording a fine view of these giant ships, the submarines, the sub-chasers, etc." Once the ship passed the lighthouse and breakwater, the harbor tour ended and the blue waters of the Pacific Ocean extended as far as the eye could see.

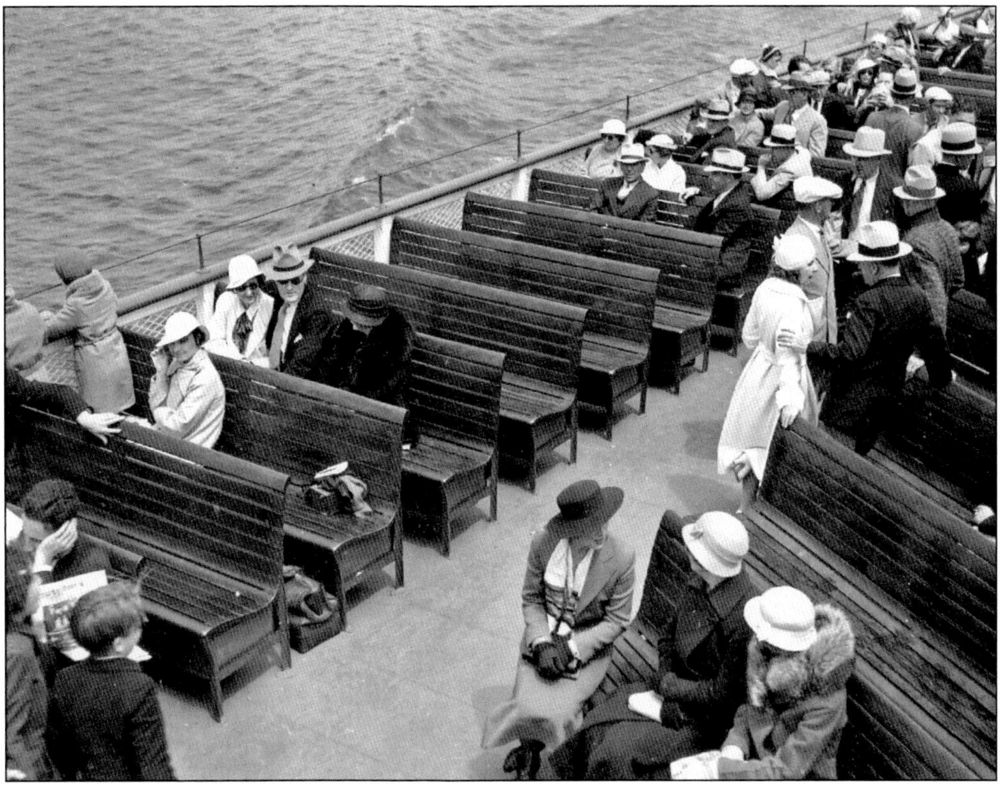

Once past the breakwater, the steamship would pick up speed and sail out to the open ocean. For two joyous hours, the passengers called the steamship home and would explore her decks, dance to the orchestra, and enjoy the sights and sounds of the sea.

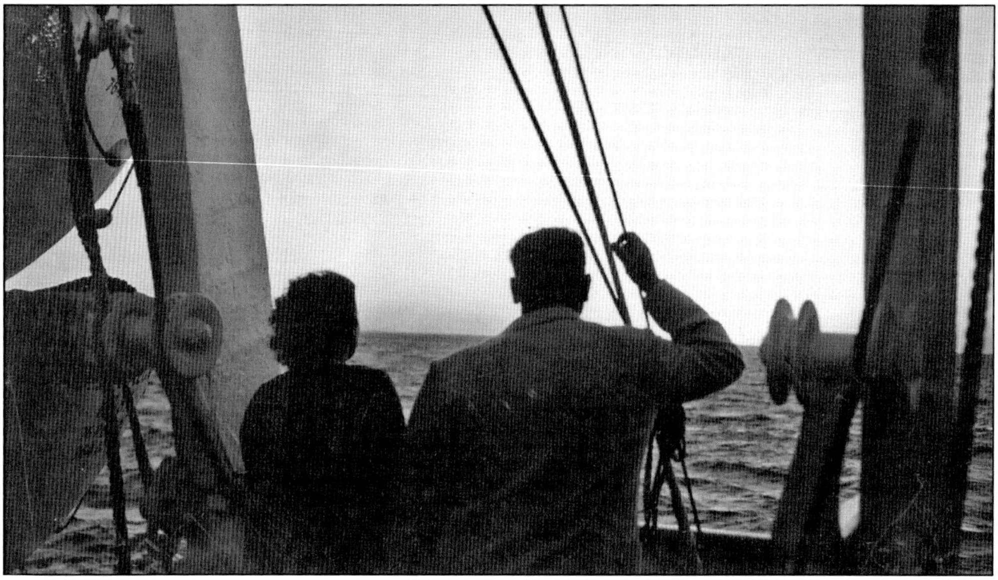

Common sights during the crossing included freight ships and sailing vessels, interesting birds such as pelicans and cormorants, and marine life such as dolphins, seals, flying fish, and the lucky passenger might even spot a whale. Seaplanes were a common sight as well. As early as 1919, seaplanes offered trips to Catalina Island. The Douglas Dolphins, of Wilmington-Catalina Airlines, were often seen buzzing overhead of the steamer during the crossing.

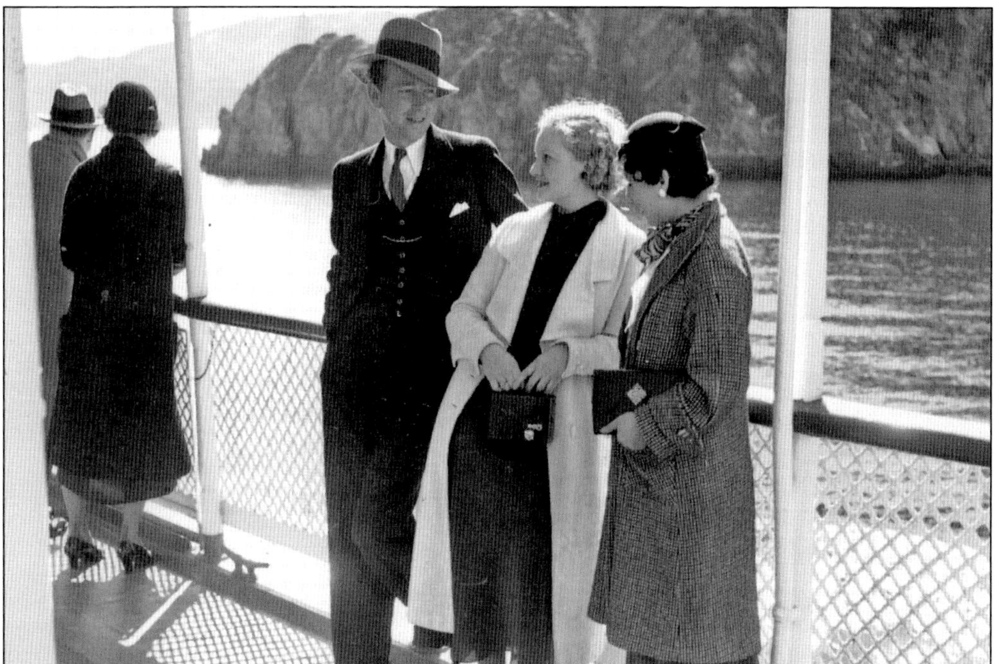

Passengers enjoyed relaxing aboard one of Wilmington Transportation Company's comfortable steamships as it crossed the San Pedro Channel. Yet, if a passenger wanted more action they could explore the decks of the ship, watch the wonders of the steam engines, play shuffleboard, grab a snack, or venture down to the ballroom and dance their way across the channel.

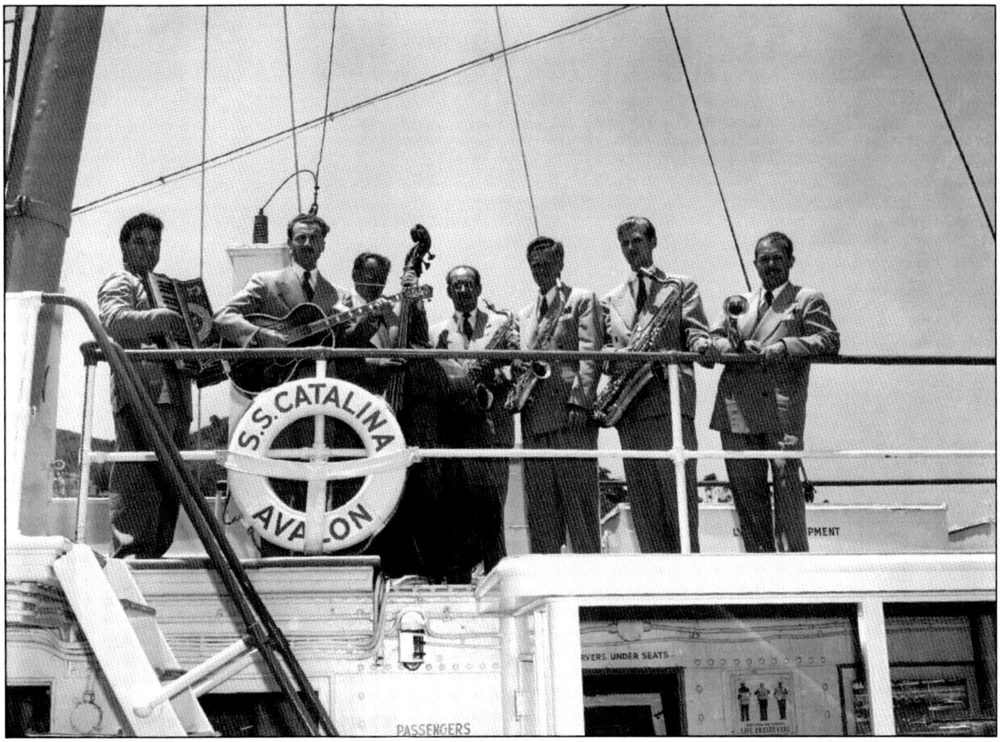

Each of the steamships in the Wilmington Transportation Company fleet traveled with an orchestra. The orchestra played in the Catalina terminal while passengers boarded the ships, and once the vessel passed the Los Angeles Harbor breakwater it would start playing in the ballroom of the ship. The orchestra entertained passengers throughout their journey and are often remembered fondly for making the trip to Catalina so exciting.

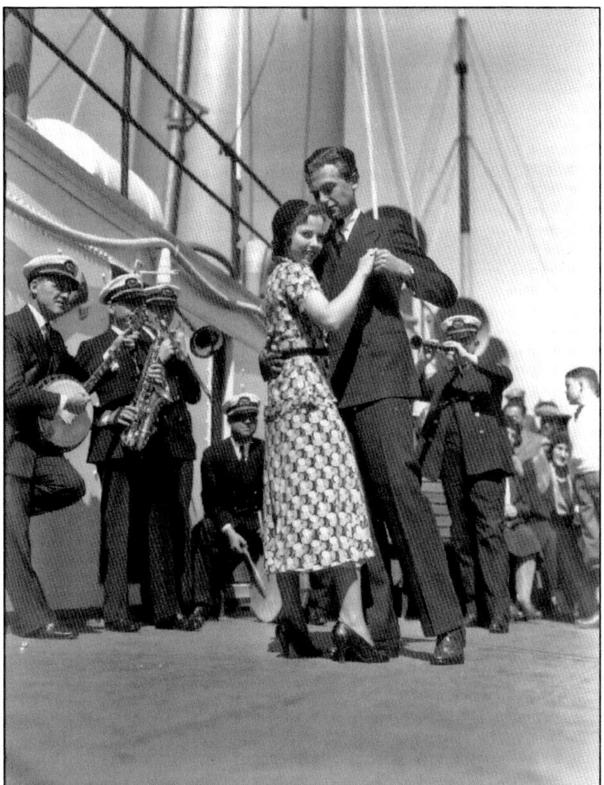

Couples dance as the orchestra plays on the top deck of the steamship. Passengers could dance their way across the channel and once on the island they could dance all night in the Casino ballroom. (Courtesy of the Santa Catalina Island Company.)

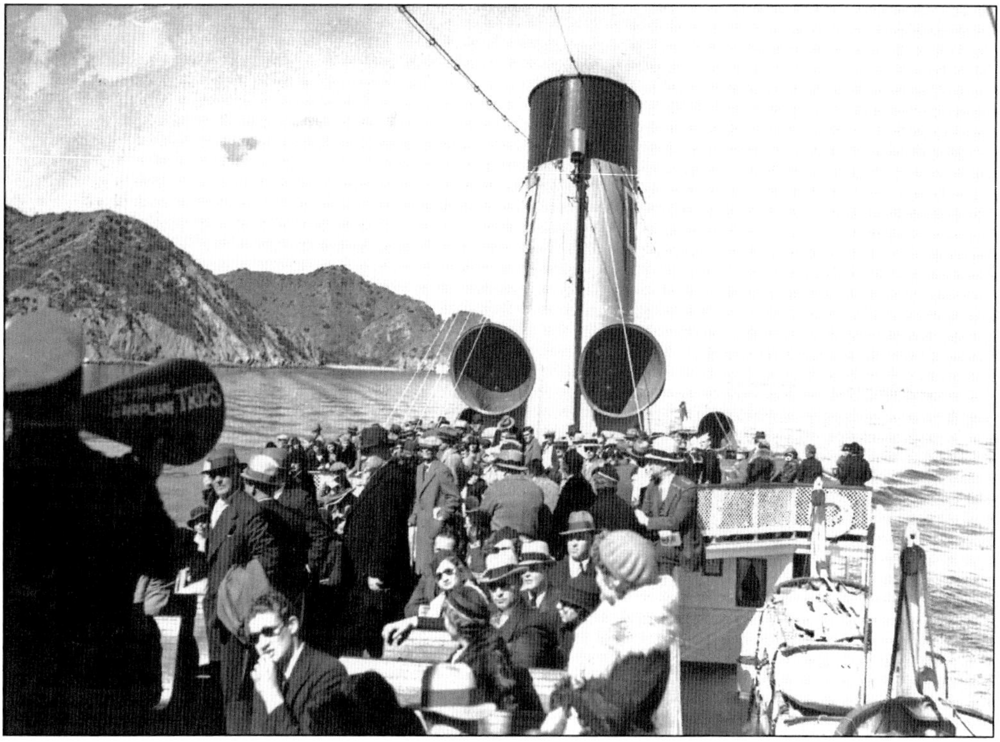

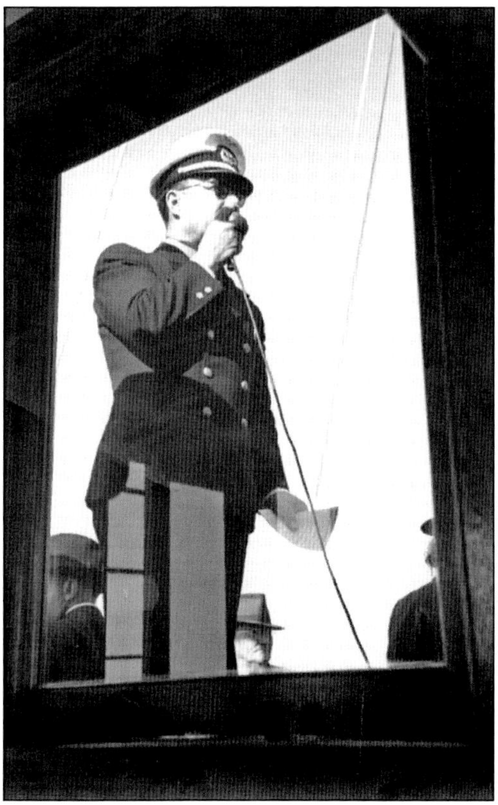

Once the steamer reached the island, it would sail down the coast from Long Point to Avalon and a spieler would give passengers information on the island's history and points of interest. The crew asked that not everyone move to one side of the ship at once to listen to the spiel. The SS *Catalina* was particularly top heavy and it was unsafe for everyone to be on one side of the ship. Therefore, the spieler would announce that the speakers would be turned off on the port side of the ship so locals and frequent travelers could sit on the port side while visitors enjoyed the views on the starboard side.

Peter Adargo was born on Catalina Island in 1899. His father worked with the Banning family and Peter grew up fishing and hunting all over the island. Peter started working on the steamships as a speiler in 1919. He spoke to millions of people, acquainting them with Los Angeles Harbor and the history of Catalina Island. He was known to many as "Mr. Catalina," or "The Voice," as he was the chief announcer on the *Catalina* for many years.

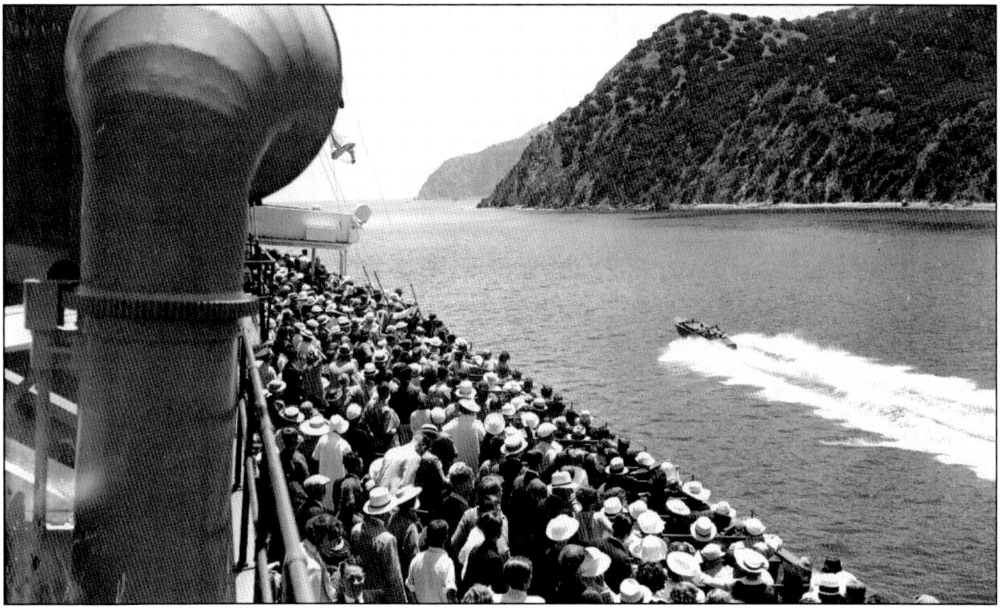

Steamer greetings were a standing tradition in Avalon and the *Miss Catalina* speedboats played an important role during the 1920s, 1930s, 1940s, and 1950s. When a steamer approached the bay, the *Miss Catalina* speedboats would race out to greet the steamer. They offered visitors fast and fun rides for 36 years.

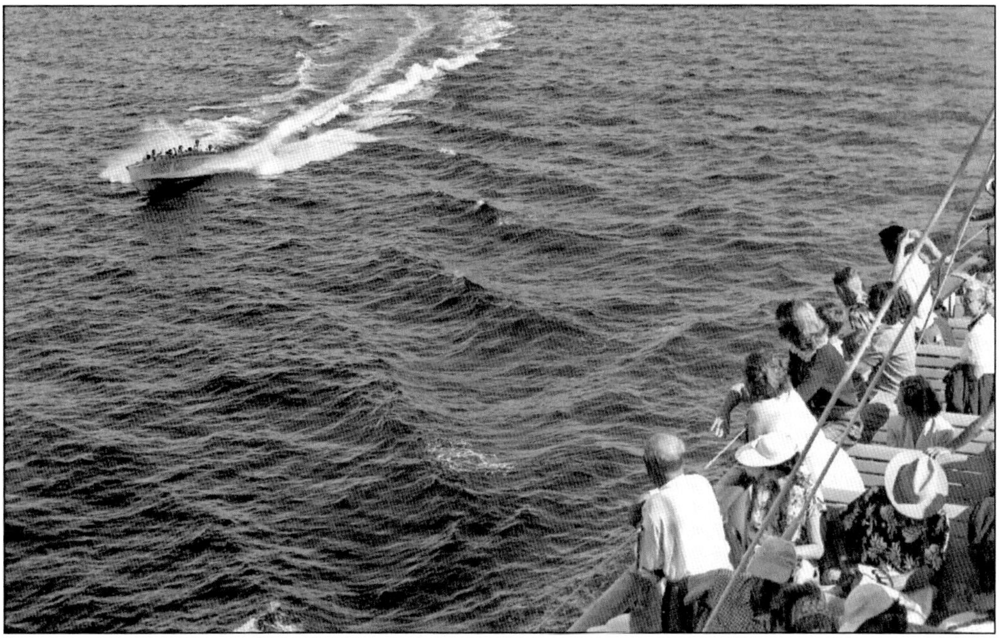

The *Miss Catalina* speedboats "Meet the Steamer" trip was so popular that boats would make two trips out to greet the steamer and take reservations for these trips. The speedboats would first meet the steamer over the horizon, long before she reached the island. They would circle around the ship, blowing their sirens and jumping the wake of the steamer. The second trip met the steamer during her cruise from Long Point. It was quite exciting for the steamship passengers and a thrill for the speedboat passengers.

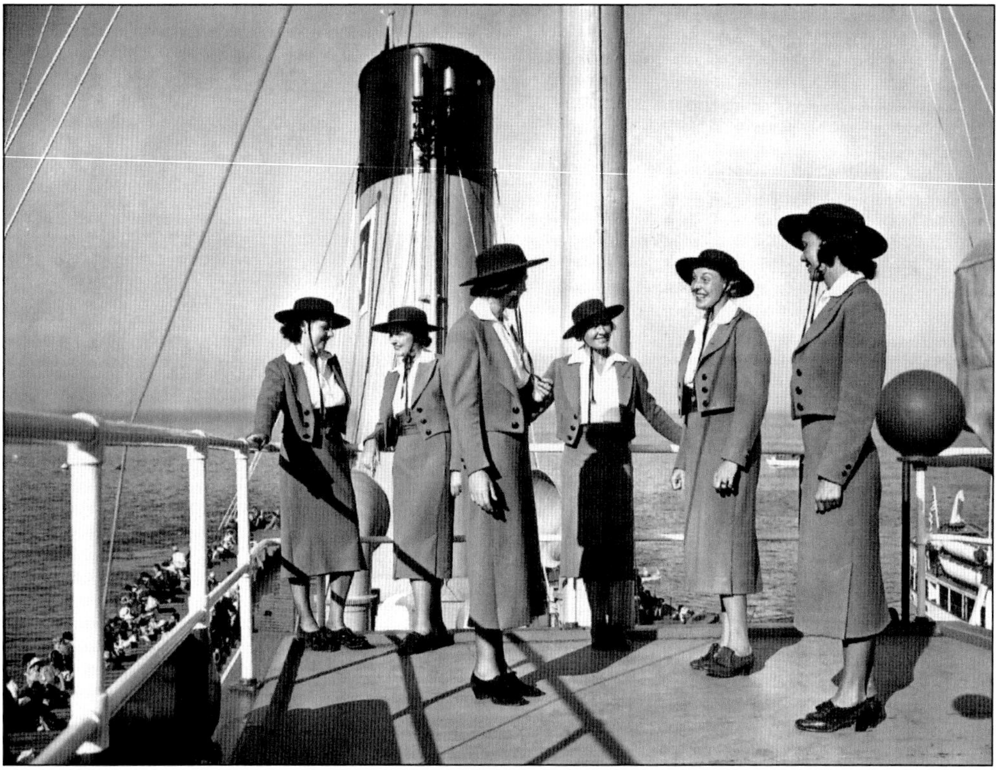

The couriers accompanied passengers on the steamship to answer questions and provide information to those who were interested. Kathleen Lane served as a courier on steamships during the 1935 and 1936 seasons. She remembers, "Our main purpose was to make the passengers comfortable and acquaint them with the things that could be done while they were on the island." In order to accomplish this task, couriers received very thorough training. They toured the entire island and the tours were explained in detail.

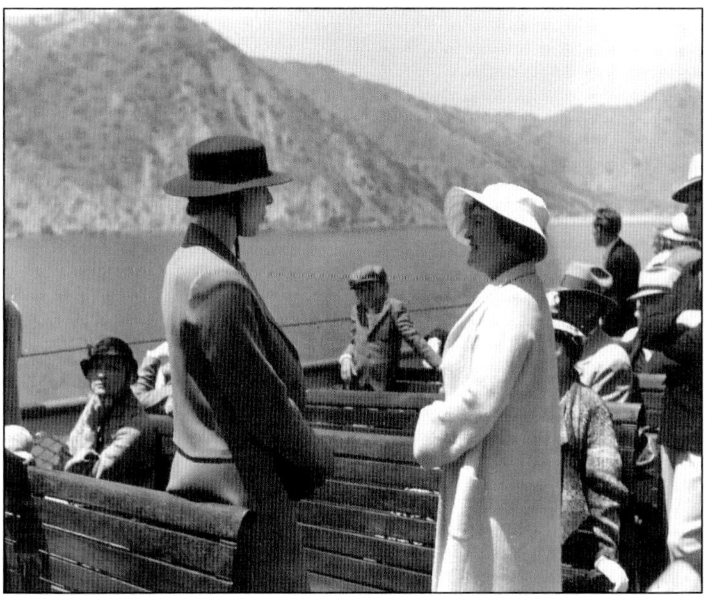

Jean Crow also served as a Courier on both the *Avalon* and the *Catalina*. She remembers that the couriers also worked on the island, "Two or three girls were designated to spend the summer in Avalon. We were stationed at different sites around town to provide information to visitors. Some evenings were spent at the Casino and during the day we would talk to visitors at the Bird Park or the Island Villas."

During the 1930s, Philip K. Wrigley introduced an Early California theme to the city of Avalon. He redesigned Crescent Avenue, planted palm and olive trees, built the El Encanto Marketplace, introduced new staff uniforms, and hired troubadours to play throughout town. The troubadours often delighted passengers on the steamships as well. This Early California theme was part of Wrigley's marketing plan for Catalina Island and it enhanced the look and feel of Avalon.

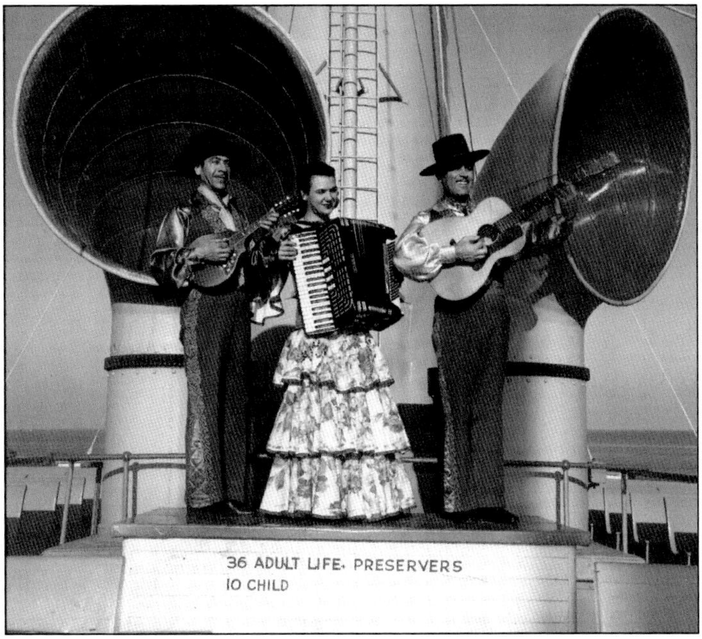

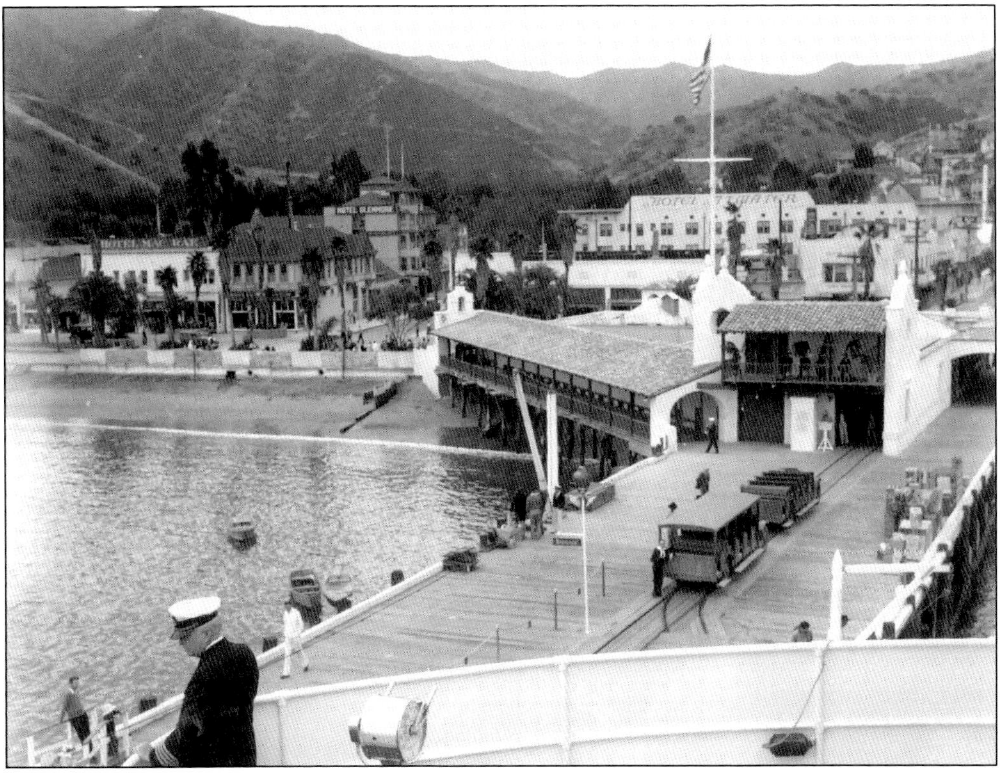

As a steamship approached Avalon Bay it would slowly dock at the steamer pier located at the center of the bay and town. This photograph shows a steamer docking at the pier with an officer observing from the bridge deck to make sure it is properly berthed.

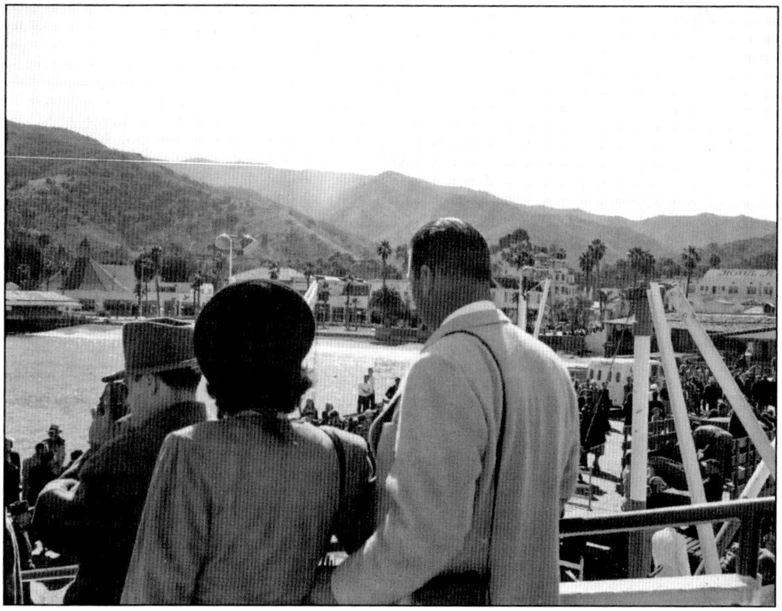

Once the steamer docked, the gangplank would be attached and passengers would begin to disembark. Travelers were transformed into visitors as they stepped off the boat and onto the steamer pier. They immediately began to take in the sights of Avalon and marvel at the beautiful Pacific isle.

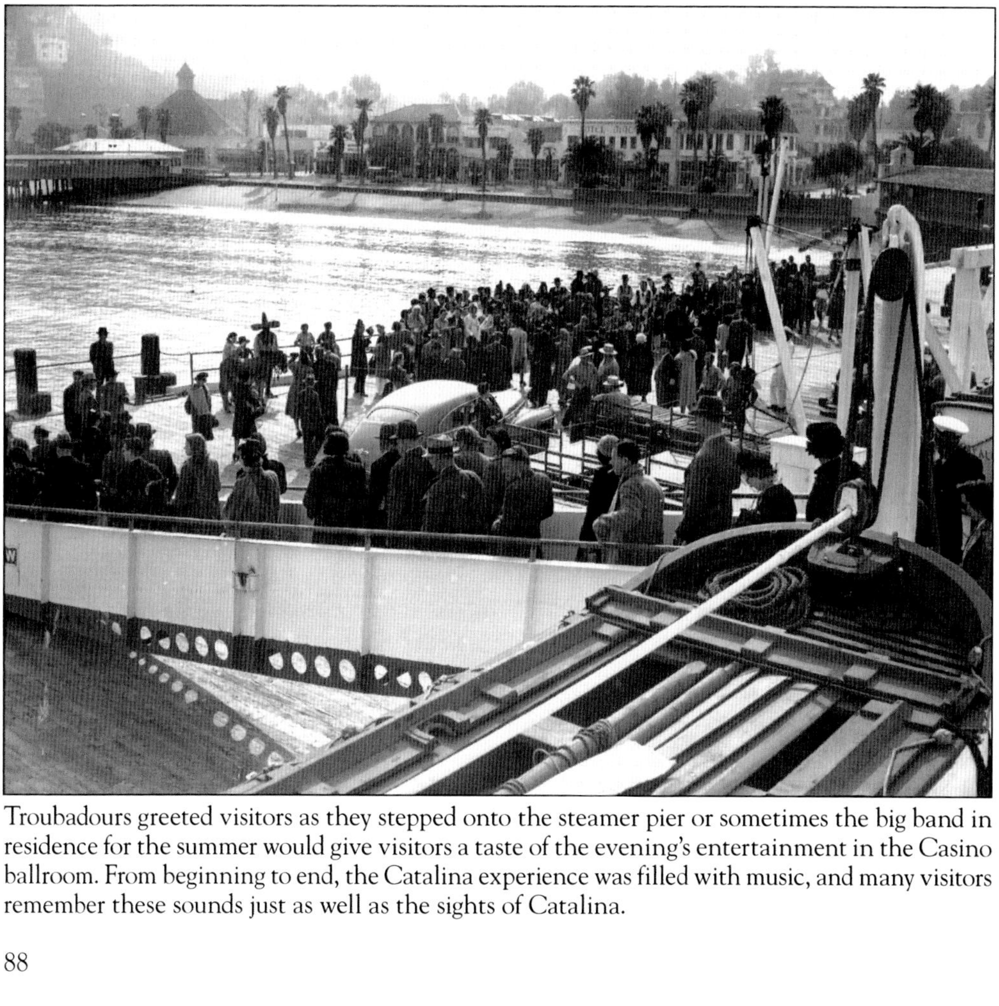

Troubadours greeted visitors as they stepped onto the steamer pier or sometimes the big band in residence for the summer would give visitors a taste of the evening's entertainment in the Casino ballroom. From beginning to end, the Catalina experience was filled with music, and many visitors remember these sounds just as well as the sights of Catalina.

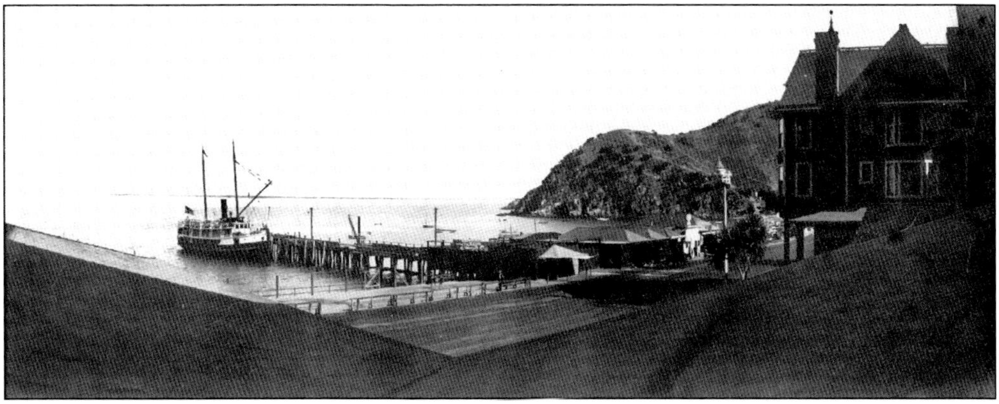

The steamer pier was originally built in 1887 by George Shatto, who had just purchased Catalina Island and intended to develop a resort community. To accomplish this goal, he first built the pier and a hotel. For over 80 years, the steamer pier was the main access point to Avalon and Catalina Island. It was changed many times over the years and became increasingly bigger as the size of the ships and visitation increased.

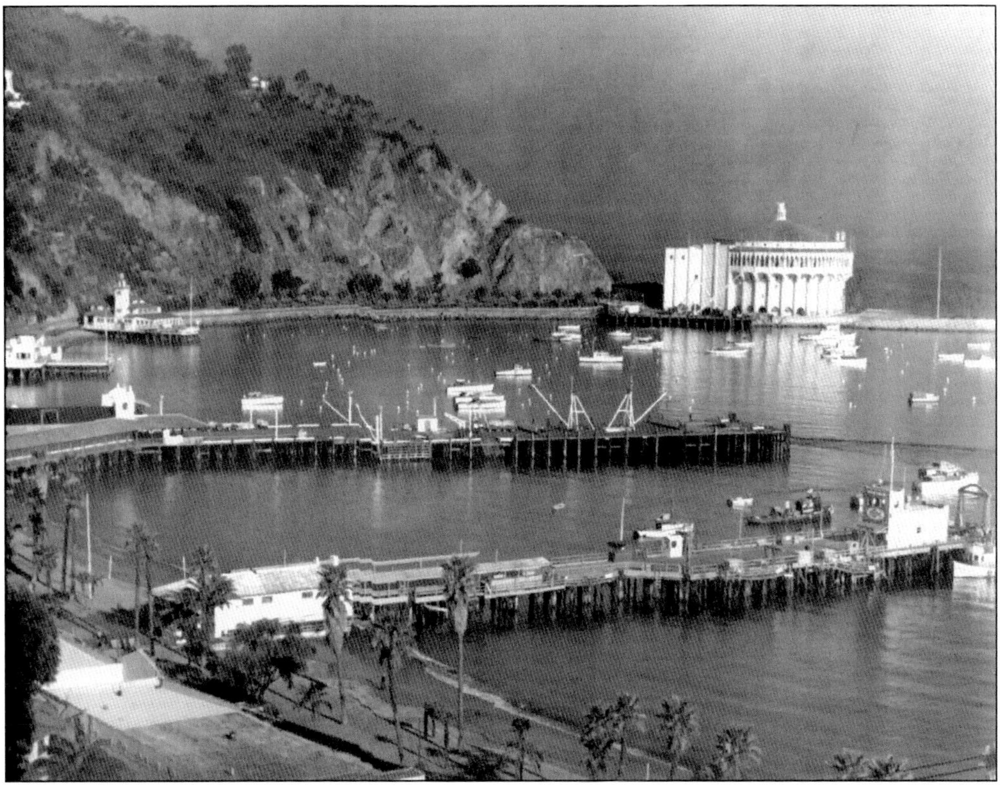

In 1909, the steamer pier was joined by the Pleasure Pier, which was initially utilized by fishermen and other pleasure launches and has served as a landing for glass-bottom and other tour boats over the years. The steamer pier continued to grow in size over the years and could accommodate steamships on either side. It remained the primary access to Avalon and Catalina Island until the mid-1960s, when it was dismantled. The Cabrillo Mole was built to replace the steamer pier on the south side of Avalon Bay.

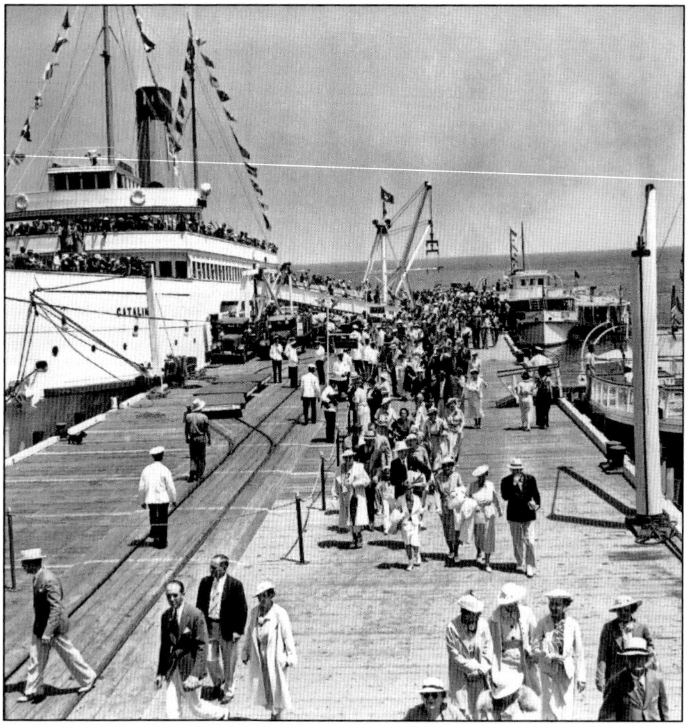

As passengers disembarked the steamship, they walked the length of the steamer pier and took in the initial sights and sounds of Catalina Island. There was much activity on the pier, including troubadours, docked glass-bottom boats, hotel trams, baggage carts, and stevedores.

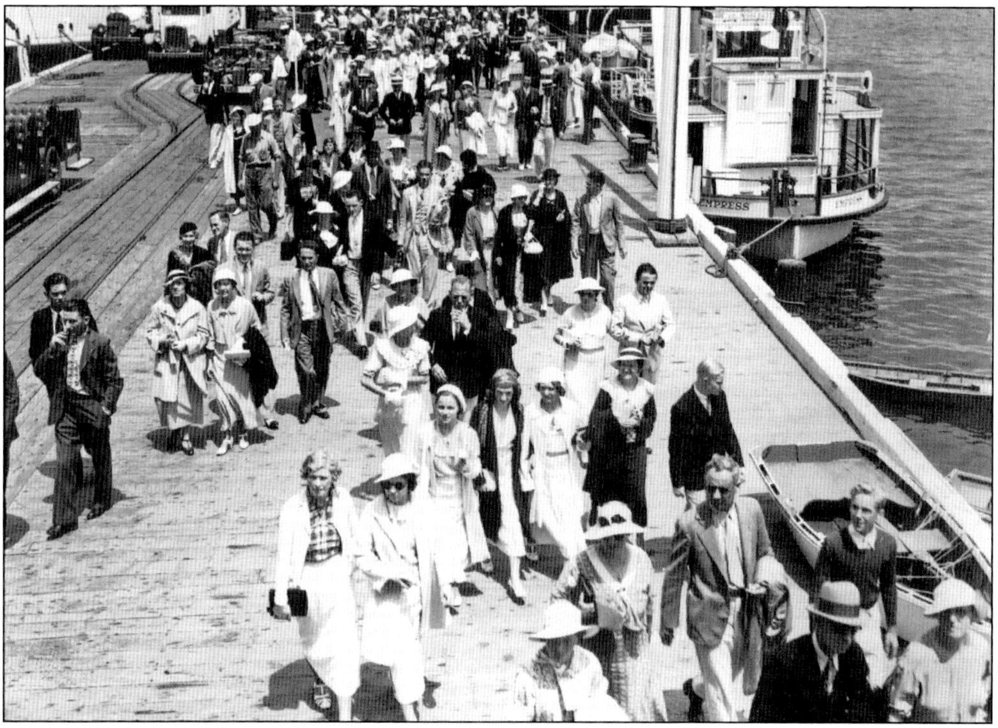

It took a long time for the average 1,000 passengers to disembark the steamships during the summer season. Passengers were led off the steamer pier, through the steamer landing, and into the center of Avalon where they would be greeted by hundreds of island residents and visitors.

Five

The Steamer Greeting

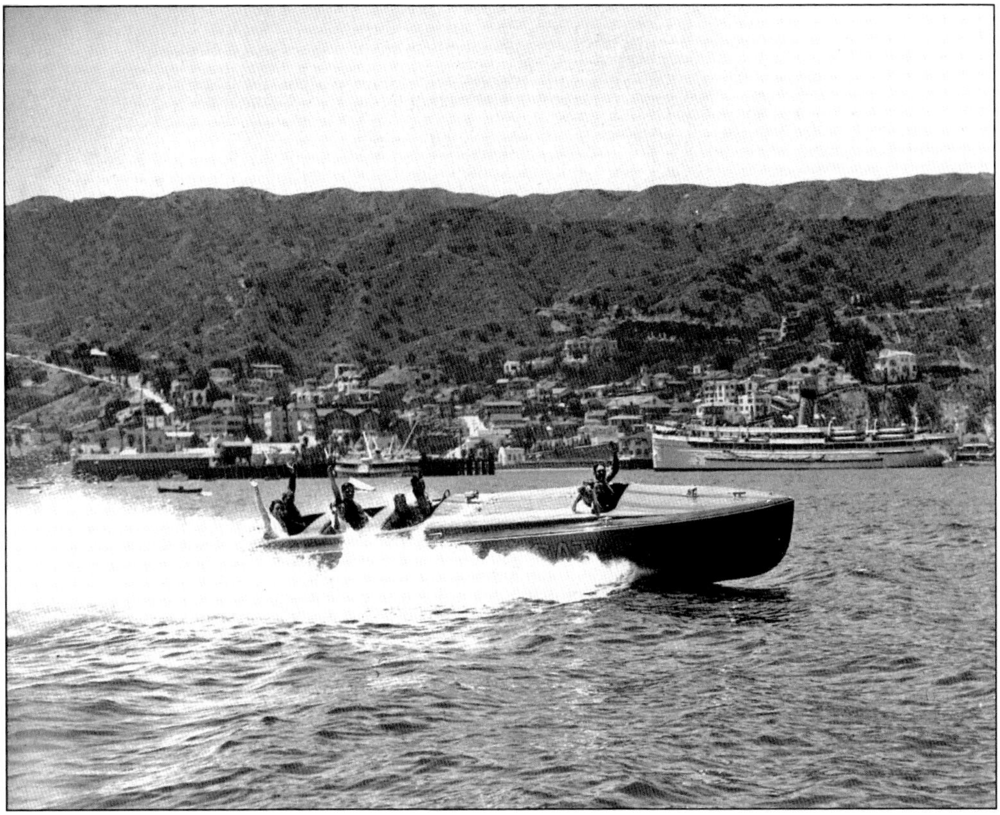

As Catalina Island began to develop as a tourist destination at the beginning of the 20th century, the small community of Avalon became the center of tourist activities. Residents were always looking for ways to enhance the visitor experience and offering a spectacular welcome when travelers stepped off the steamships was the perfect way to show their hospitality. This festive welcome quickly became a tradition known as the "steamer greeting." The earliest images of steamer greetings are seen in postcards, as "running of the gauntlet," and diving for coins appear on them as early as 1900. By the mid-1930s, the greeting included *Miss Catalina* speedboats circling the ship as it approached the bay, children yelling to "throw a coin" and then diving to the ocean bottom as the steamer docked at the pier, and hundreds of people singing as passengers disembarked. The steamer greeting, in all its forms, continued until the mid-1960s when the pier was removed. However, memories of it are strong and live in the hearts of visitors and residents.

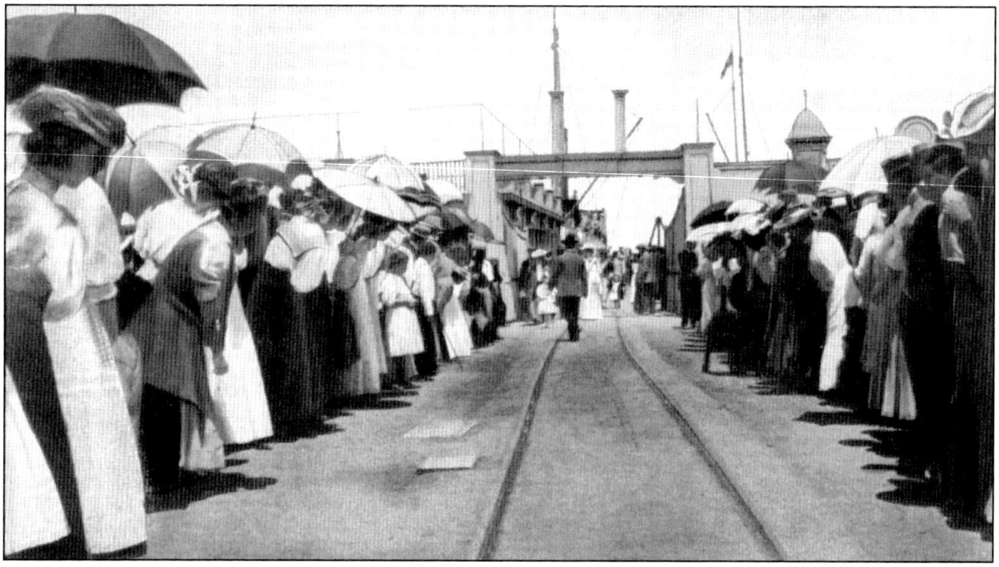

"Running the gauntlet" was one of the first known steamer greeting activities and referred to passengers walking off the steamer pier upon their arrival in Avalon. Residents and visitors lined the sides of the pier to offer a friendly welcome and passengers would have to pass through this gauntlet of people to begin their adventure in Avalon.

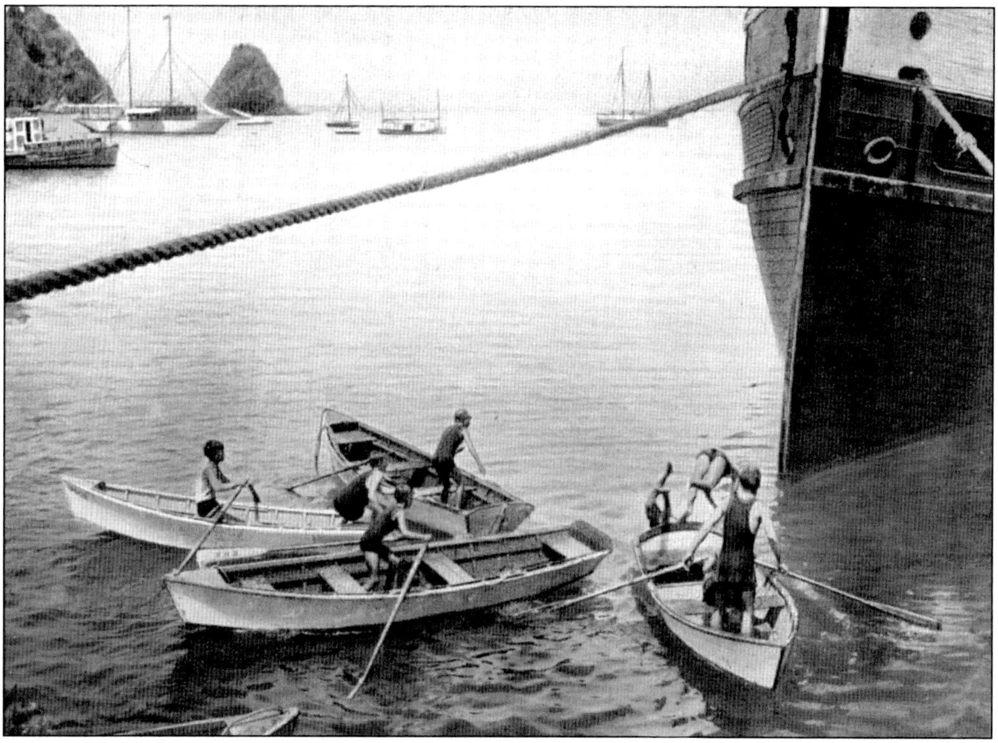

Diving for coins was part of these early steamer greetings and a popular activity for the town's children. As the ship docked at the pier, children would row or swim out to the ship and yell up to the passengers, "Throw a coin!" Passengers would toss their change and the children would dive to the ocean floor to retrieve them.

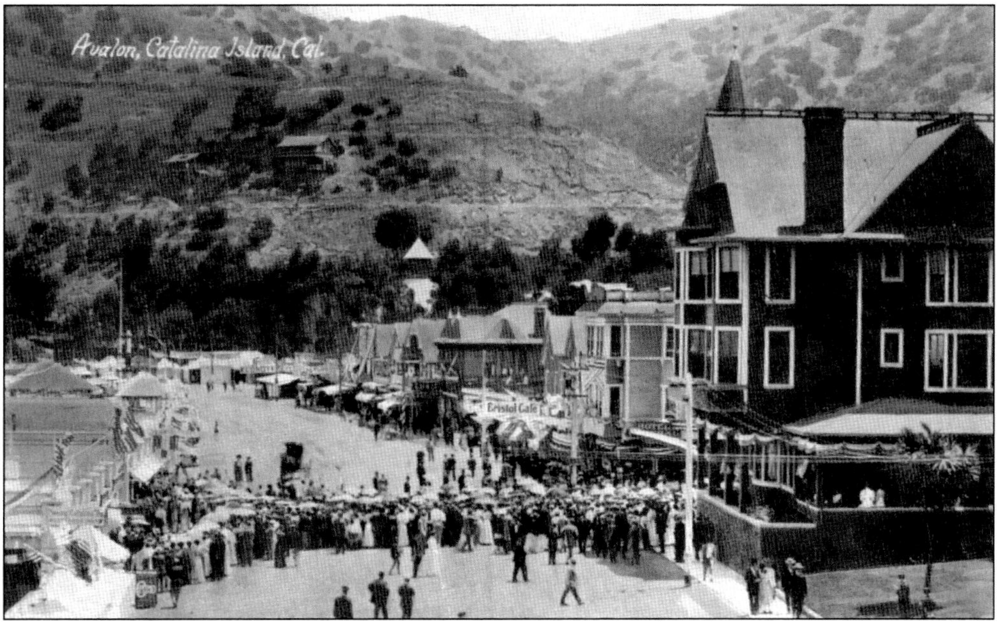

One of the earliest mentions of the steamer greeting appeared in the *Los Angeles Times* in 1894. The article described, "Avalon was gay with bunting on Saturday, and people flocked to the wharf to welcome the first arrival of the steamer Falcon after the regular opening of the season. Enlivening strains of music from the porch of the Hotel Metropole gave further evidence that the summer's festivities on the island had begun early and auspiciously."

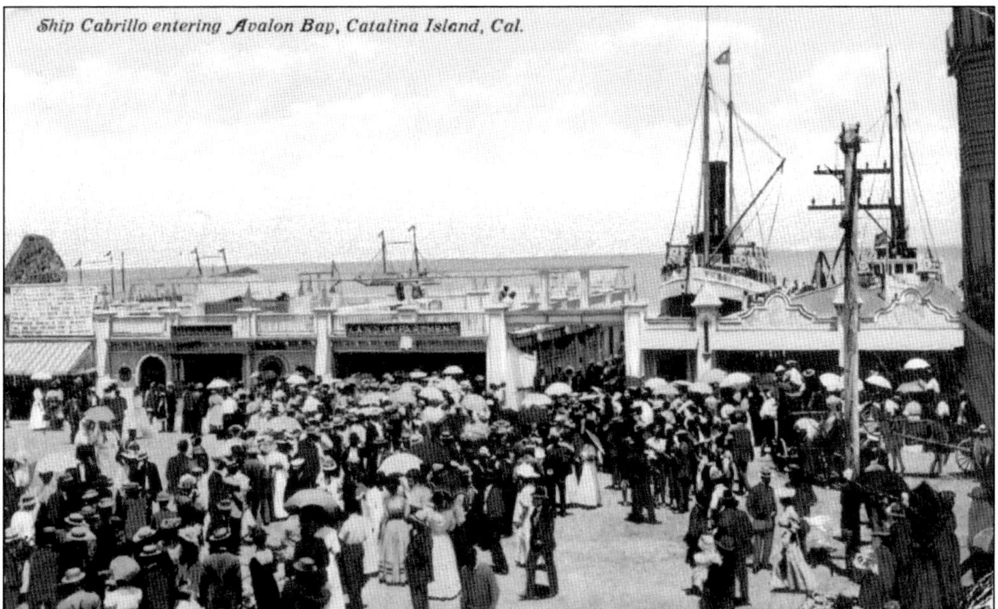

The steamer greetings quickly became a popular activity for the island's residents and visitors. Once passengers disembarked the ships, they were quickly transformed into visitors and they often wanted to participate in the next steamer greeting to give the subsequent group of passengers the same welcome they had received.

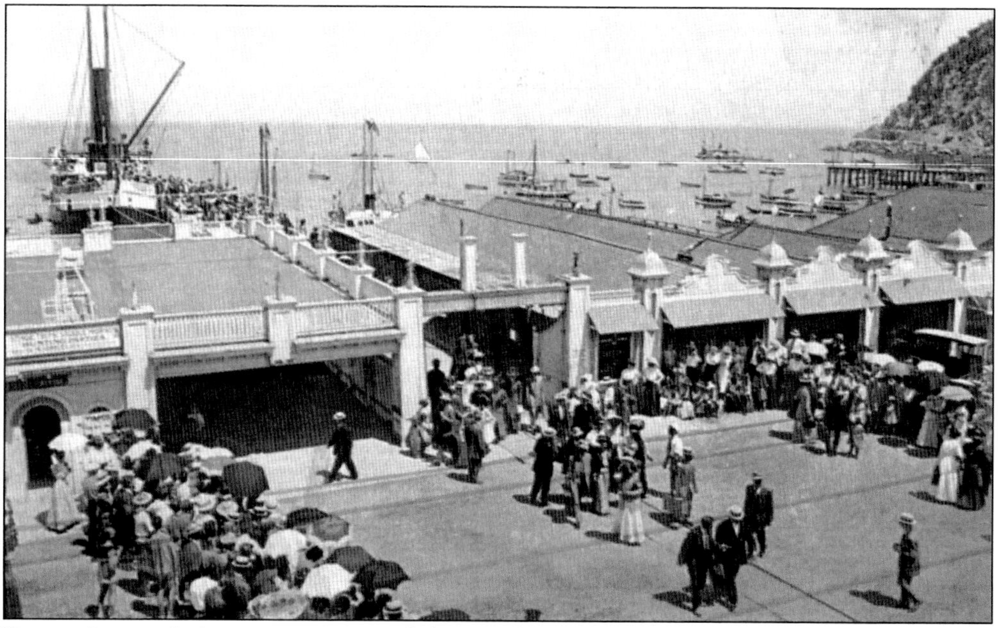

During those early days, passengers traveled to Catalina Island in their finest clothes. This postcard of an early steamer greeting shows the gentlemen disembarking the ship dressed in suits and hats and the ladies are wearing full length skirts and carrying parasols. It was quite an affair.

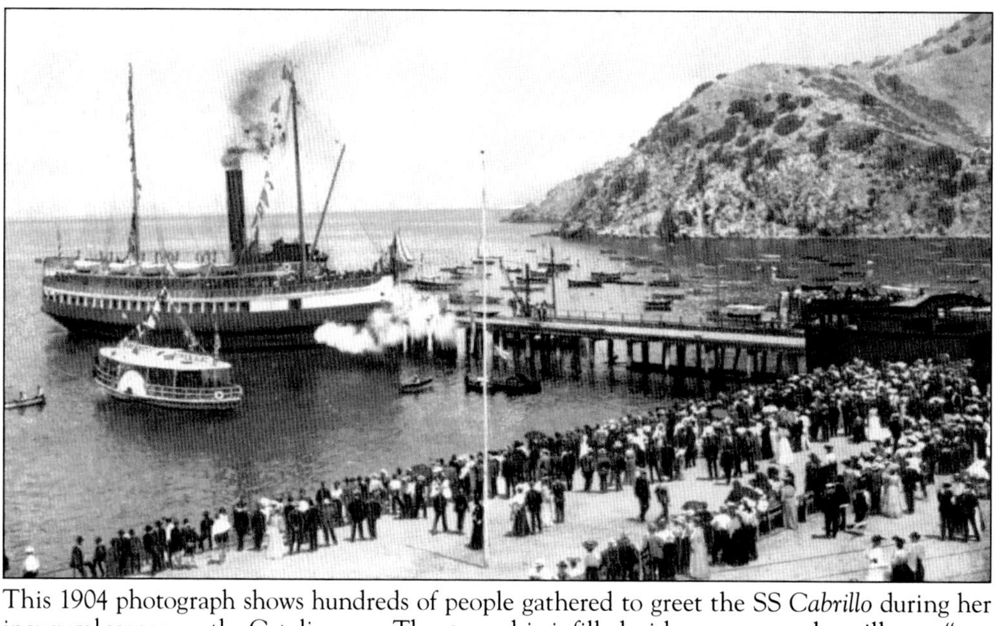

This 1904 photograph shows hundreds of people gathered to greet the SS *Cabrillo* during her inaugural season on the Catalina run. The steamship is filled with passengers who will soon "run the gauntlet" and be welcomed to Avalon.

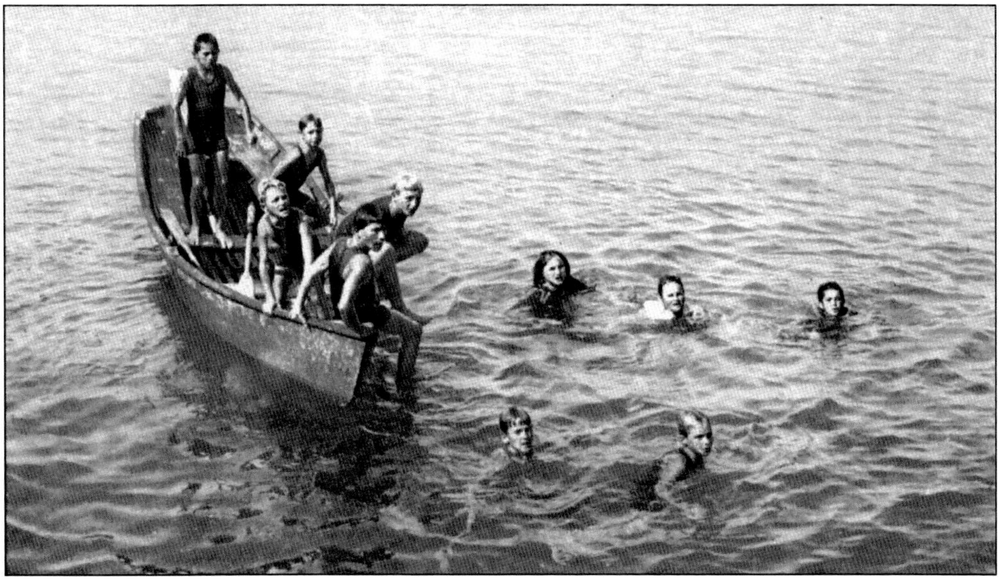

Coin diving was a tradition unique to Catalina Island. Since it took a long time for the sometimes thousands of passengers to disembark the ship, children and young adults would swim out and entertain the passengers as they waited to get off. Coin diving was quite lucrative and the divers had many tricks for storing their gains.

Island resident Chuck Liddell dove for coins as a child and remembers that on a good summer day there would be up to 25 divers in the water. He recalls that "basically there were three places where we would put our money; it was either in your mouth, your trunks, or you'd put it in your mask." Coin diving could be quite competitive and children of all ages participated. Liddell remembers that during the 1950s, young children could make up to $3 per day and older kids could pull in up to $10 per day.

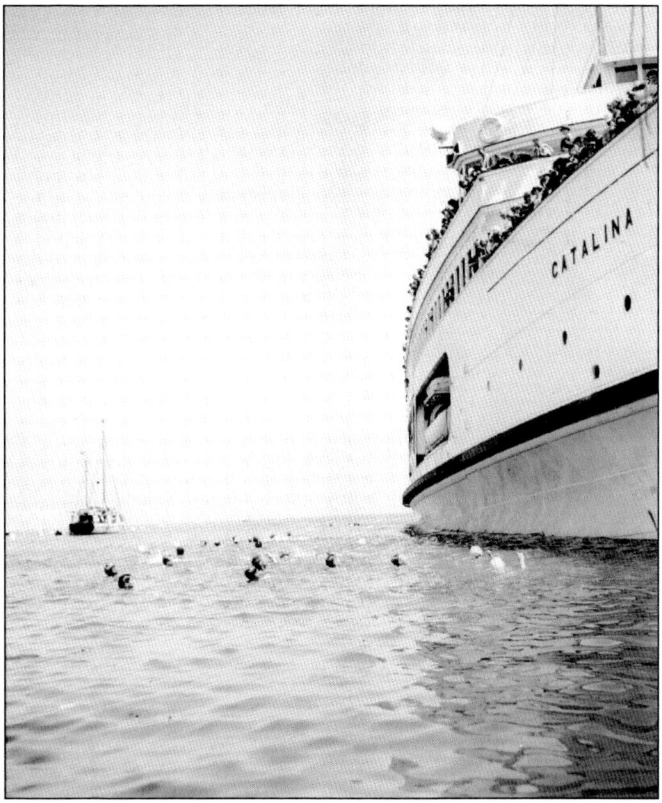

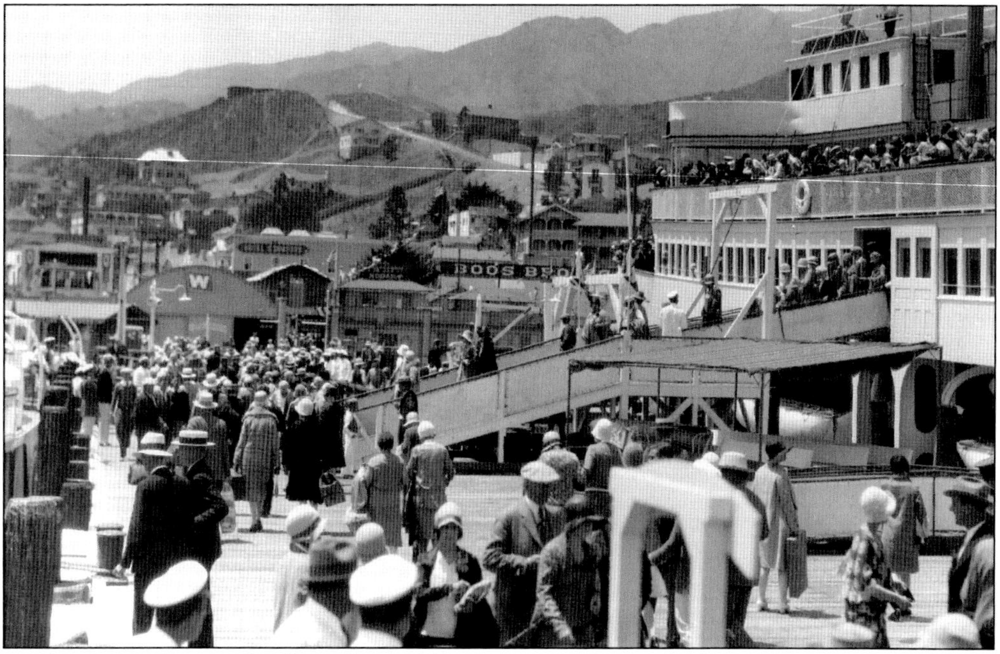

By the 1920s, thousands of people would arrive in Avalon each day during the busy summer season. The SS *Catalina* and SS *Avalon*, combined, carried up to 3,500 passengers. As visitation to the island grew, so did the activity on the steamer pier and the steamer greeting.

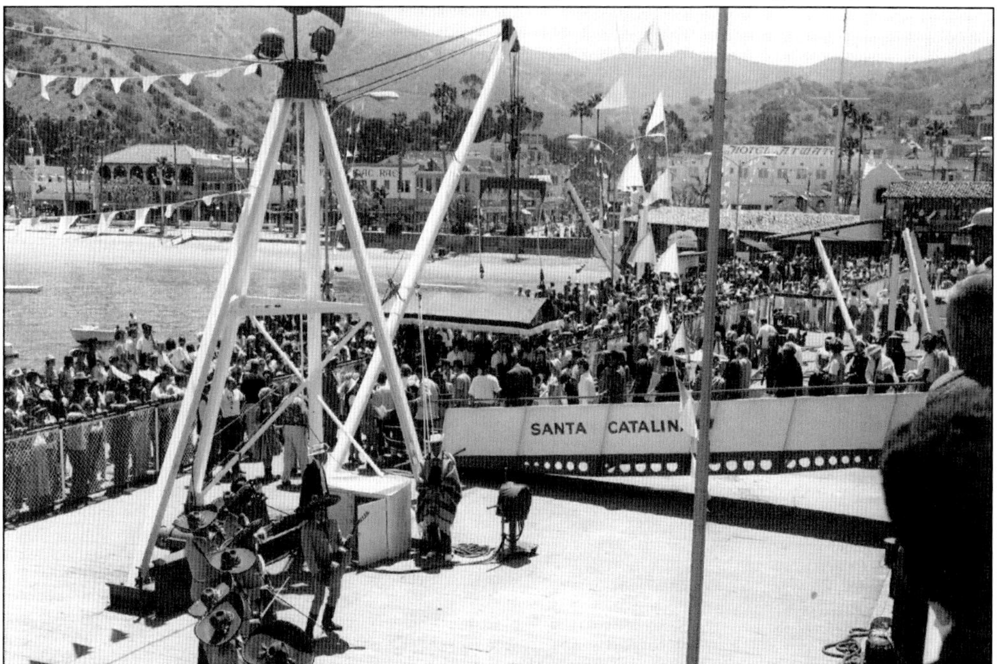

The 1920s ushered in a significant expansion in the steamer greeting. The *Miss Catalina* speedboats would race out to greet the ship long before she reached Avalon Bay, and while she docked at the steamer pier, the Chimes Tower would play and children dove for coins. Once the passengers stepped off the ship, troubadours or a big band often greeted them.

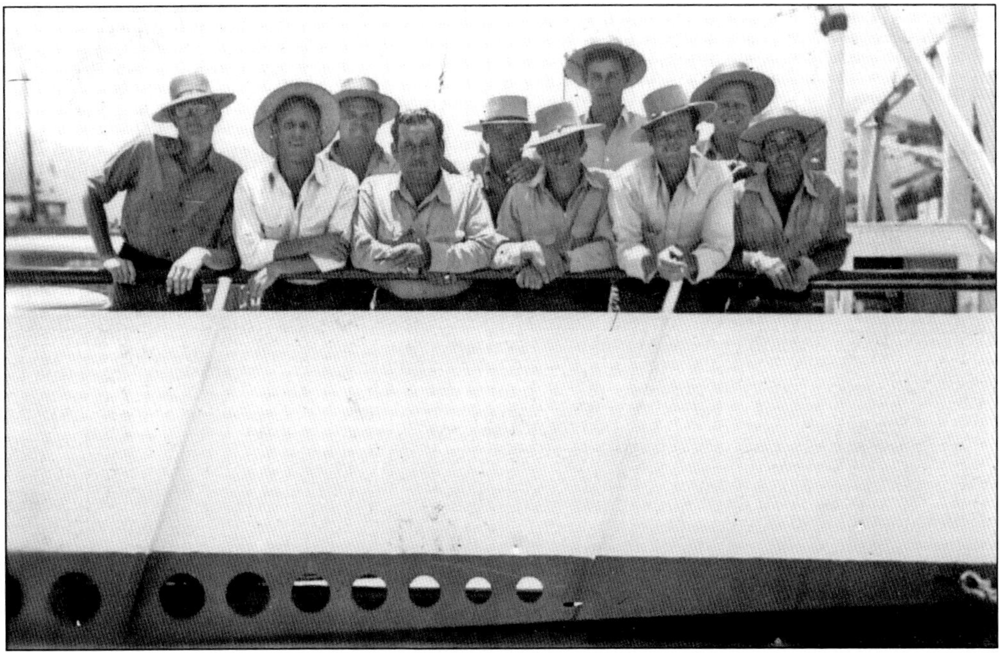

Among the activity on the steamer pier the stevedores were pressed to handle all of the luggage and freight. Silas Hathaway was a stevedore between 1936 and 1939 and he remembers that when the ship arrived at the pier they would catch the ship lines, secure her to the dock, and place the passenger ramps.

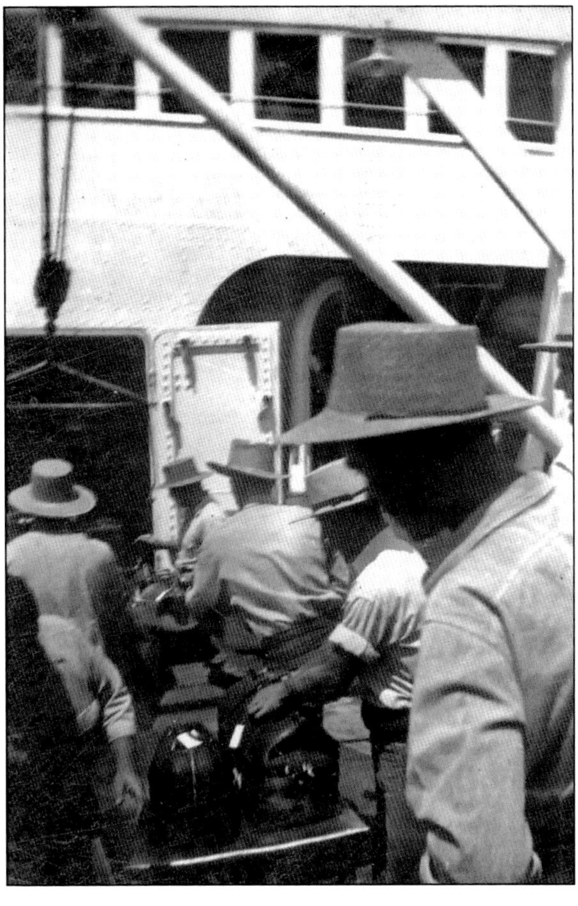

Silas also remembers, "They had a conveyer that came out of the hold of the boat and they put the baggage on first. And, after the baggage was unloaded you'd unload the freight." He recalled that it could get quite busy during a certain period in the summer when five ships would come in per day.

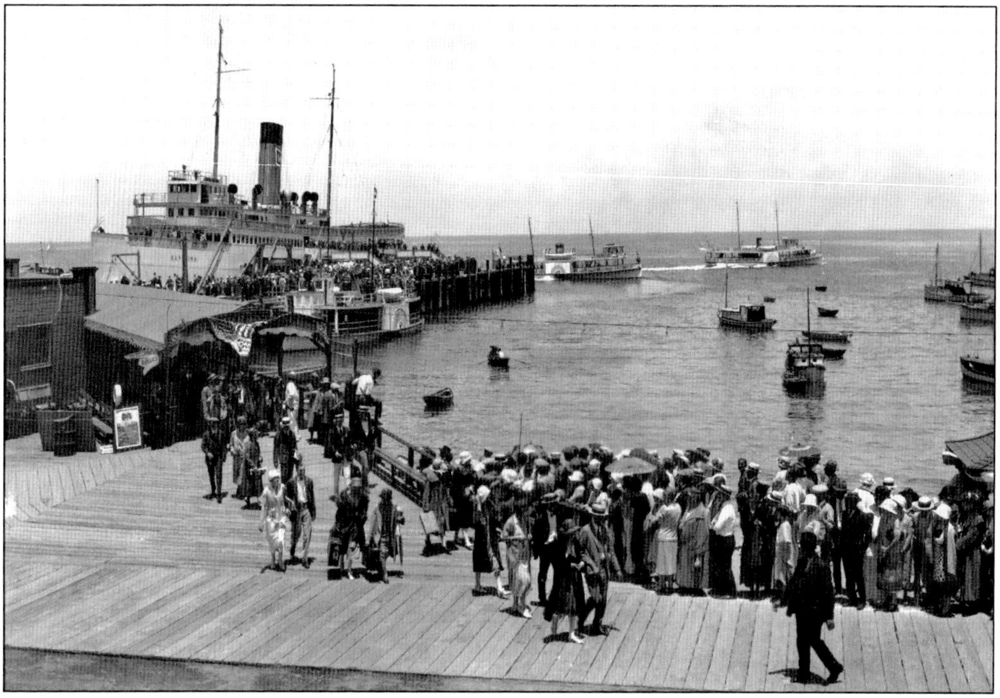

In the 1920s, a covered walkway was added to the end of the steamer pier that led passengers to the left and into Avalon. This changed the former "running of the gauntlet" as residents and visitors no longer lined both sides of the pier, but gathered on the left side to offer their greetings.

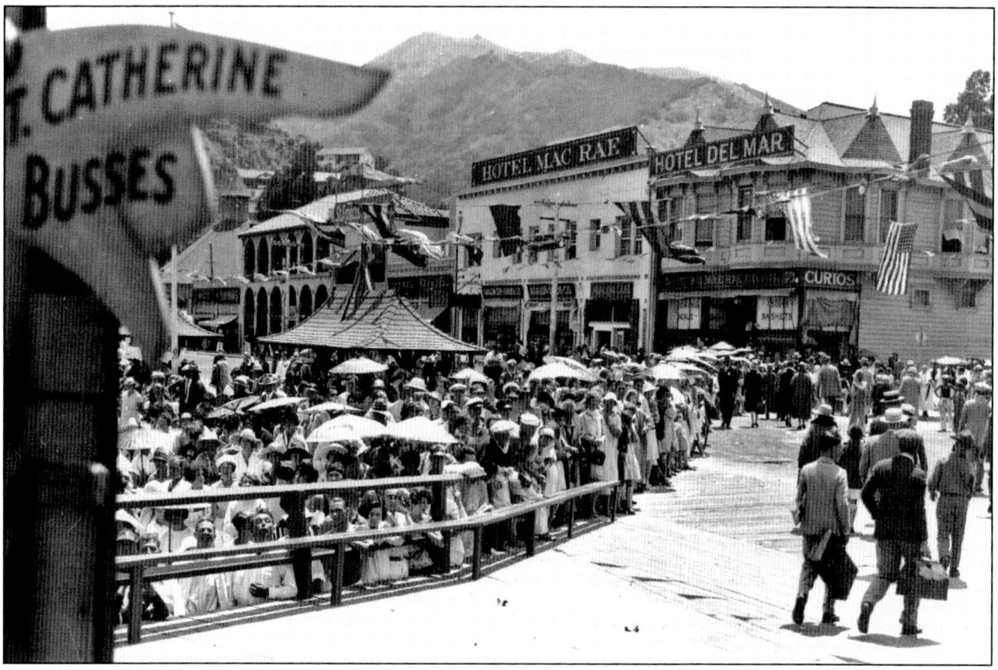

Hundreds of residents and visitors gathered at the foot of the steamer entrance to see who stepped off the steamship that day. As the island's number of visitors grew along with its popularity, the steamer greeting expanded into an elaborate welcome by the 1930s.

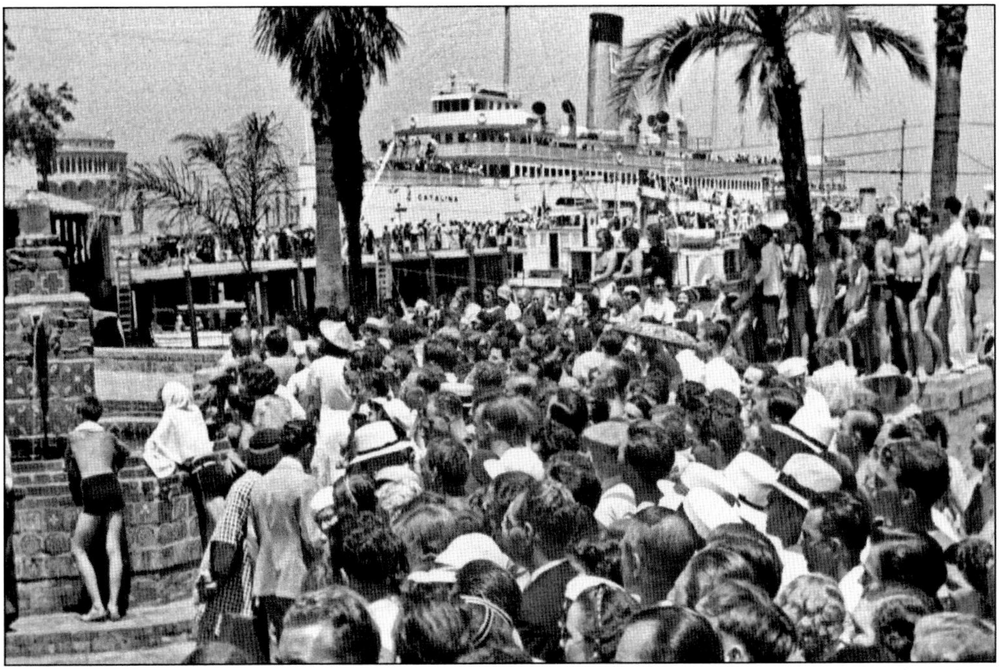

During the busy summer season, large crowds gathered to greet the steamships. Island resident Rudy Piltch remembers, "Everyone would line up to greet the steamer. There would be people sitting on the walls, standing on the fountains and they would fill up the street."

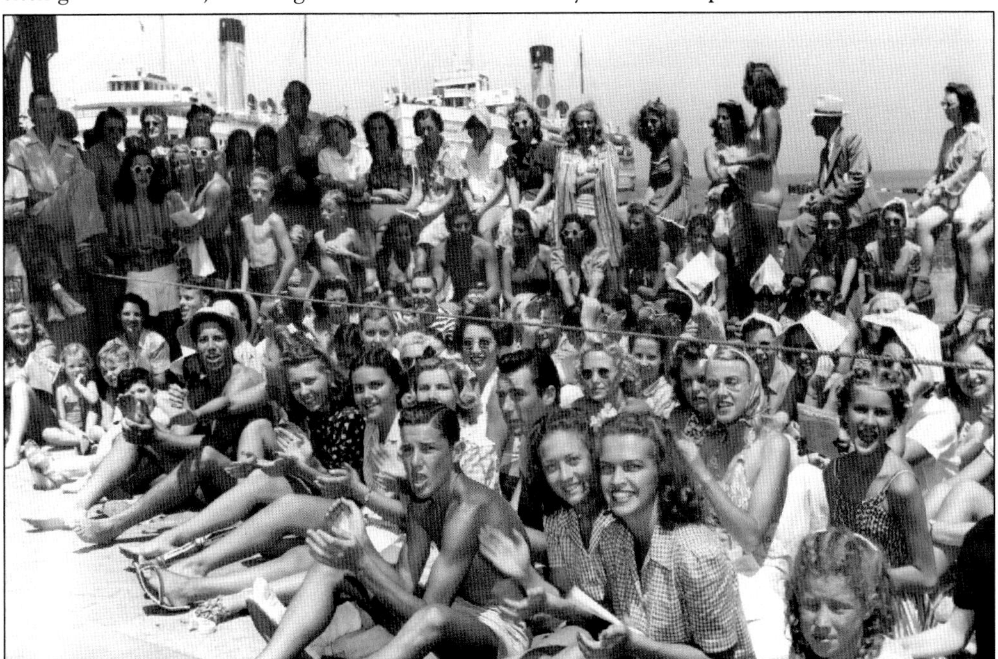

As the people gathered, an official greeter would work with the crowd and prepare them for the greeting. The greeter would lead everyone in song and organized the crowd to say "Hi Neighbor" as travelers stepped off the steamer pier. Many island residents remember Hunsey Gilner as being one of the first official greeters in Avalon.

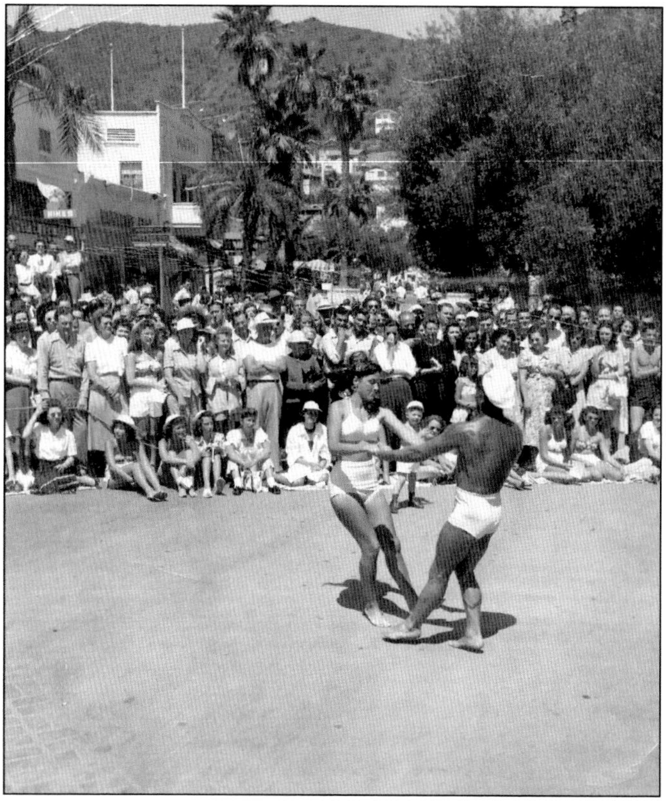

Another one of Avalon's official greeters was Duke Fishman. Duke would lead people in song, dance with members of the crowd, and was known for his friendly hazing of steamship passengers. He would often point out a gentleman as he stepped off the pier and say, "Hey mister, your suitcase is leaking," or "Hey mister, what have you got in that bag?"

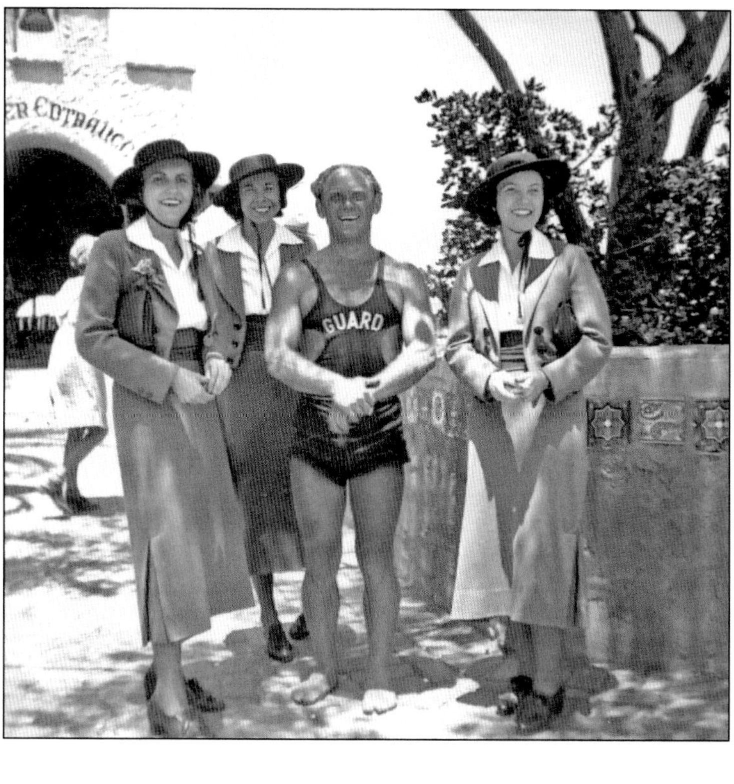

Duke Fishman was an integral part of the steamer greeting for many years. He also served as a lifeguard on the beaches in Avalon but would leave his station to greet each steamer and all those who disembarked to enjoy Catalina. Duke is pictured here with three ship couriers at the steamer entrance.

Duke Fishman was born in the Philippines and was raised in the South Seas. He lived in many parts of the world before finding a home on Catalina Island. Duke first came to the island in 1933 to work on a motion picture being filmed at the Isthmus. By the following summer season, Duke was employed as a lifeguard and official greeter and continued to entertain and protect Catalina's visitors until the mid-1960s. Duke was a true Catalina character and is remembered fondly by residents and visitors alike.

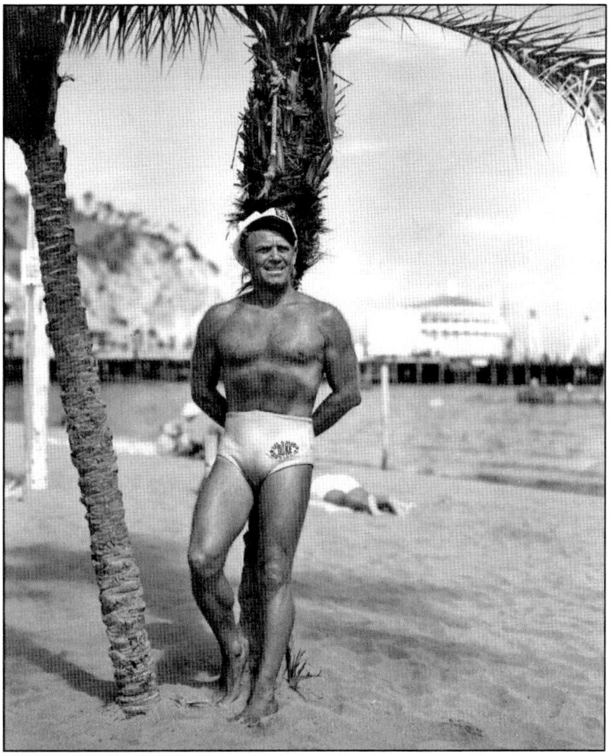

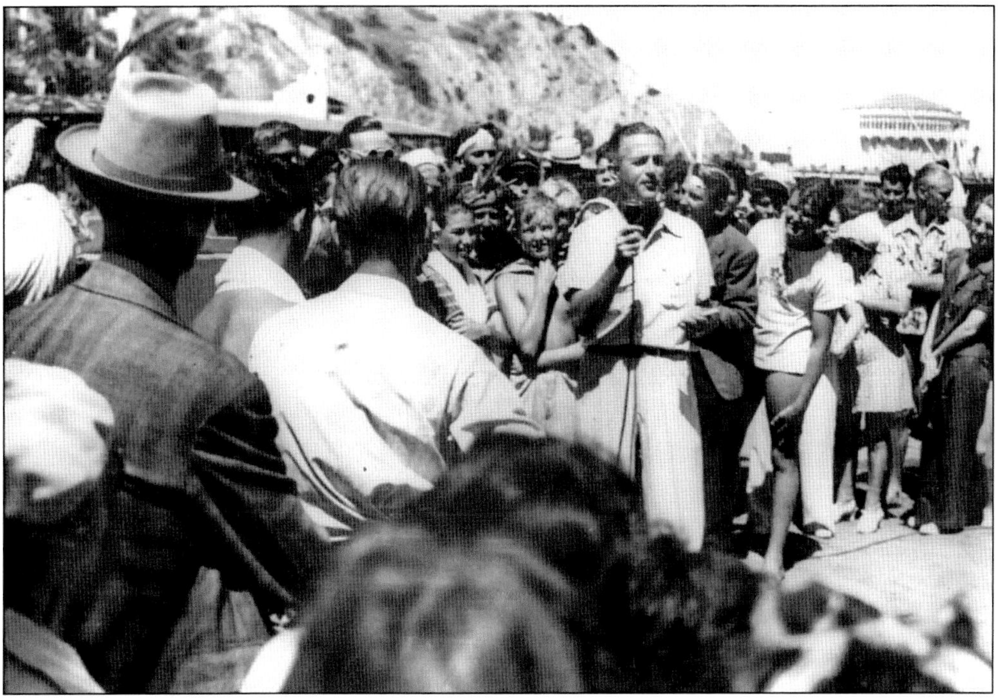

Gary Breckner was a popular radio announcer who broadcast his daily radio show from Avalon. He was involved with broadcasting the big bands from the Casino ballroom and often joined the steamer greetings by interviewing the crowd and passengers as they stepped off the steamer pier.

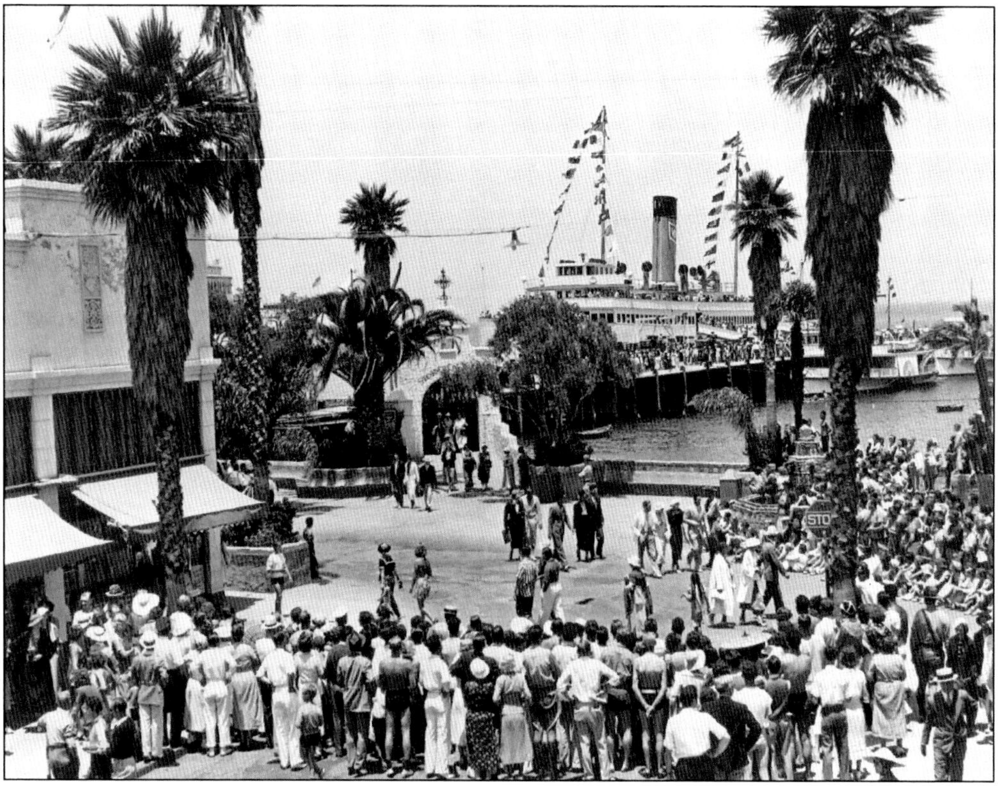

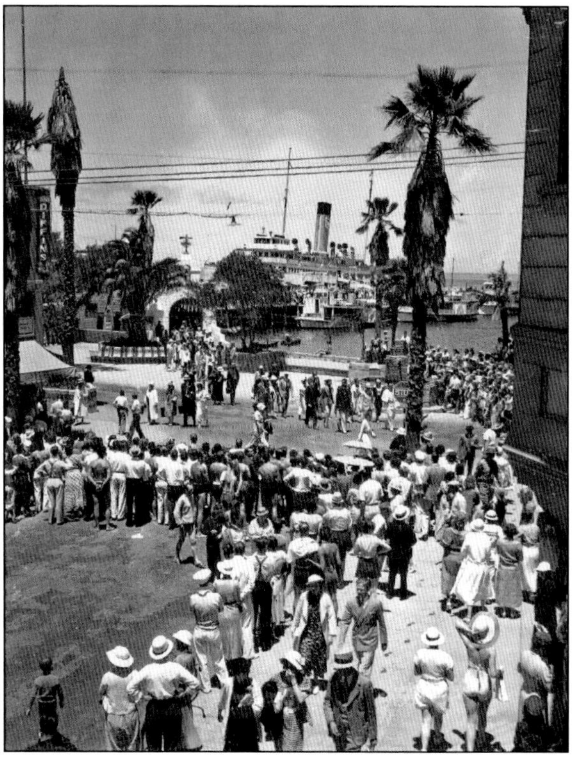

By 1940, the steamer greeting grew into an elaborate affair. Hundreds of people would gather along Crescent and Sumner Avenues to participate in this traditional welcome. As the passengers departed the steamer pier, the crowd would sing songs, yell out "Hi, Neighbor," and offer a friendly welcome to all.

The steamer greeting was just the beginning of Catalina's hospitality. Once passengers stepped into the town of Avalon, they would be treated with friendly service in every store, restaurant, and hotel. The tour guides were well known for excellent service and their extensive knowledge of the island. Everyone did their best to ensure that every visitor to Catalina had an enjoyable experience.

The Chicago Cubs traveled to Avalon each spring for over 30 years, and upon their arrival they received a spectacular welcome from the town. At the time, William Wrigley Jr. owned both the Chicago Cubs and Catalina Island and decided that the Cubs would hold their annual spring training in Avalon. The Cubs traveled by train from Chicago, leaving behind the cold weather and snow for the Mediterranean climate of Catalina.

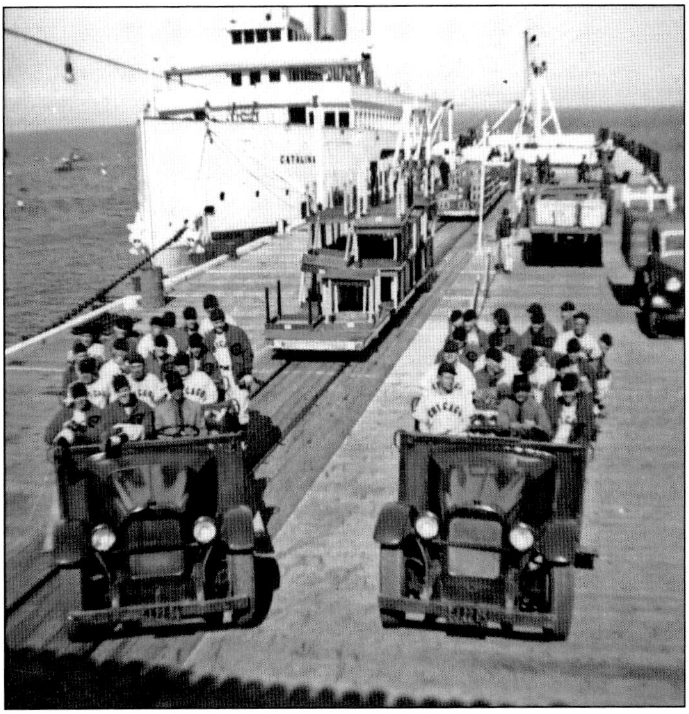

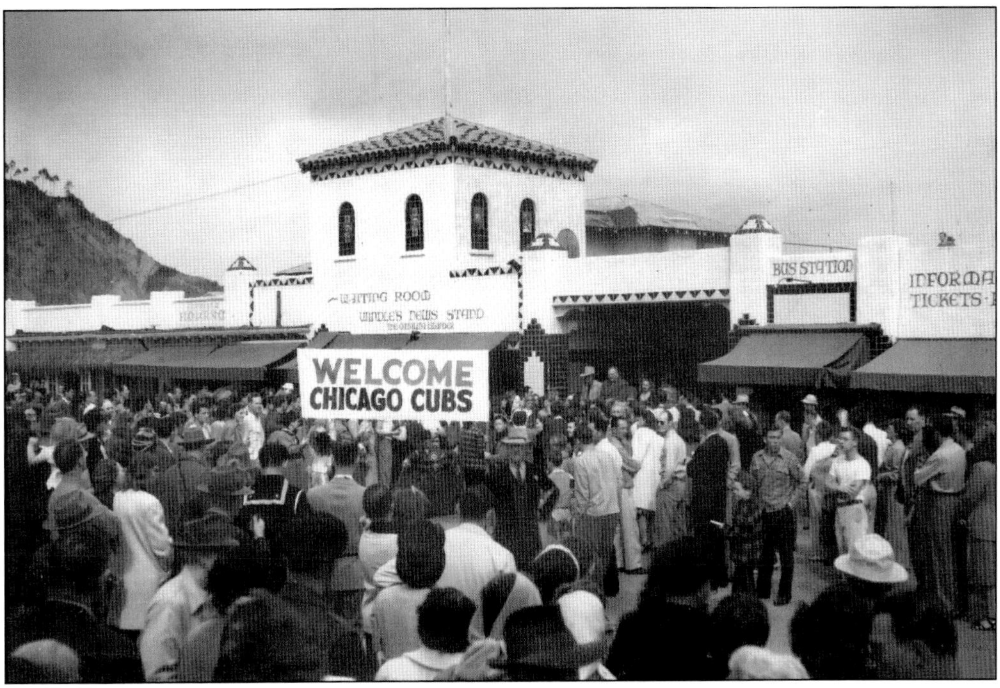

The Cubs would train each morning and then be encouraged to take full advantage of the island through golfing, fishing, hiking, and hunting. The team continued to train on Catalina Island until 1951, with the exception of the years during World War II. The players were extended every hospitality from the citizens of Avalon and considered Catalina Island to be their home away from home—and Avalon has long considered the Chicago Cubs their home team.

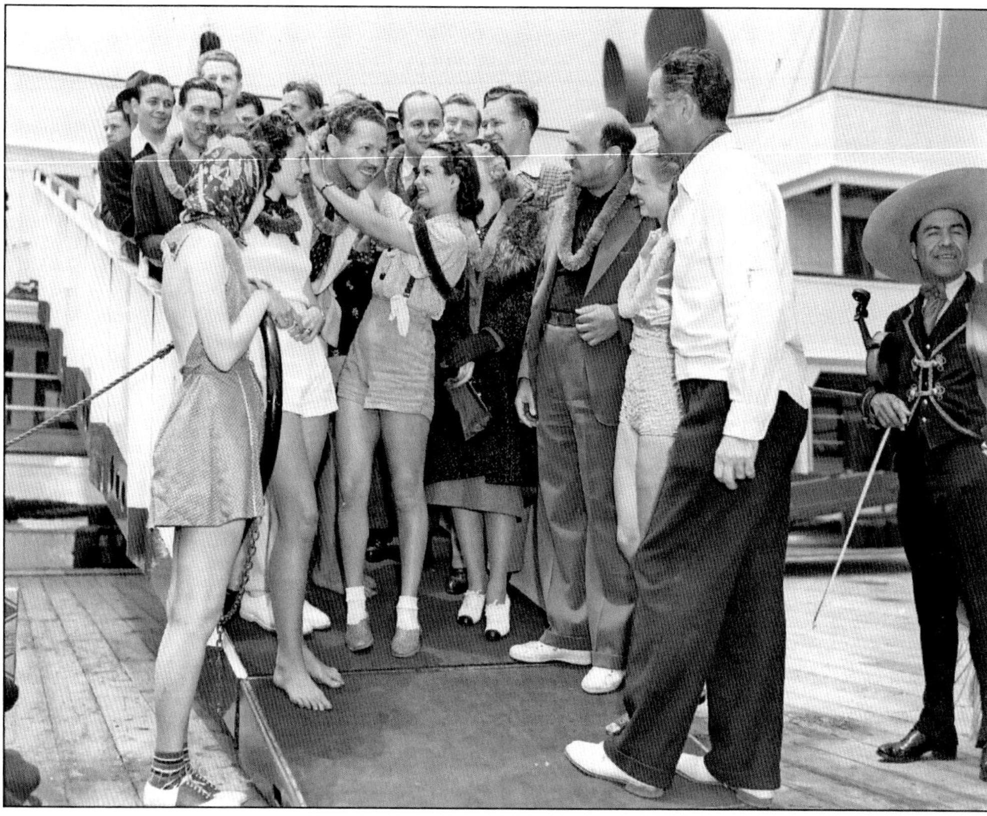

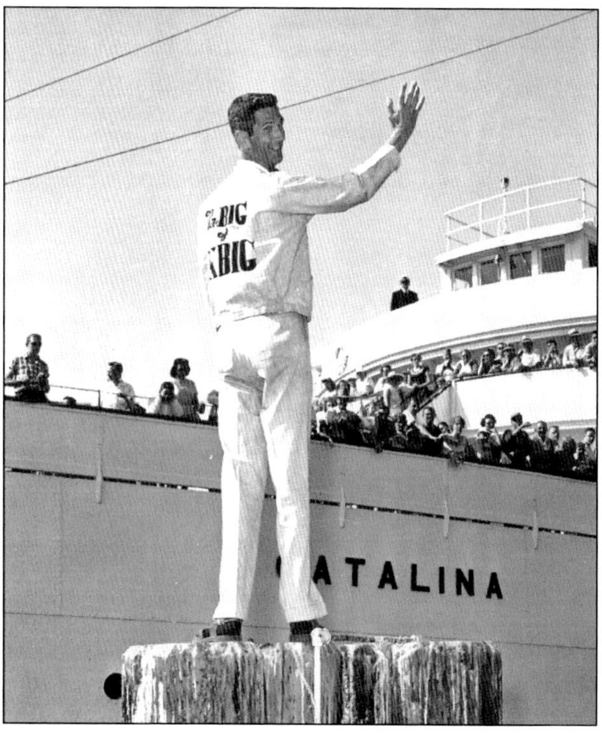

When celebrities or big bands arrived on the steamer, they would often be given a special greeting. The Roger Pryor Band is pictured here stepping off the ship to kick off the summer season in the Casino ballroom in 1938.

Carl Bailey, also known as "Mr. Big," was a radio announcer for KBIG radio station. During the 1950s, Bailey broadcast his show from Avalon and would often broadcast from the *Catalina* as it crossed the San Pedro Channel on the way to Avalon. Mr. Big had a feature on his show known as "man-on-the-deck interviews," which were broadcast shortwave from the *Catalina*. He also served as an official greeter for Avalon.

As a visit to the magic isle came to an end, visitors brought their baggage down to the steamer terminal and checked it for their return trip. It was loaded onto carts and rolled down the pier to the steamer. Once passengers arrived on the mainland, luggage was retrieved from the baggage room in the Wilmington terminal.

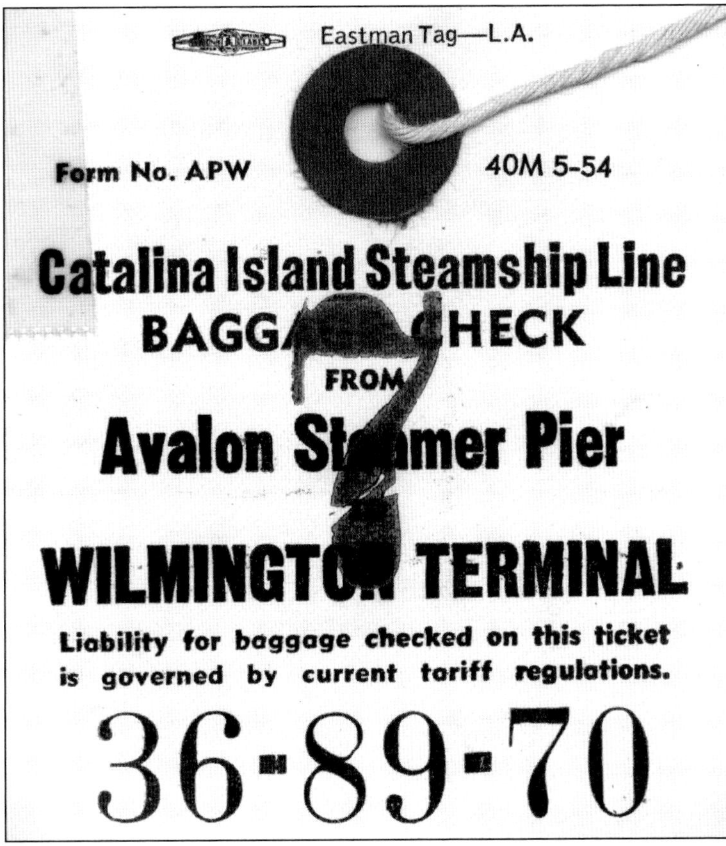

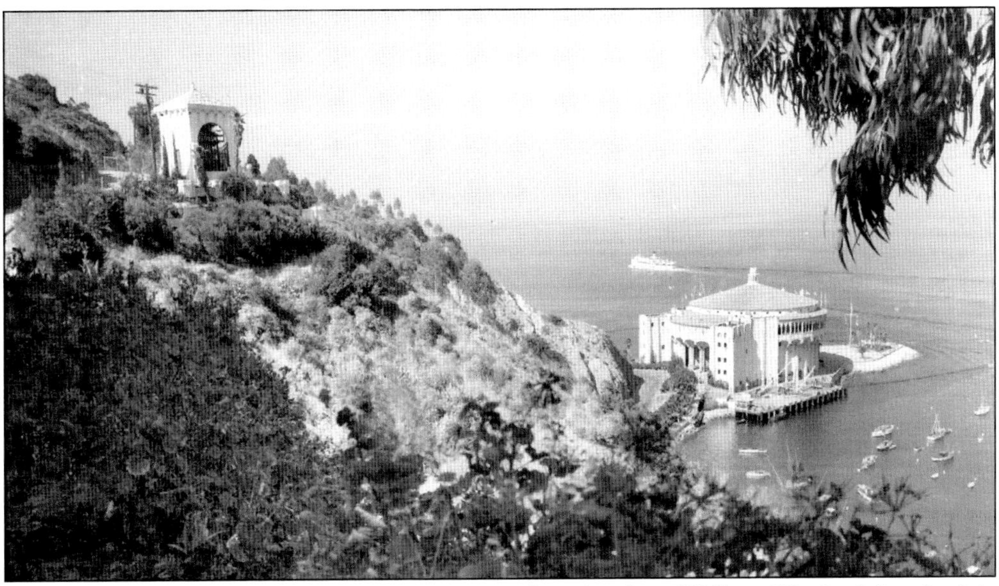

The Chimes Tower was a gift to the community of Avalon from William Wrigley Jr.'s wife, Ada Foote Wrigley. The chimes kept time for the small community for 16 hours each day. They could be played from a console on the steamer pier, and familiar songs were often played for visitors as they disembarked and loaded the steamers.

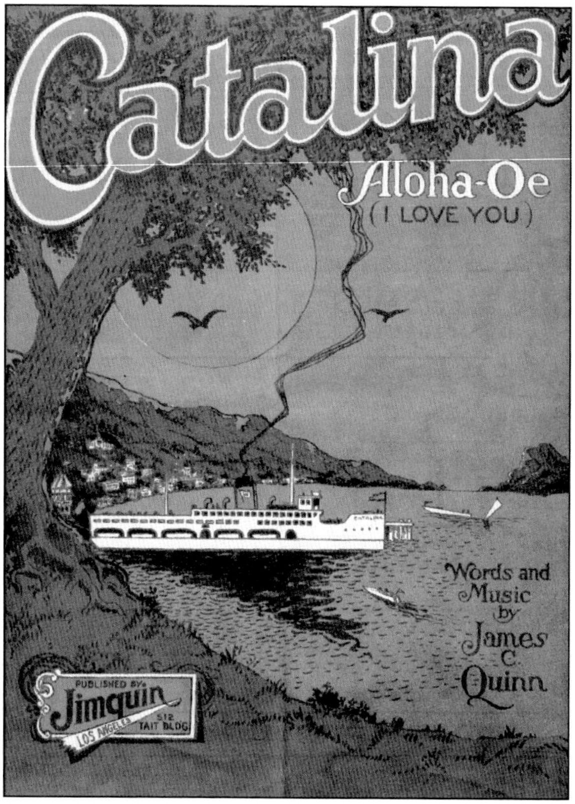

Ada Blanche Wrigley Schreiner, daughter of Philip K. Wrigley, remembers that they would often play Hawaiian music, such as "Catalina Aloha-Oe" from the Chimes Tower during the steamer farewell. Blanny also remembers that the chimes would "play the song 'Avalon' and I would cry buckets because it was always so sad to leave the island. To this day, every time I hear 'Avalon' it brings tears to my eyes."

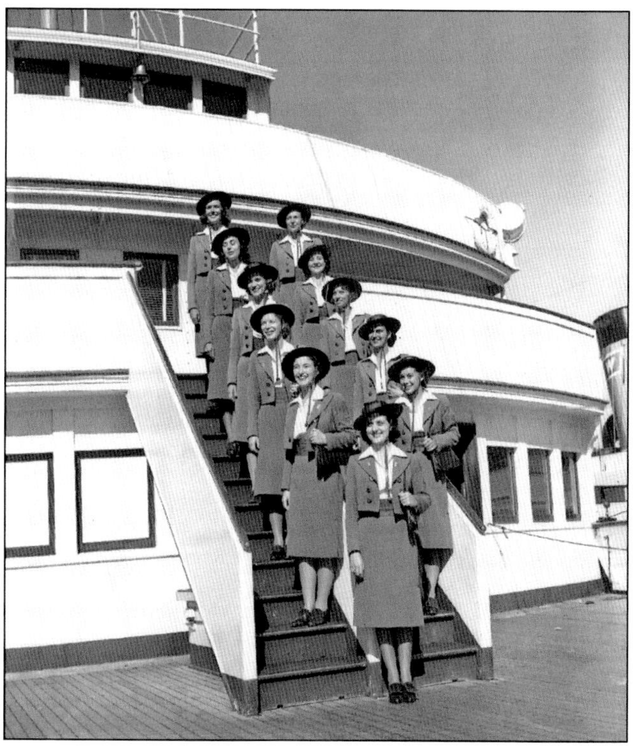

"La Golondrina" was another song that often played during the farewell. Many island residents and visitors recall that the steamship's couriers would climb the stairway leading to the bridge of the ship and wave goodbye to those on shore.

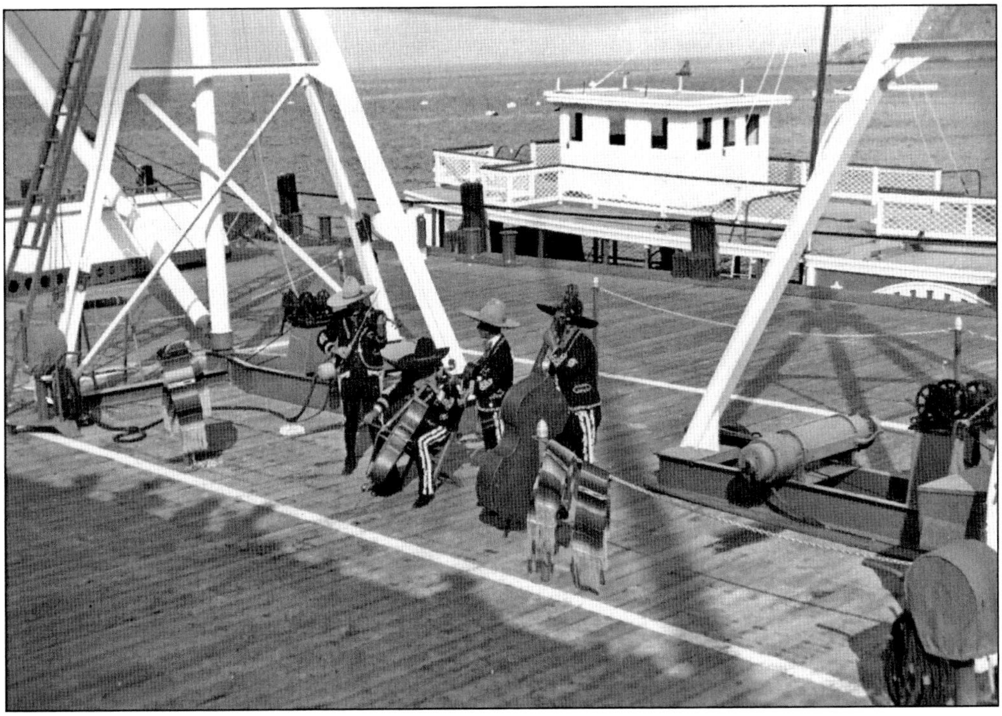

The troubadours were a significant part of the steamer greeting, but also played an important role in the farewell. They would play from the steamer pier, serenading the passengers as the ship pulled away and the Catalina Orchestra would answer them from above.

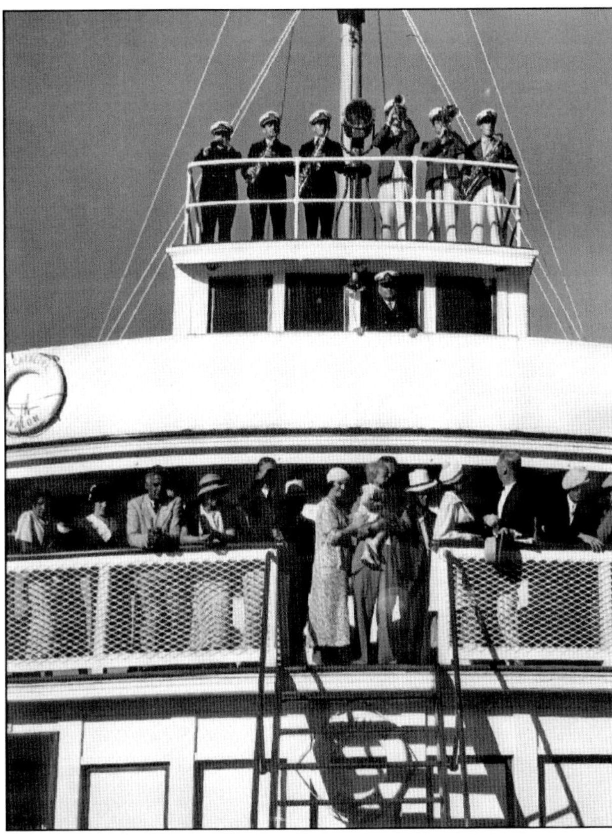

As the ship departed, the Catalina Orchestra would be on top of the wheelhouse of the ship, answering the troubadours below. Island resident Roy Rose remembers how the orchestra and troubadours would play to each other during the farewell as well as the familiar songs of the chimes tower. He recalls, "You would see tears streaming down people's faces. It was so beautiful the way it was all done as the steamer backed out of the harbor." (Courtesy of the Santa Catalina Island Company.)

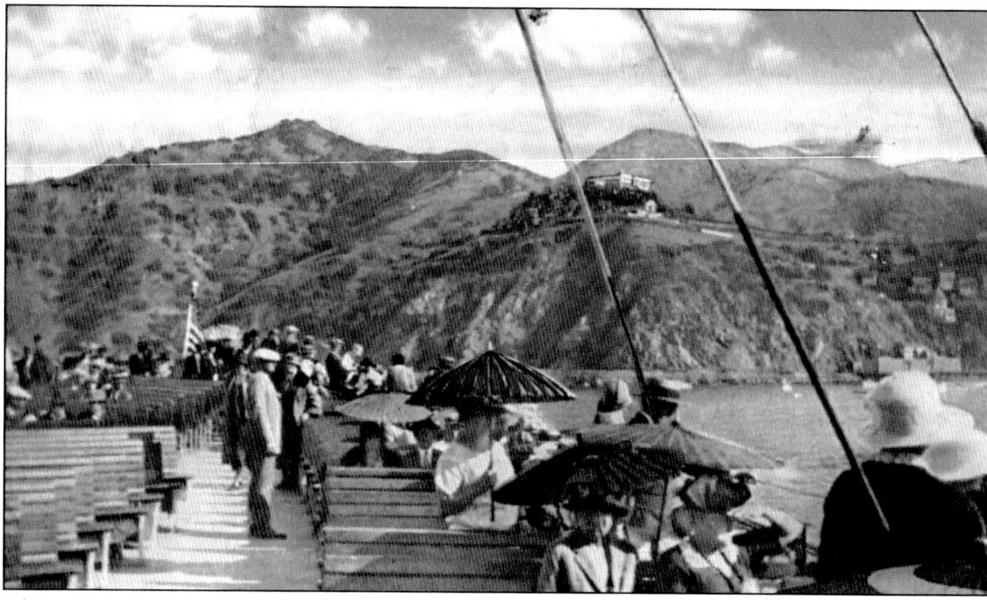

The steamship would depart in sweet sorrow from the bay and begin her journey back to the mainland. This postcard from the 1920s shows passengers taking one last look at the beautiful town of Avalon from the top deck of a ship. Their time on the island may have ended, but their Catalina experience continued.

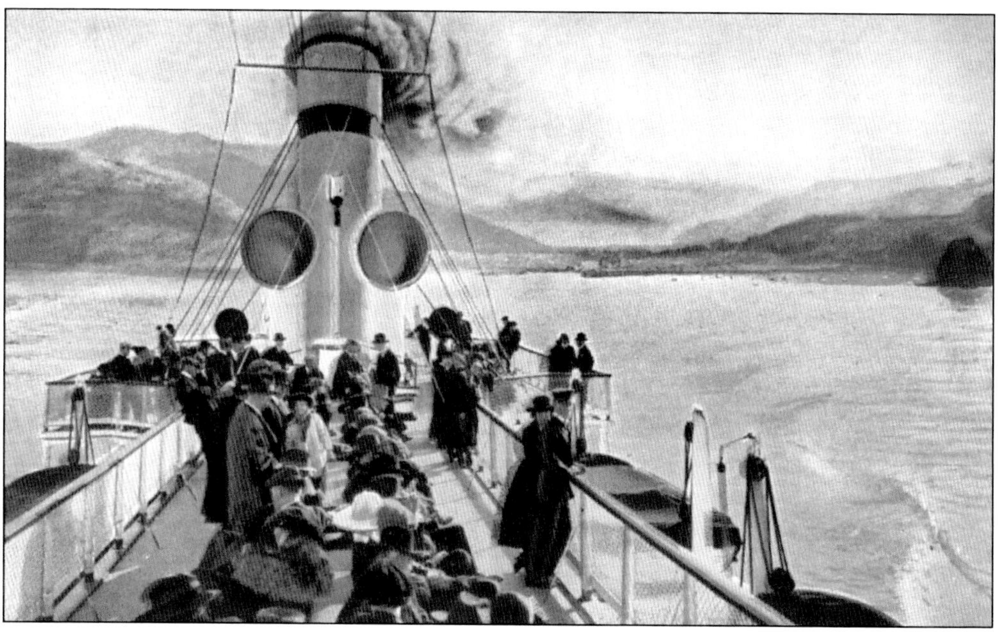

Passengers enjoyed the return trip across the San Pedro Channel as they would again be captivated by the sights and sounds of the sea and entertained by the ship's orchestra. During the two-hour crossing, passengers would explore the ship, marvel at the engines, grab a snack, and relax after a long day of sightseeing.

Six

FILLING THE VOID

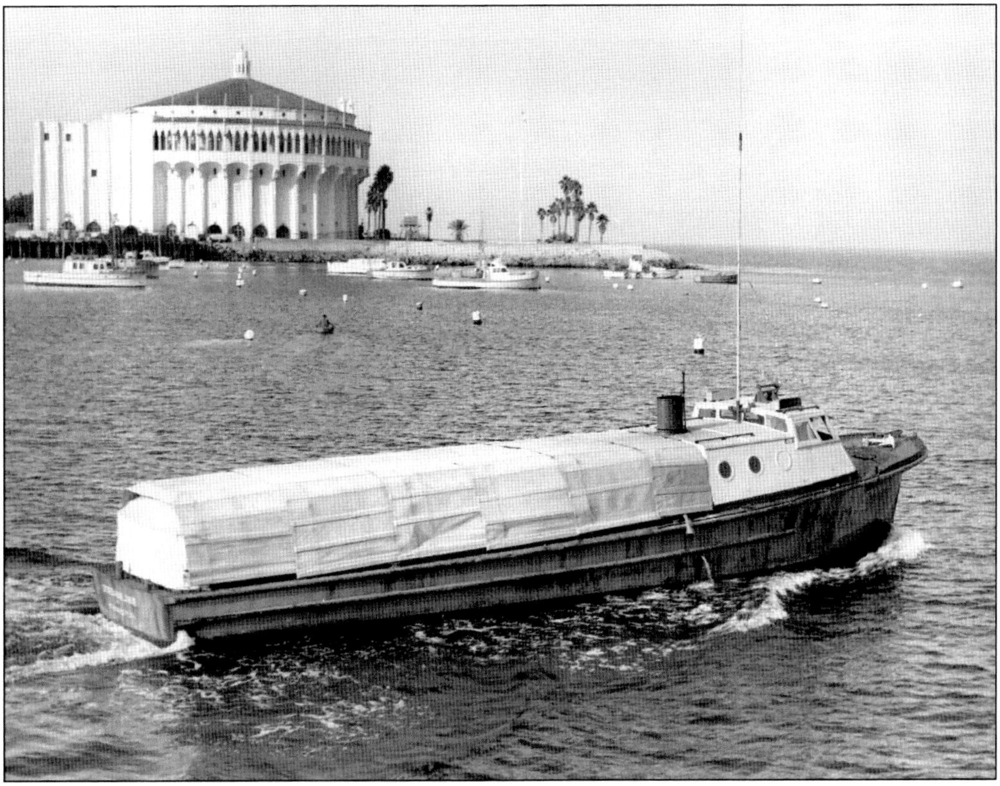

The first glimpse of the end of Catalina's romantic steamer era began with the onset of World War II. For the first time in many years, regularly scheduled passenger service to Catalina had ceased and island residents and visitors had to look for other options. During the war, the SS *Avalon* remained the primary mode of limited transportation to the island, however water taxis were also employed as cross-channel carriers. After the war, the Santa Catalina Island Company established the Island Boat Service to operate small cross-channel vessels. These boats supplemented the steamships and ensured that Catalina Island would never again be without passenger service. Island Boat Service and other independent operators placed several different vessels on the Catalina run during this time. The boats described in this chapter filled a void in Catalina Island's transportation history between regularly scheduled steamship passenger service and the small, fast, and reliable fleet that serves the island today. (Courtesy of Santa Catalina Island Company.)

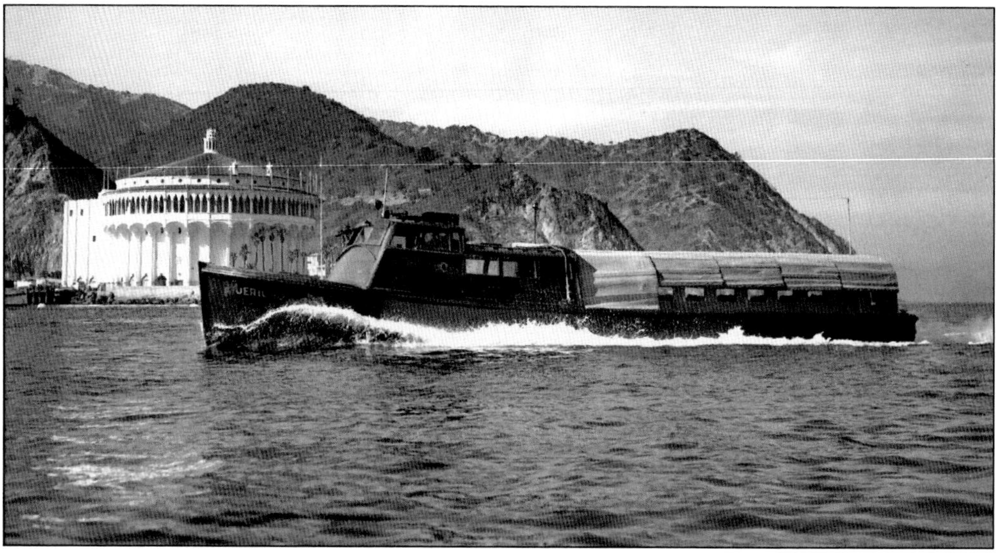

The 49-foot *Jericho* was built in Los Angeles in 1942 as a water taxi. Island resident Roy Rose remembers, "The first water taxis had roll top curtains and were open in the back. The fumes from the engines would come into the boat and people would get carbon monoxide poisoning. It was a rough, dark crossing." (Courtesy of Santa Catalina Island Company.)

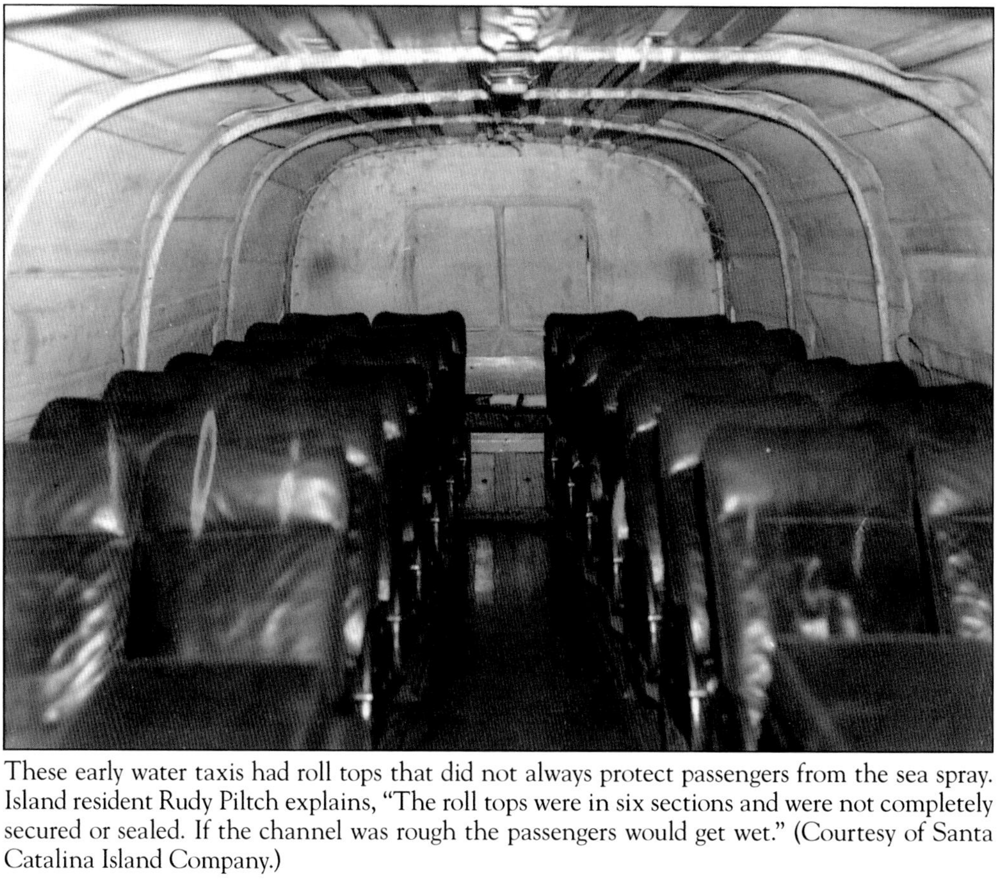

These early water taxis had roll tops that did not always protect passengers from the sea spray. Island resident Rudy Piltch explains, "The roll tops were in six sections and were not completely secured or sealed. If the channel was rough the passengers would get wet." (Courtesy of Santa Catalina Island Company.)

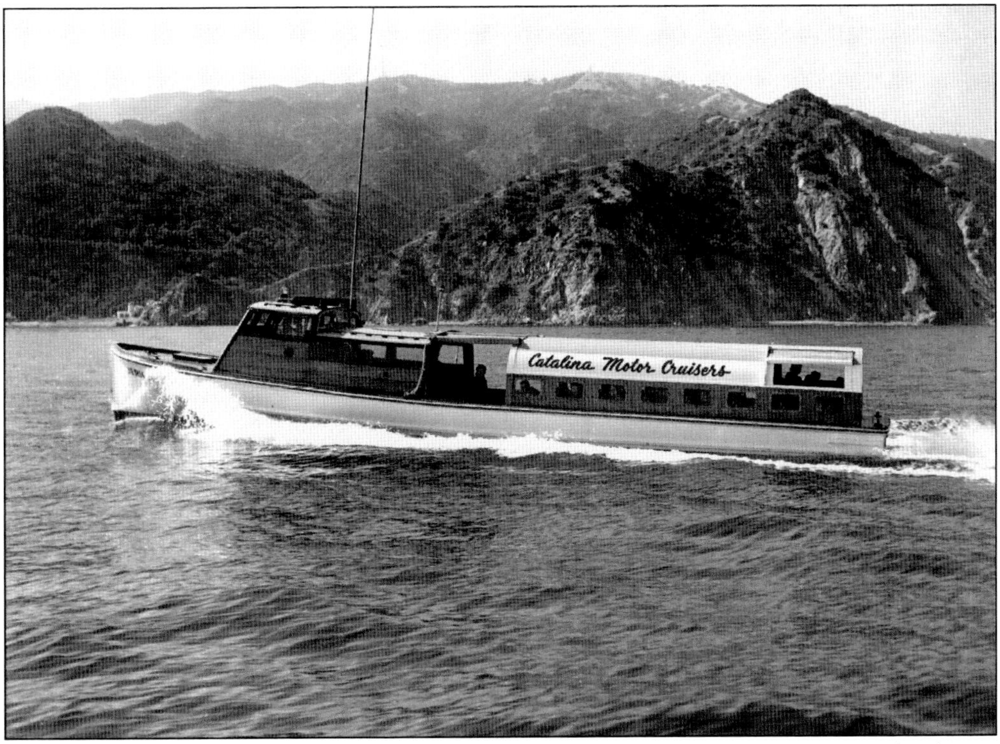

After World War II, Island Boat Service purchased the *Jericho* for the Catalina run. Island Boat Service installed a permanent cabin, replacing the former roll top that greatly increased passenger comfort. The *Jericho* continued to serve on the Catalina run for several more years.

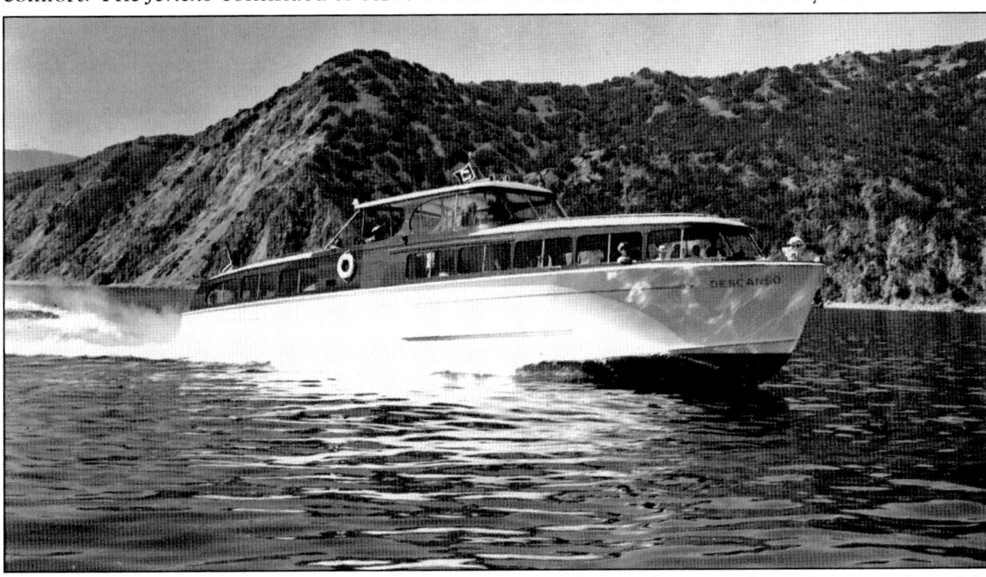

The *Descanso* was built for the Coast Guard in 1943. The 63-foot vessel was later purchased by the Santa Catalina Island Company as a tour boat. It was meant to augment the *Blanche W* as a tour boat for the Seal Rocks Cruise, but was soon pushed into cross-channel service. Her gasoline engines were replaced by diesel engines and she was placed on the Catalina run by Island Boat Service. (Courtesy of Santa Catalina Island Company.)

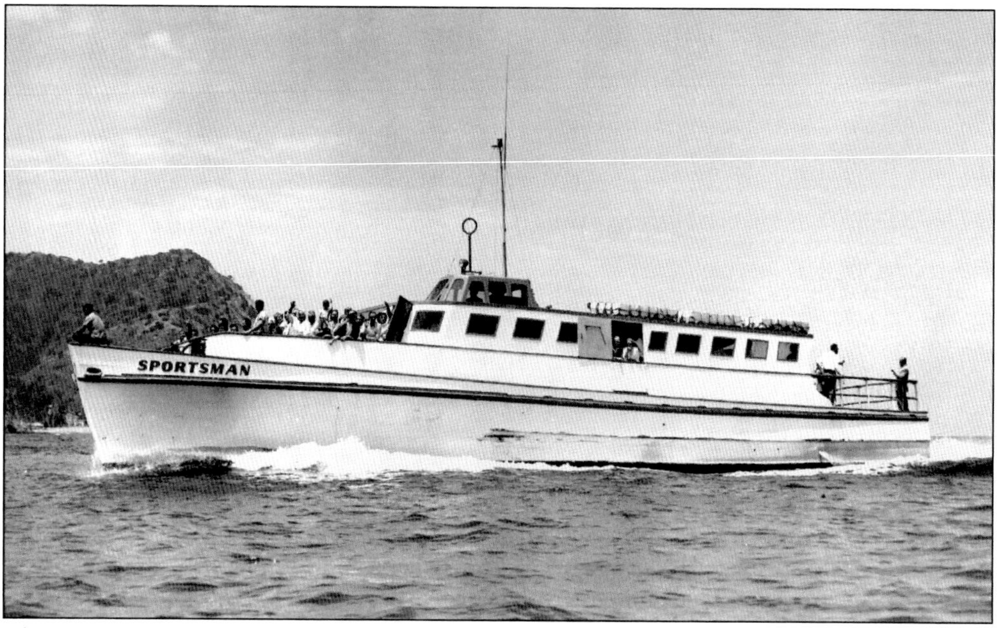

The *Sportsman* was launched in 1942 as a Coast Guard Deep Water Air Sea Rescue Boat. Island Boat Service purchased the 83-foot vessel for use on Catalina Island. She was converted for passenger use and diesel engines were installed. The *Sportsman* was placed on the Catalina run and crossed the channel in 2 hours and 20 minutes.

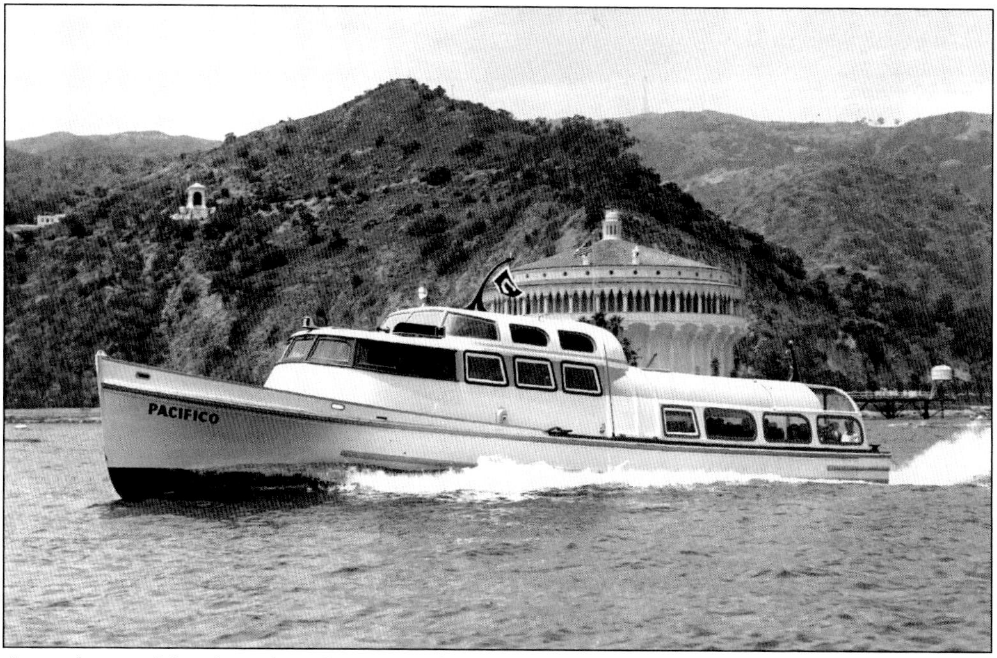

According to Island resident Doug Bombard, "The *Pacifico* was the best riding boat in the channel at that time." She was built as a water taxi and operated on the Catalina run by Island Boat Service. It was equipped with a converted 500-horsepower Ford tank engine and carried 48 passengers. She had leather seats, deluxe appointments, and was fast, making the crossing in less than two hours. (Courtesy of Santa Catalina Island Company.)

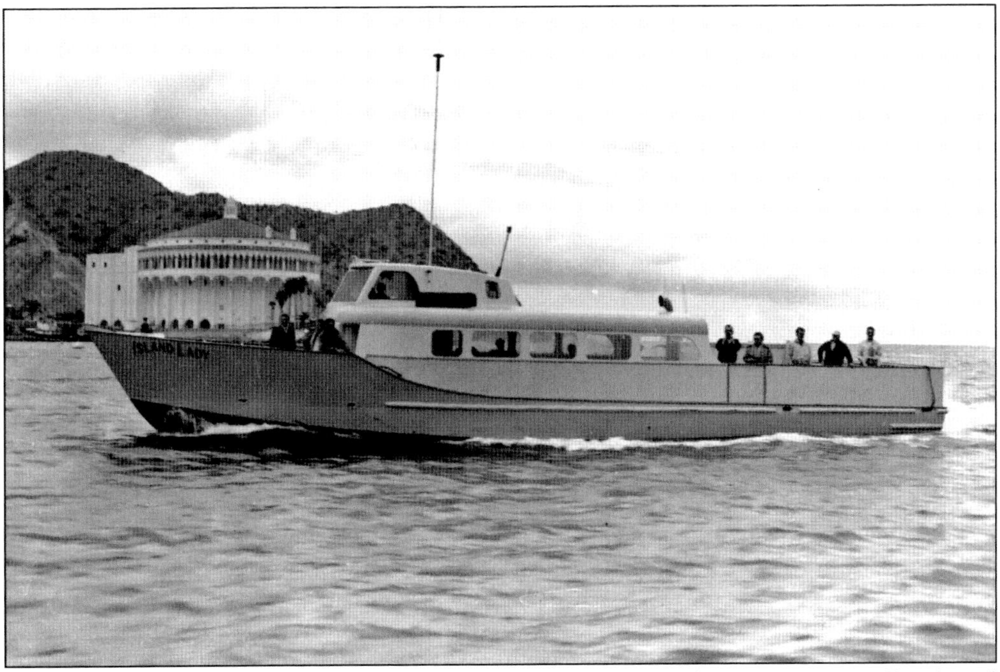

The *Island Lady* was the first boat to operate on the Catalina run between Newport Beach and Avalon. She began operating shortly after World War II and provided service to the island until the early 1950s.

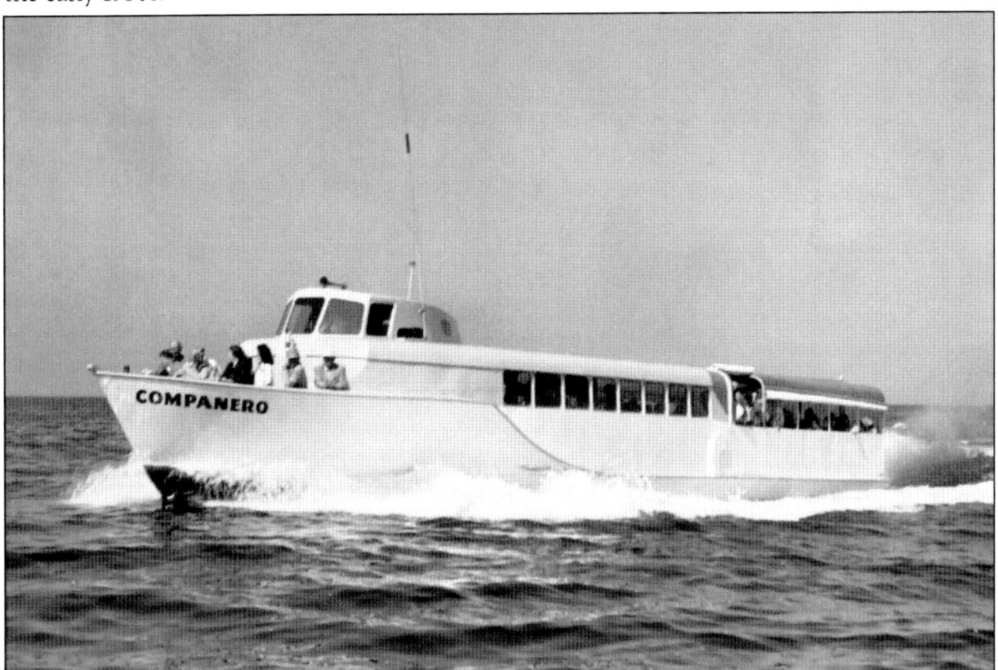

The *Island Lady* later returned to Catalina under the operation of Island Boat Service with a new look and a new name. The *Companero*'s passenger cabins were redesigned and she operated as a fill-in boat on the Catalina run during the 1950s. (Courtesy of Santa Catalina Island Company.)

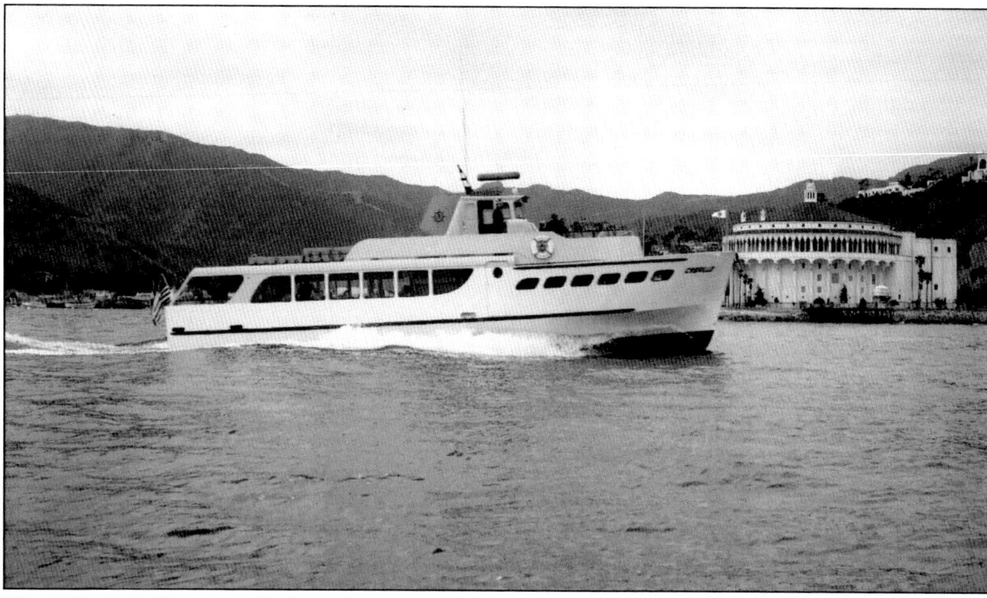

The MV *Cabrillo* was a 65-foot aluminum boat built in San Diego for Island Boat Service. The motor vessel was an attempt by Philip K. Wrigley and the Santa Catalina Island Company to introduce a new line of small, fast boats designed to cross the channel. The *Cabrillo* had lounge-style seating, cocktail tables, and a full bar. She could accommodate 140 passengers.

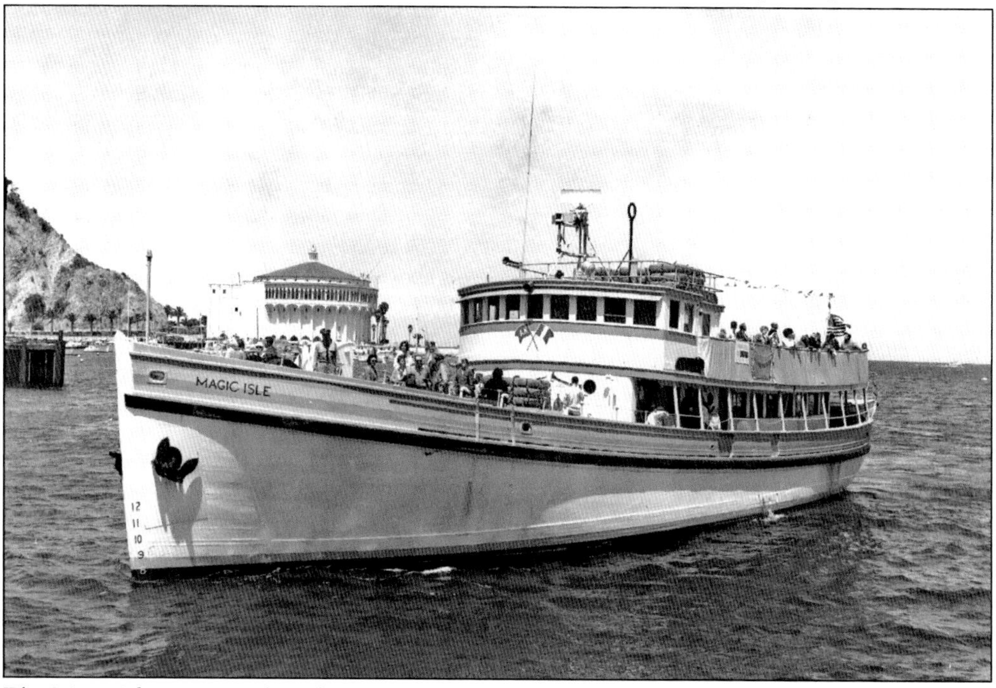

The *Magic Isle* was a 107-foot, former military ship that was introduced to the Catalina run by a privately owned competitor. She was built in Washington in 1943 and used to supply the Pacific Islands during World War II. The *Magic Isle* was owned and operated by Howard and Les Thuet. Many island residents fondly referred to the *Magic Isle* as the "Tragic Pile" as it did not offer the smoothest or most comfortable ride across the channel.

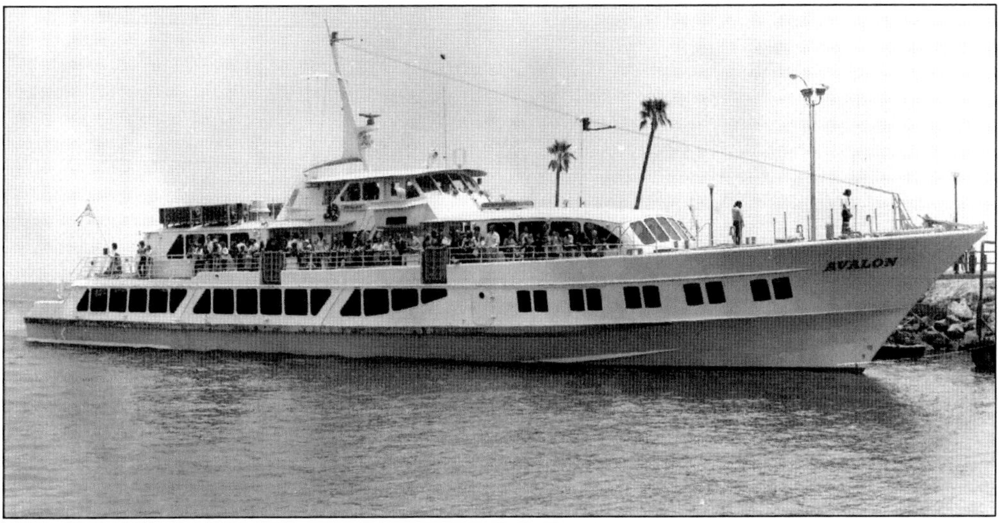

The GT *Avalon* was a 160-foot aluminum cruise vessel built in San Pedro. According to an article in the *Catalina Islander* in 1970, "the GT *Avalon* was designed for rapid, luxurious cross channel transportation." The *Avalon* had fully appointed lounges, a snack bar, piped in music, and had a dance deck. She could accommodate 500 passengers.

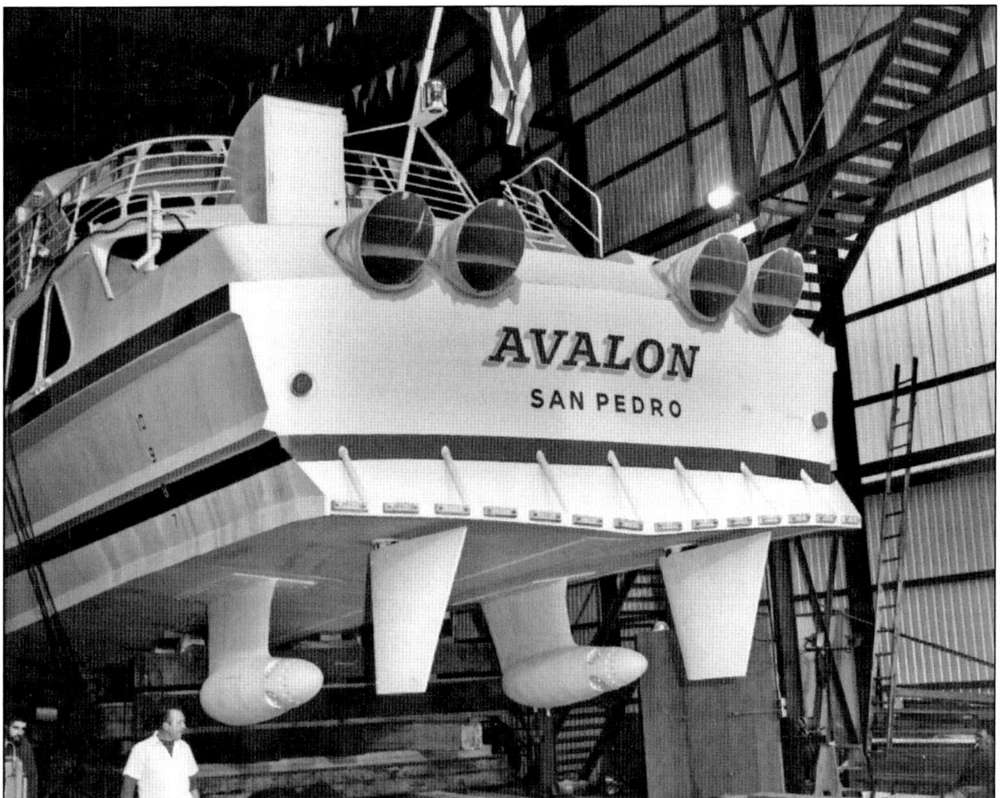

The privately operated *Avalon* served on the Catalina run for only part of one season. The vessel was later damaged when she hit a rock during a private charter off the coast of Palos Verdes. Today, the *Avalon* can be found providing dinner cruises off the coast of Hawaii.

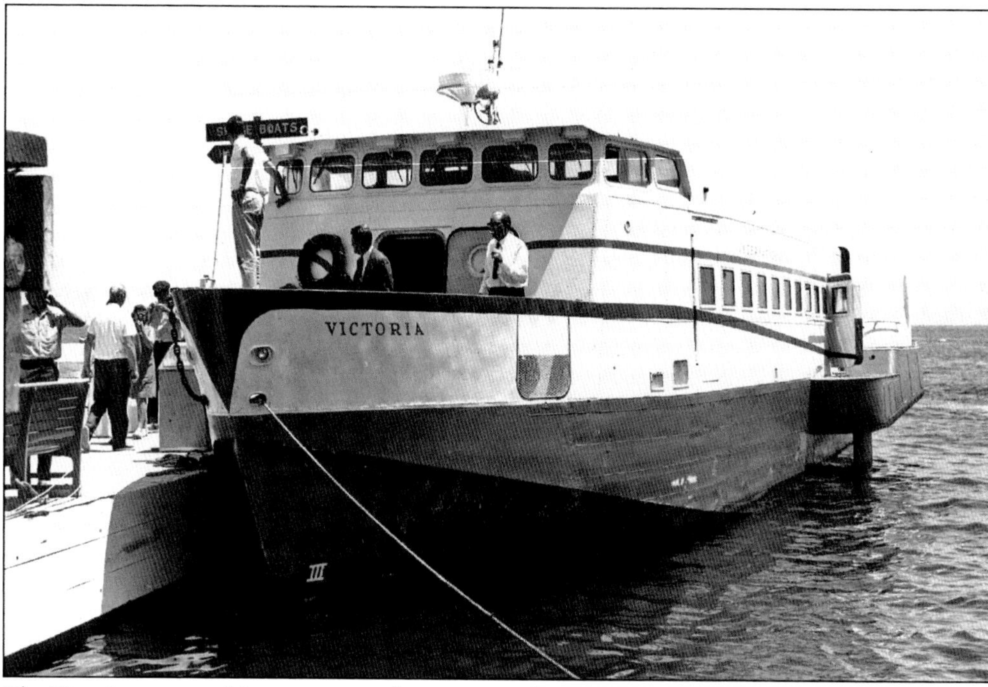

The *Victoria* was one of the most unique boats to provide passenger service to Catalina Island. She was a submerged foil hydrofoil vessel and the only one to successfully operate on the Catalina run. The government owned the *Victoria* and was testing her new technology. It was brought to Catalina in 1969 and operated for several months during that season. A gear box on the boat later malfunctioned and she was taken off the run. The operators felt that they had proved their point that a hydrofoil could successfully navigate the San Pedro Channel and decided not to rebuild the gear, thus her short, but innovative time on the Catalina run ended. (Courtesy of Santa Catalina Island Company.)

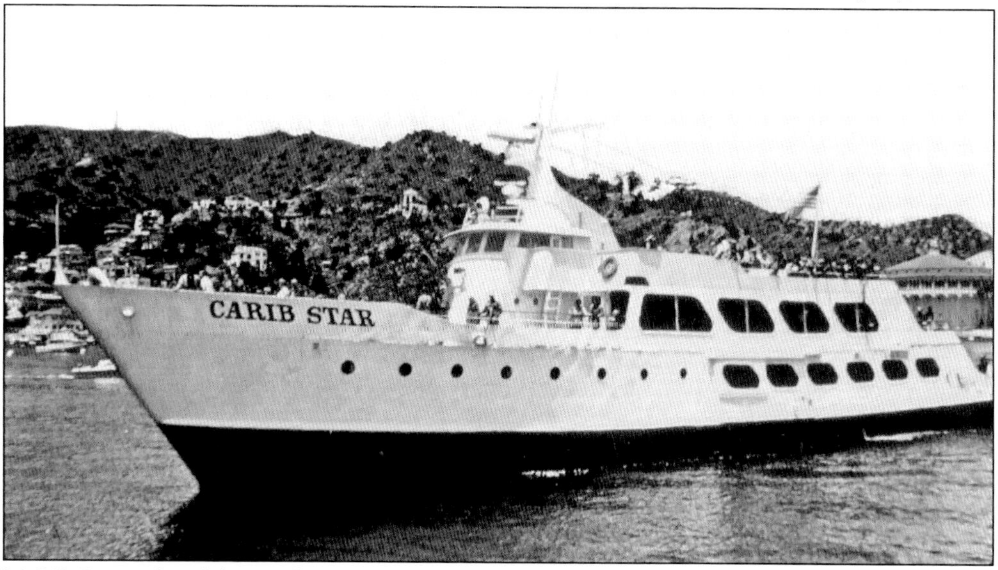

M.G.R.S. introduced the *Carib Star* as a companion boat to the SS *Catalina* in 1974. She was operated between San Pedro and Avalon. On April 10, 1975, there was an explosion aboard her while docked in Los Angeles Harbor. She was partially sunk, but was salvaged and taken to San Francisco.

Seven

FAST, RELIABLE SERVICE

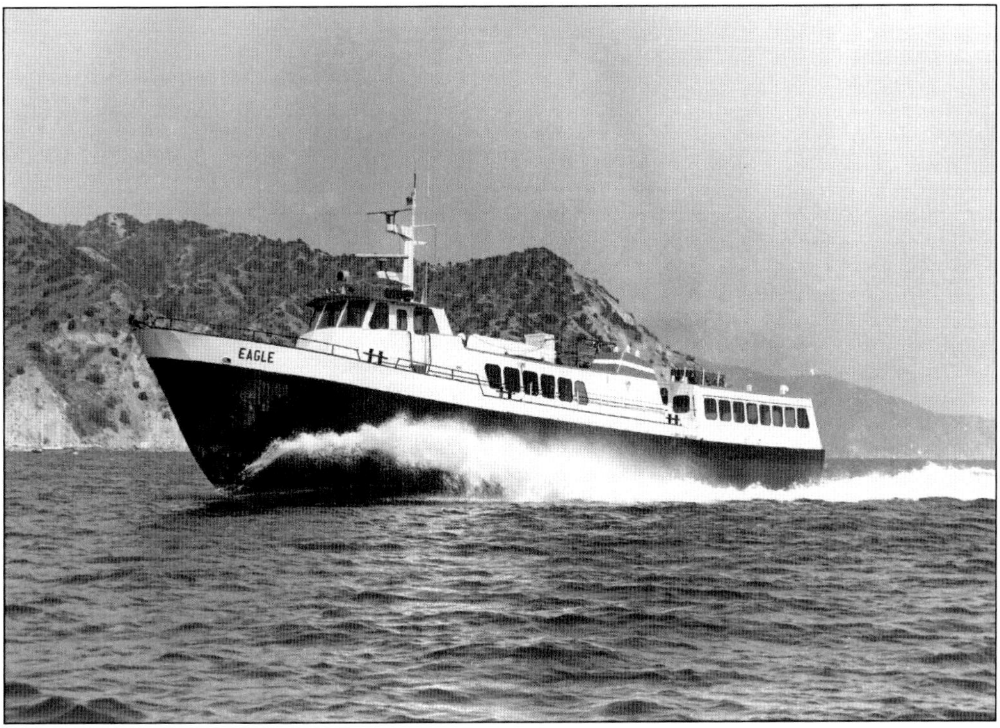

The 1970s ushered in a new era of smaller boats that provided regularly scheduled passenger service to Catalina Island. This trend echoed the advances in maritime technology and the changing economy of Avalon. Catalina Cruises introduced their new service in 1970 and were the first post-steamer group to honor a commitment to provide frequent, reliable, comfortable, and affordable service. Catalina Cruises was a subsidiary of Crowley Maritime, a worldwide maritime company operating out of Los Angeles Harbor. They saw the need for consistent passenger service to Catalina Island and filled it with Catalina Cruises. Catalina Cruises served the island faithfully for many years and was later joined by Catalina Express in 1981. Catalina Channel Express was founded by Doug Bombard with the help of his son Greg and friend Tom Rutter. Initially they were looking for a way to bring guests to the Two Harbors Resort at the Isthmus of Catalina. They purchased a sportfishing boat that they converted into a passenger vessel for the Catalina run. Catalina Express has since grown to a fleet of eight modern high-speed vessels, each built specifically for the Catalina run. Today, Catalina Express provides the most reliable, frequent, and fastest service to Catalina Island available.

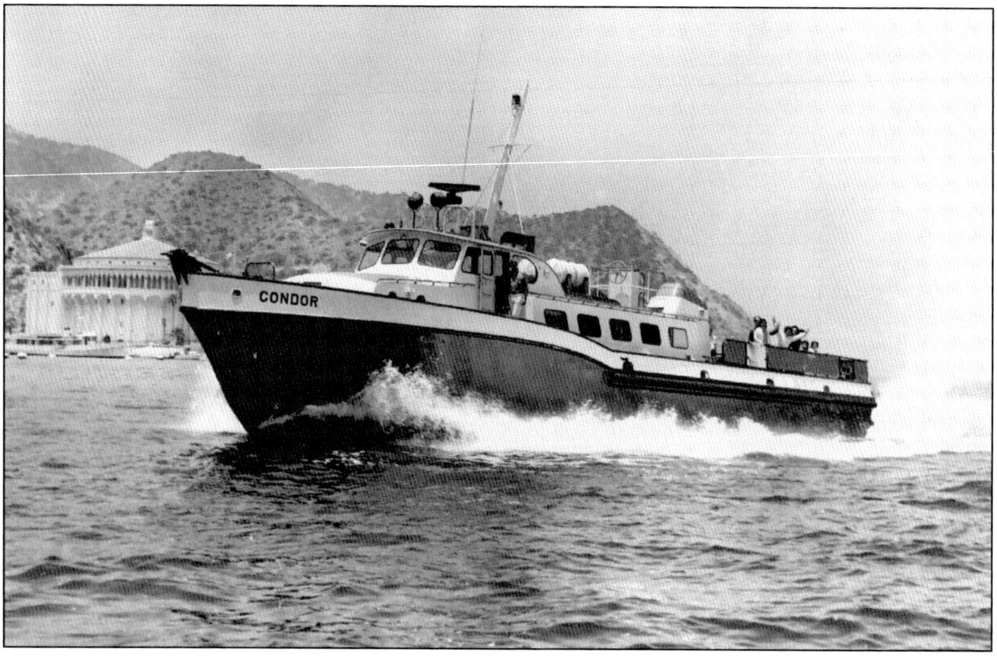

Catalina Cruises commenced their operation by introducing two quality steel-hull boats, the *Condor* and the *Eagle,* to the Catalina run. Both vessels were originally built as crew boats employed by oil companies to bring employees to their oil rigs. The *Condor* and the *Eagle* served the island on a regular schedule throughout their inaugural season and residents and visitors began to frequent their service.

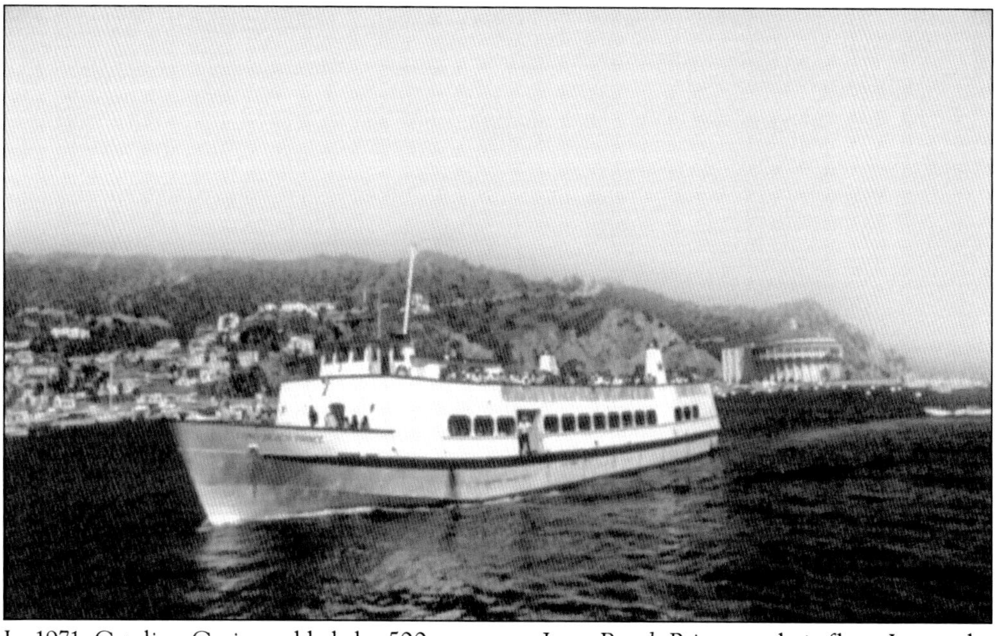

In 1971, Catalina Cruises added the 500-passenger *Long Beach Prince* to their fleet. It was the first vessel built specifically for the Catalina run by Catalina Cruises and quickly became the standard of the fleet. The *Prince* was 132 feet in length, double-decked, with glass enclosing the lower deck. She had large windows, a snack bar, a sound system, and padded benches.

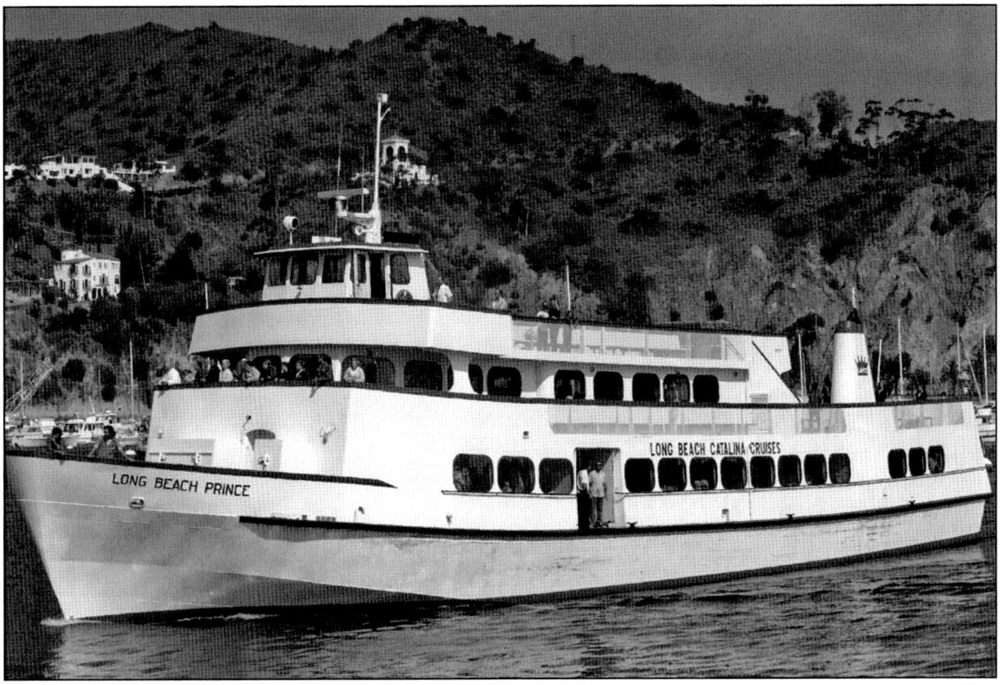

A third, upper deck was later added to the *Long Beach Prince*, increasing her capacity to 700 passengers. The Catalina Cruises fleet could now accommodate up to 1,000 passengers and was becoming an increasingly popular service among island residents and visitors. And as their popularity grew, so did the size of the Catalina Cruises fleet.

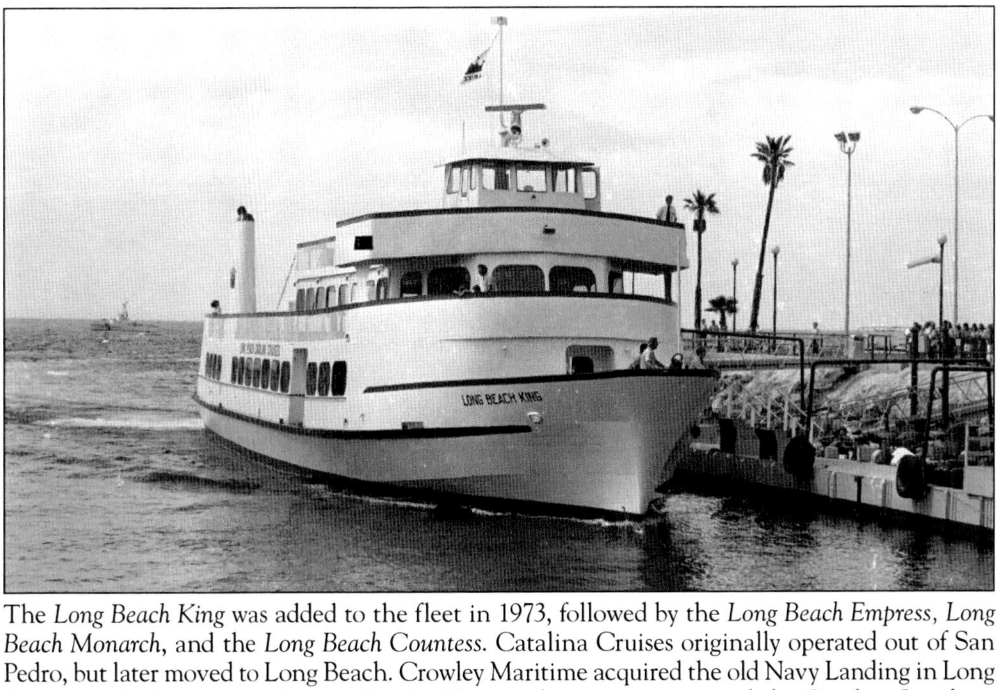

The *Long Beach King* was added to the fleet in 1973, followed by the *Long Beach Empress*, *Long Beach Monarch*, and the *Long Beach Countess*. Catalina Cruises originally operated out of San Pedro, but later moved to Long Beach. Crowley Maritime acquired the old Navy Landing in Long Beach and built a terminal and office buildings. The site was renamed the Catalina Landing. (Courtesy of Santa Catalina Island Company.)

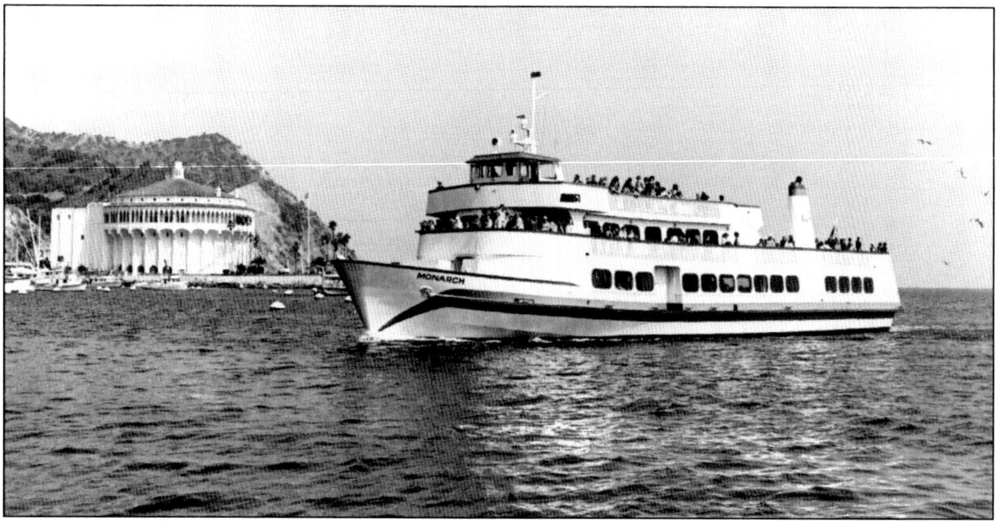

The *Long Beach King, Empress, Monarch,* and *Countess* were all sister ships taken from the same design. They were 134-foot, triple-decked boats that carried over 800 passengers across the San Pedro Channel in two hours. With these boats, Catalina Cruises provided a reliable, regularly scheduled service to Catalina for 25 years. Crowley Maritime Corporation later sold Catalina Cruises to Ray Handy and Bruce Voss in 1997. The *Long Beach King* and *Countess* still provide passenger service to Catalina Island under the operation of Catalina Classic Cruises. (Courtesy of Santa Catalina Island Company.)

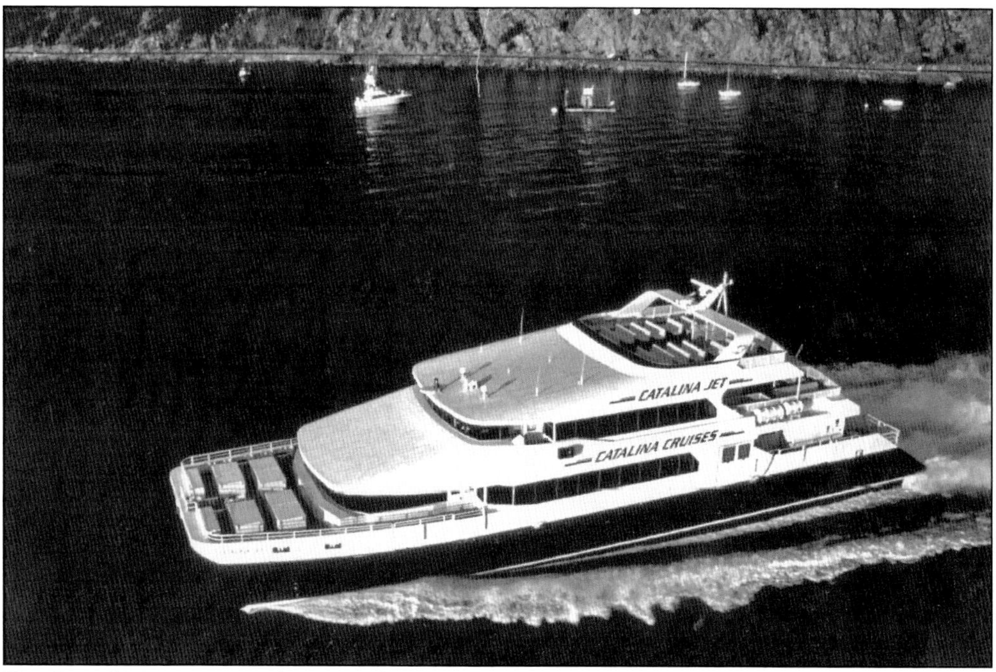

Handy and Voss continued to provide consistent passenger service to the island and sought to increase their level of service by introducing the *Catalina Jet* in 1999. The high-speed catamaran had a water-jet system and crossed the channel in just over one hour, carrying up to 450 passengers. The *Catalina Jet* served on the Catalina run until Catalina Cruises ceased operations in 2001. (Courtesy of Catalina Express.)

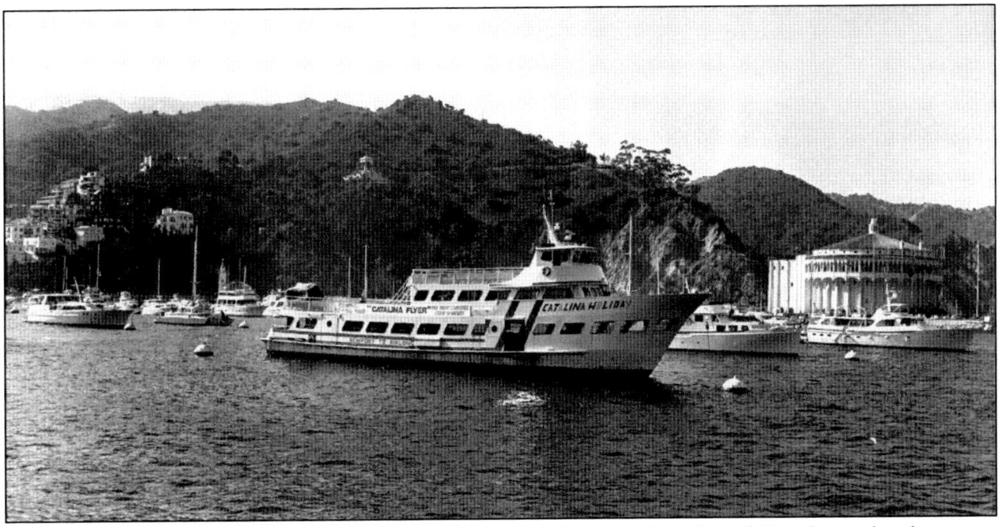

The certificate to operate passenger service between Newport Beach and Catalina Island went to auction in the mid-1950s and was purchased by Phil Tozer. Tozer established Catalina Passenger Service and introduced the *Island Holiday* to the Catalina run. She served passengers from the mid-1950s until 1978 when she was replaced by the *Catalina Holiday*.

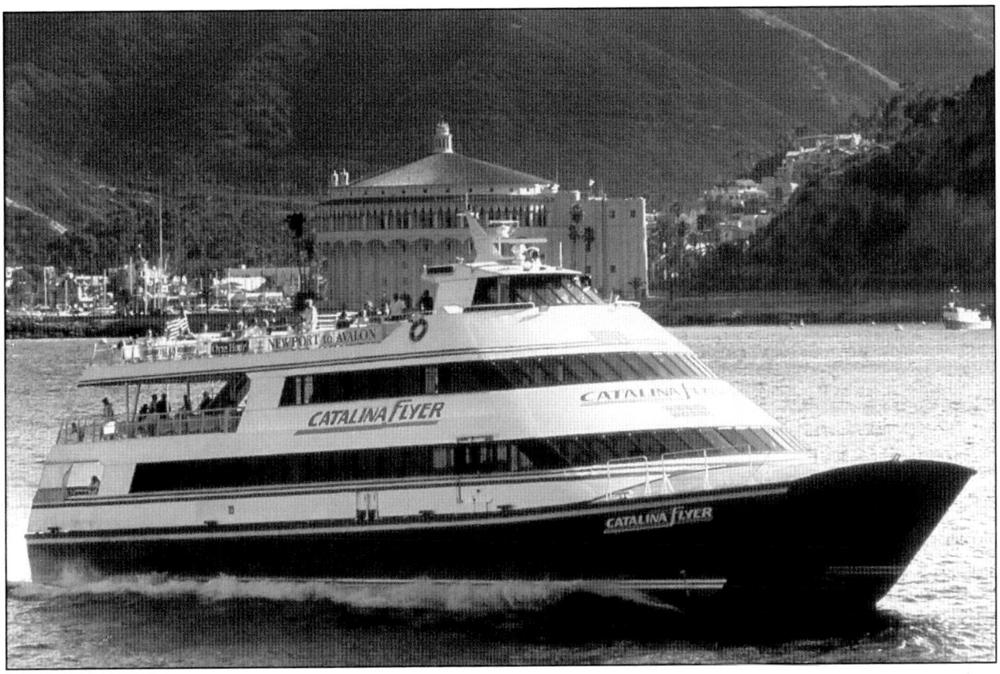

The *Catalina Holiday* served on the Catalina run from 1978 until 1988 when the *Catalina Flyer* replaced her. The *Flyer* is a large catamaran with a capacity to carry 500 passengers. She makes daily trips to Avalon throughout the year and operates on the longest-running passenger use certificate for the Catalina run. Other single boat operations providing service to Catalina Island include the *Catalina Explorer*, which operates out of Long Beach, and the *Marina Flyer*, operating out of Marina del Rey. (Courtesy of Catalina Passenger Service.)

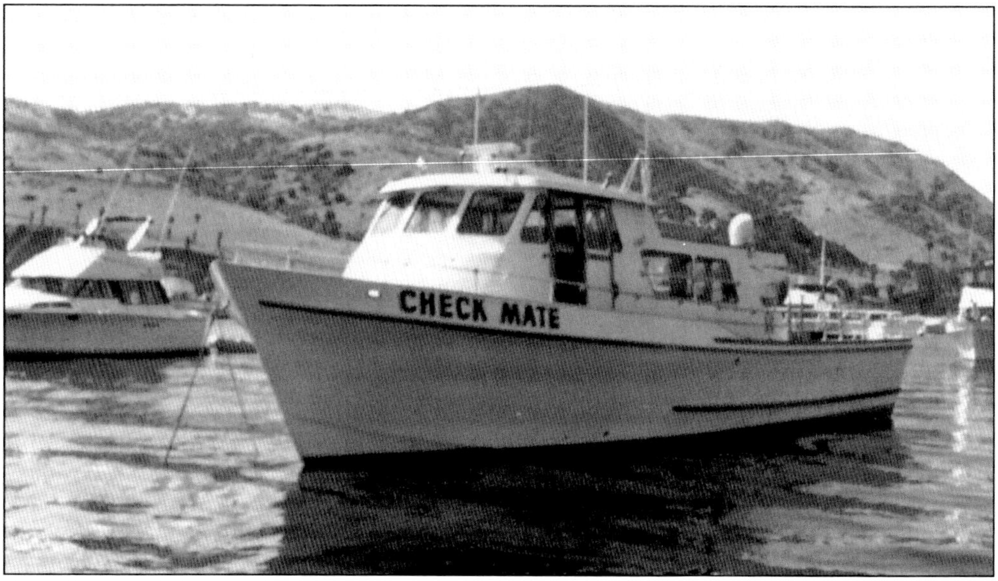

Doug Bombard, the founder of Catalina Channel Express, was looking for a way to bring hunters, guests, and other commuters to the Two Harbors Resort for their hunting program and archery camps. Previously, hunters and visitors arrived by seaplane, but the seaplane service ended and Bombard needed a fast, convenient way for visitors to access Two Harbors. Doug and his son Greg purchased a sportfishing boat that previously operated out of Portland, Oregon. In 1981, the *Check Mate* was converted for passenger service, repowered, and renamed the *Catalina Express.* (Courtesy of Catalina Express.)

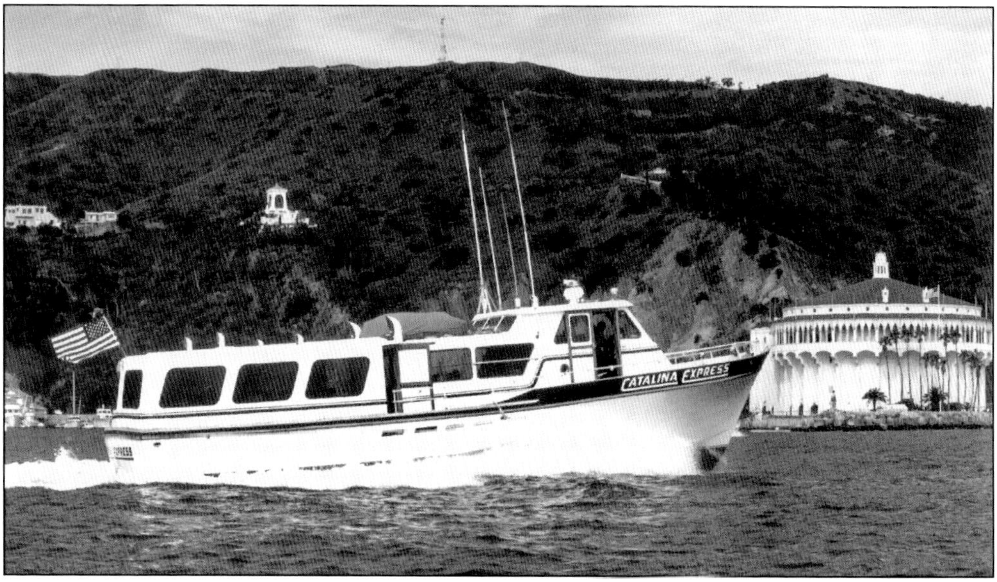

Doug Bombard designed a passenger cabin for the vessel, a roll-control system was installed, and airline-type seating was added. In fact, the airline seats were purchased from Continental Airlines. The *Catalina Express* was 56-feet long with two Detroit engines, each with 450 horsepower. She crossed the channel in one and a half hours with 55 passengers. The vessel was placed on a year-round, regular schedule, making multiple trips to the island each day from San Pedro. (Courtesy of Catalina Express.)

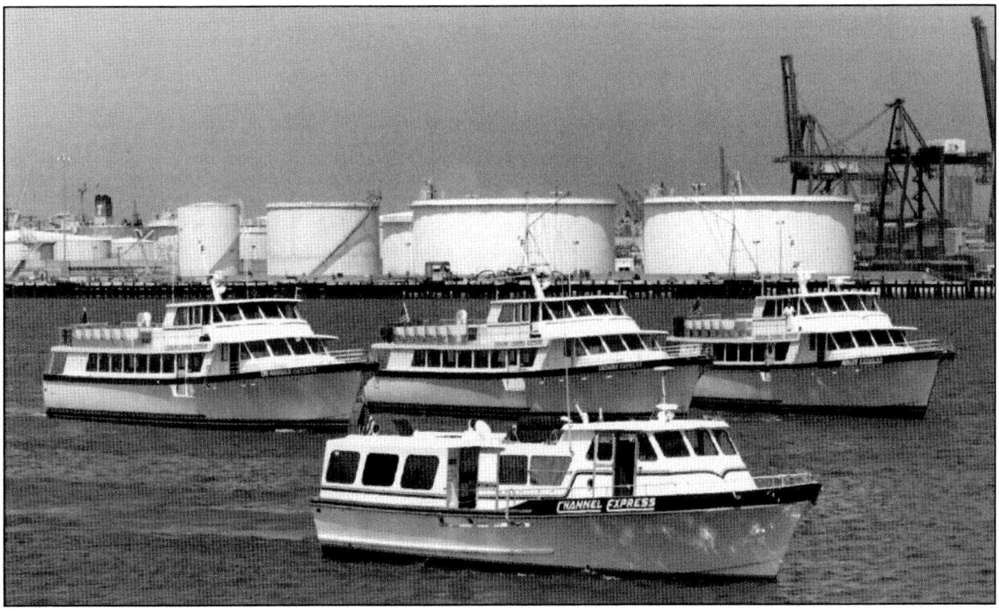

The fast, reliable service offered by Catalina Express quickly became popular among island residents. Not since the days of seaplane service had any cross-channel carrier catered to the needs of islanders. People saw that they could rely on the regular schedule and for the first time it was convenient to travel to the mainland and back on the same day. The popularity of the service grew, and by 1983 Catalina Express added the *Avalon Express* to the run. This was the first of many 149-passenger boats to join the Catalina Express fleet. The *Catalina Express* and the *Two Harbors Express* followed her in 1985. (Courtesy of Catalina Express.)

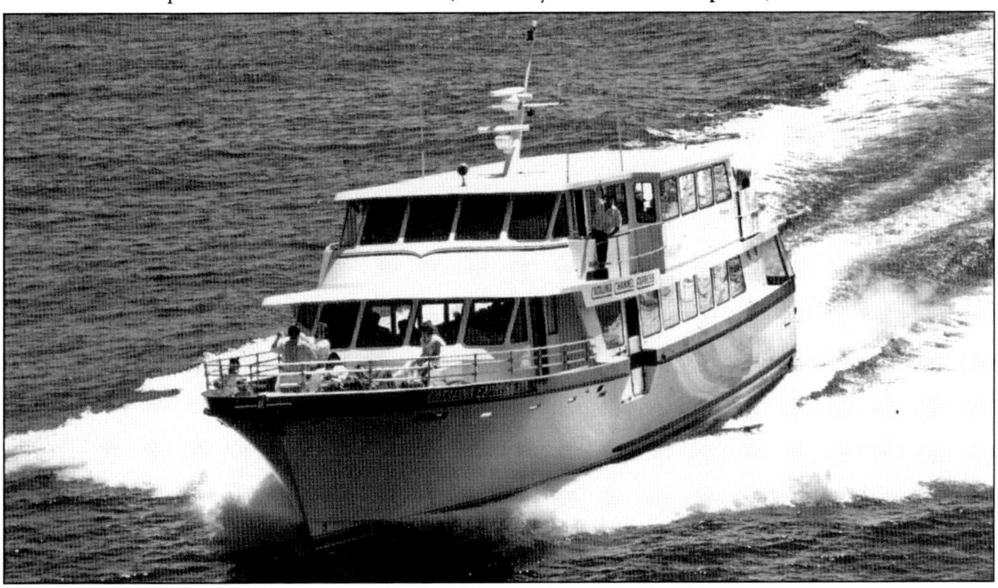

The *Catalina Express* and *Two Harbors Express* were sister ships made from the same plans. Both ships were 90 feet in length with a capacity for 149 passengers. The *Catalina Express* replaced the original *Check Mate* and was equipped with twin-screw engines, each with 930 horsepower, as was the *Two Harbors Express*. Both ships crossed the channel in about an hour and a half. (Courtesy of Catalina Express.)

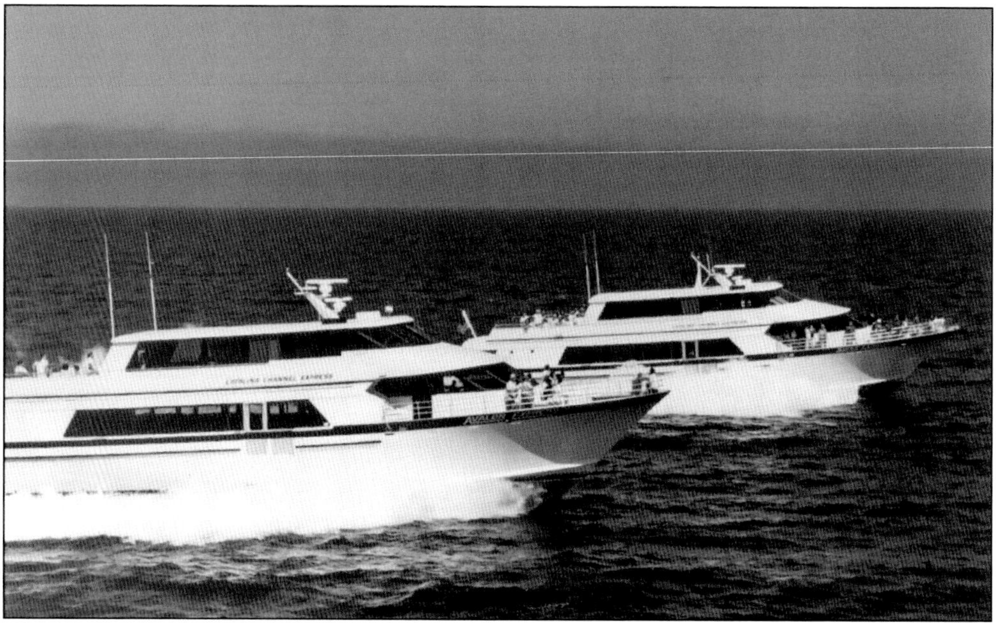

The *Super Express* was added to the fleet in 1988, followed by her sister ship, the *Avalon Express*, in 1989. Both were 95 feet in length, equipped with twin-screw engines that had 2,200 horsepower, carried the traditional 149 passengers, and could cross the channel in one hour. The vessels were the first to operate out of the Catalina Express's new terminal, known as the Catalina Express Port, at the bow of the *Queen Mary* in Long Beach. (Courtesy of Catalina Express.)

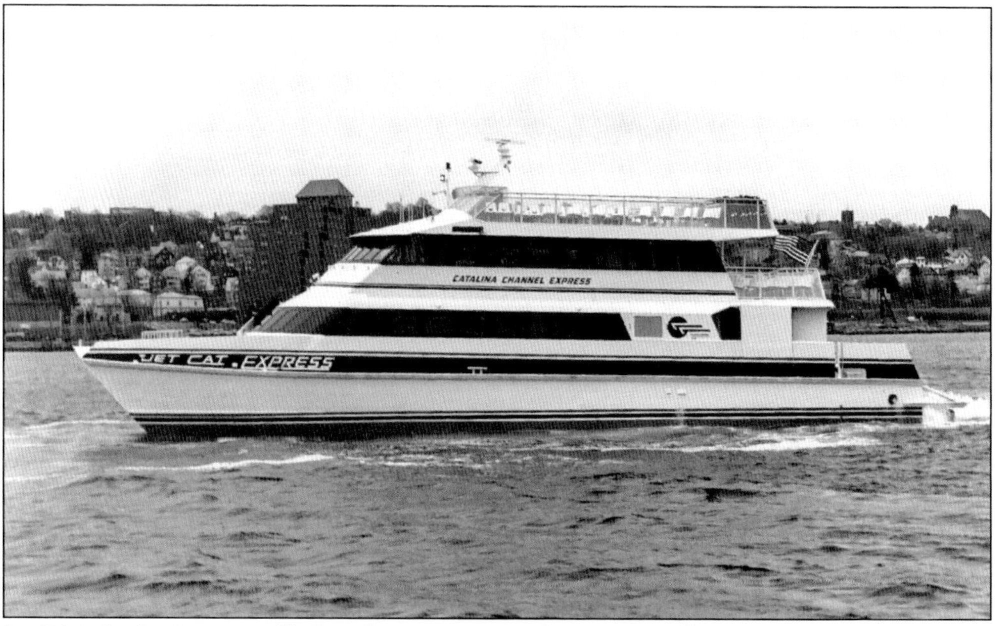

In 1991, the *Jet Cat* was added to the growing Catalina Express fleet. The catamaran was 102 feet in length, carried 360 passengers, and crossed the channel in one hour. It was the first vessel powered by a water-jet system to serve on the Catalina run, which is a large turbine that forces water through a nozzle that creates thrust. Two 149-passenger vessels later replaced the *Jet Cat* in 1994. (Courtesy of Catalina Express.)

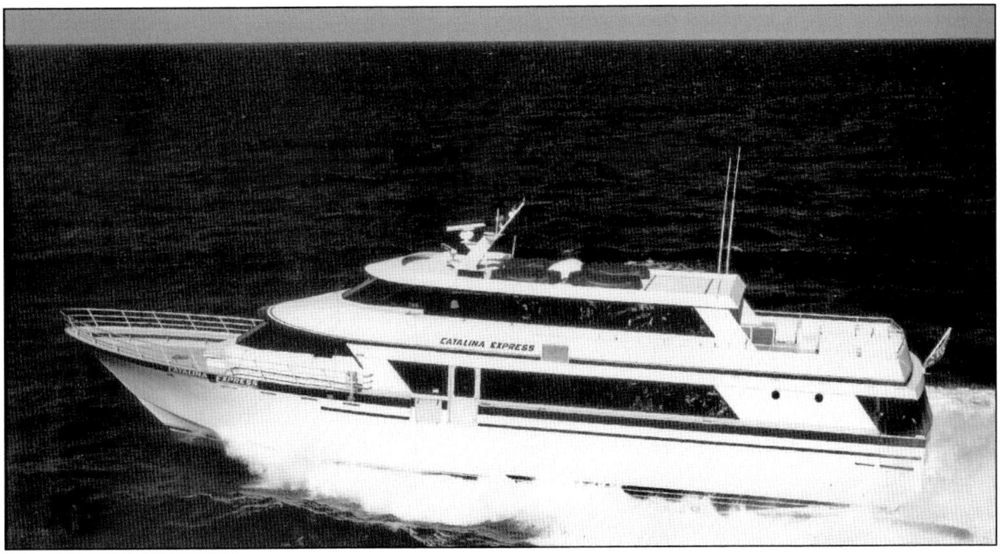

The *Catalina Express* and *Islander Express* replaced the *Jet Cat* on the Catalina Express fleet. Both vessels were 100 feet in length and were equipped with twin-screw engines, each with 2,335 horsepower. The boats could cross the channel in one hour at 32 knots. (Courtesy of Catalina Express.)

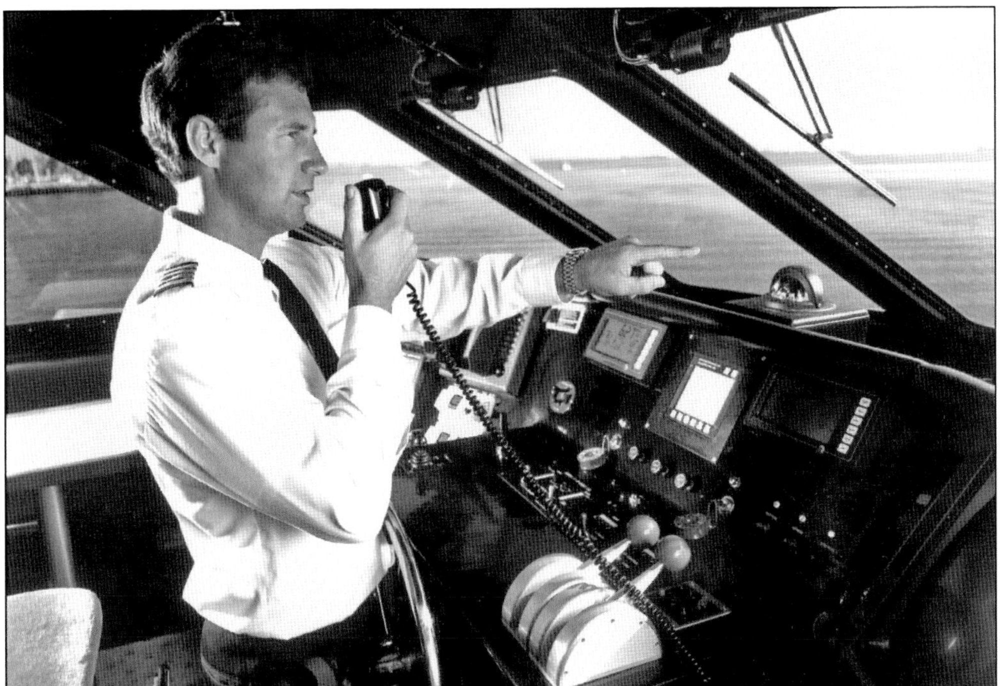

Catalina Express employs over 400 people during the height of the busy summer season. Each employee and crew member plays an important role in providing customers with an enjoyable experience. According to president Greg Bombard, "From the reservations agent to the captain and his crew, our goal is to offer passengers more than just a boat ride but a total travel experience. Our repeat business and increasing passenger loads over the years are proof that it works." Chris Ryan, senior captain for the Catalina Express fleet, is pictured here navigating through Long Beach Harbor on his way to Avalon. (Courtesy of Catalina Express.)

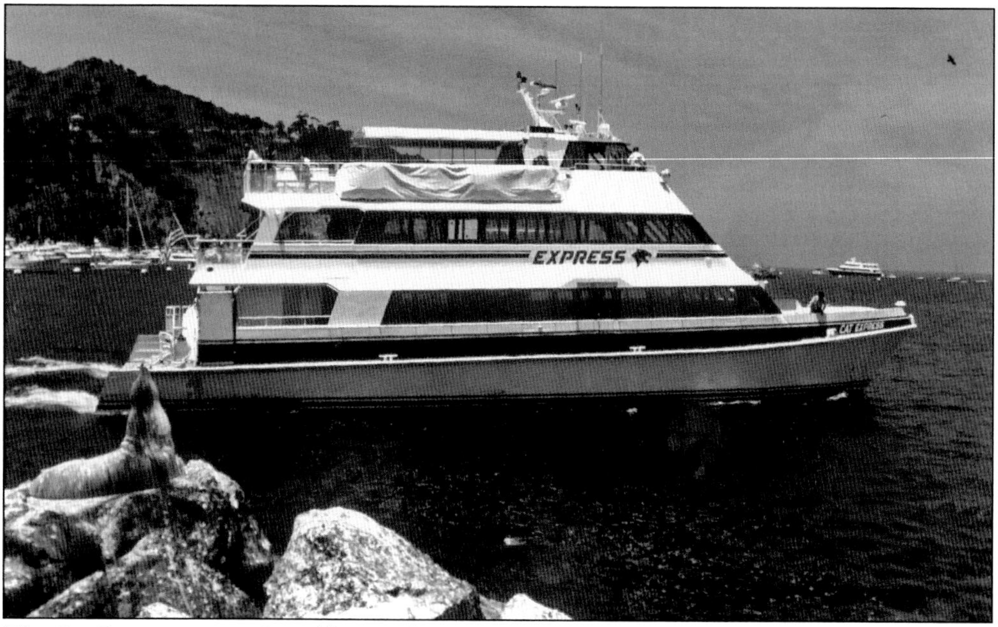

The *Cat Express* was purchased by Catalina Express in 1997 in an effort to increase the capacity of their fleet. It had previously operated out of Seward, Alaska, as a tour boat. The vessel is 97 feet in length, has the capacity for 365 passengers, and is equipped with twin-screw diesel engines, each with 1,800 horsepower. The *Cat Express* still serves on the Catalina run today. (Courtesy of Catalina Express.)

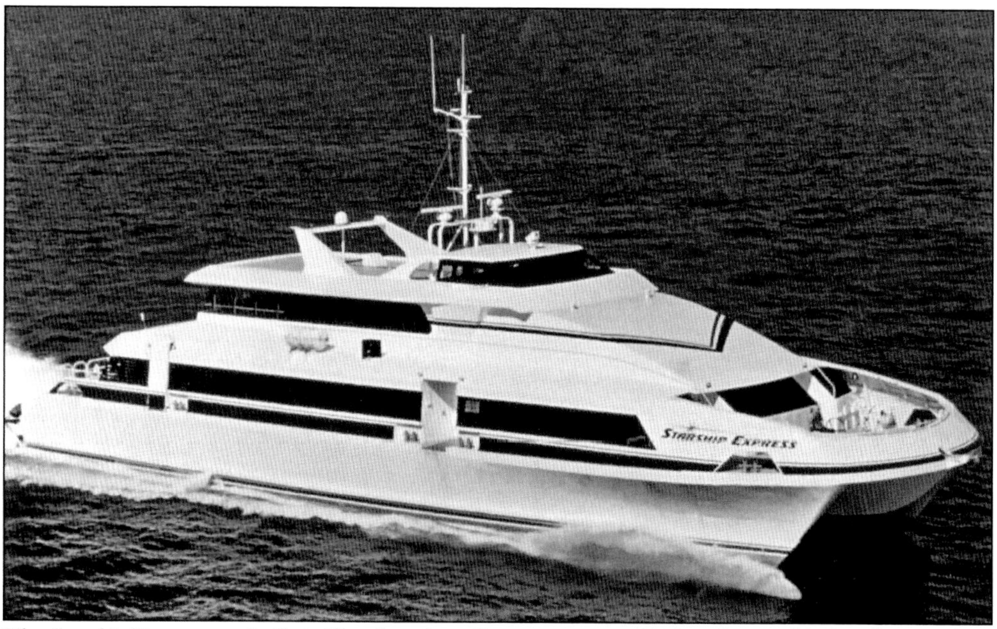

The *Starship Express* was built in New London, Connecticut, in 1999 and was added to the Catalina Express fleet that same year. The *Starship* is a high-speed, water-jet catamaran and is powered by two 3,110-horsepower engines. The 134-foot vessel carries up to 300 passengers and crosses the channel in less than an hour at speeds up to 37 knots. The *Starship Express* is a smooth riding, fast boat and is a current favorite on the Catalina run. (Courtesy of Catalina Express.)

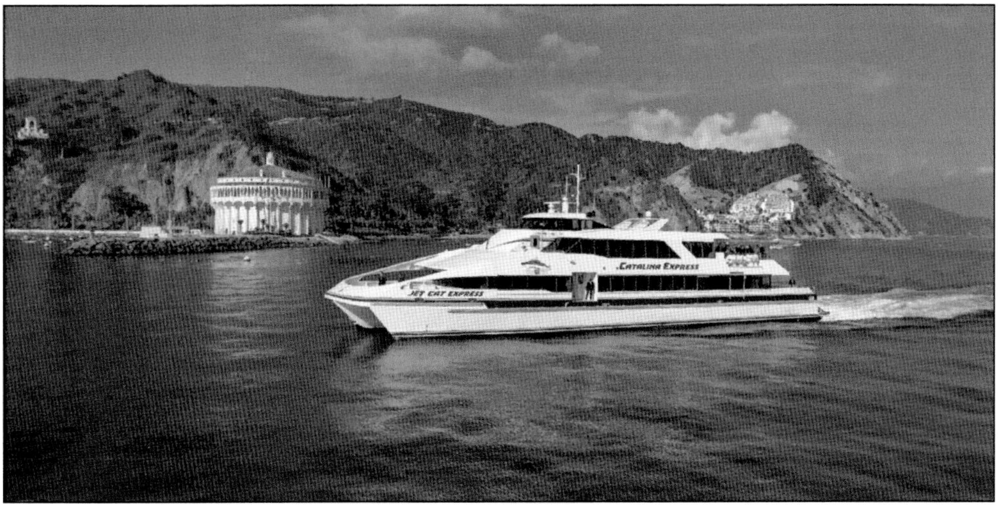

The *Jet Cat* was added to the Catalina Express fleet in 2001. The catamaran is propelled by four 2,335-horsepower diesel engines driving four water jets. The *Jet Cat* is 145 feet long and carries 381 passengers across the channel in less than an hour at speeds up to 39 knots. (Courtesy of Catalina Express.)

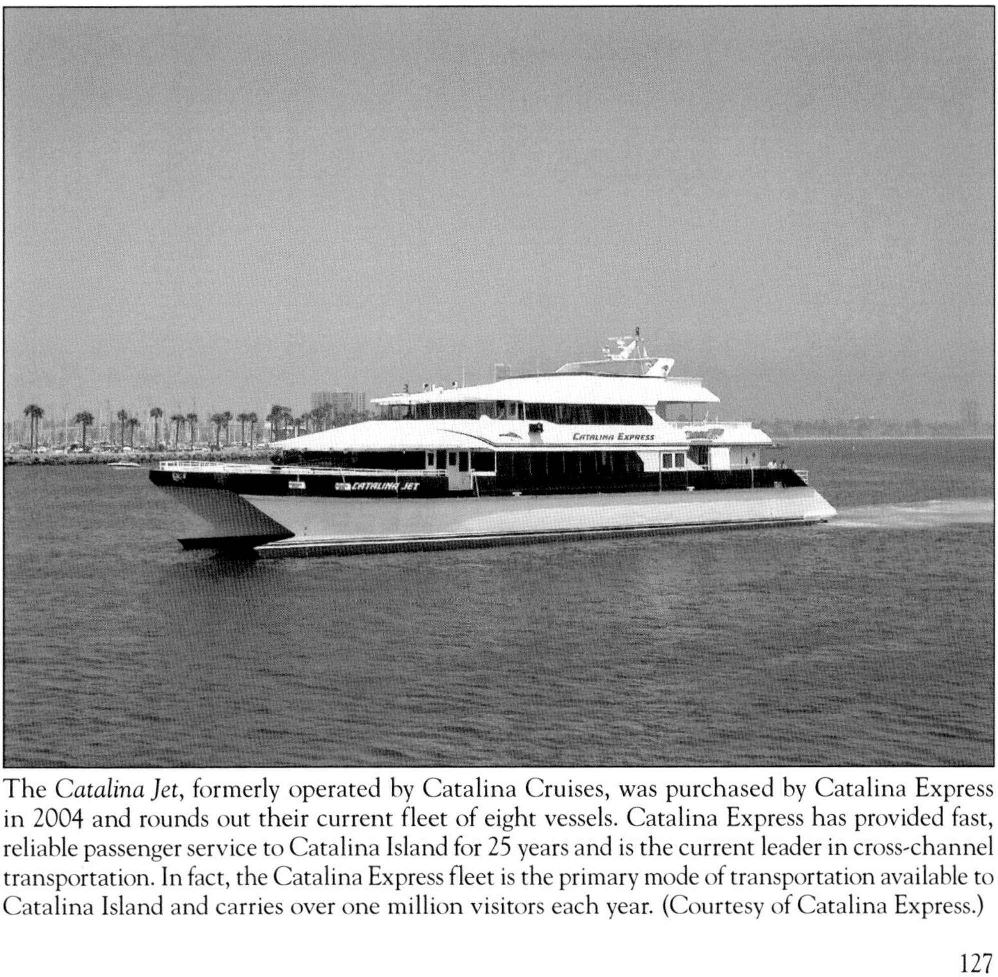

The *Catalina Jet*, formerly operated by Catalina Cruises, was purchased by Catalina Express in 2004 and rounds out their current fleet of eight vessels. Catalina Express has provided fast, reliable passenger service to Catalina Island for 25 years and is the current leader in cross-channel transportation. In fact, the Catalina Express fleet is the primary mode of transportation available to Catalina Island and carries over one million visitors each year. (Courtesy of Catalina Express.)